The Bible and the Flag

The Bible and the Flag

Protestant missions and British imperialism in the nineteenth and twentieth centuries

Brian Stanley

APOLLOS is an imprint of Inter-Varsity Press
38 De Montfort Street, Leicester LE1 7GP, England.

First published 1990

British Library Cataloguing in Publication Data
Stanley, Brian, *1953–*
    The Bible and the flag: Protestant missions and
    British imperialism in the nineteenth and twentieth centuries.
    1. Christian missions, history
    266′.009

ISBN 0–85111–412–1

Set in Baskerville
Typeset in Great Britain by Avocet Robinson, Buckingham
Printed in Great Britain by
Dotesios Printers Ltd, Trowbridge, Wiltshire

Contents

	Preface	7
	List of abbreviations	9
1	Christianity and the anti-colonial reaction	11
2	What is imperialism?	33
3	The gospel for the globe	55
4	The claims of humanity, 1792 to 1860	85
5	From protection to annexation, 1860 to 1895	111
6	Missions and the nationalist revolutions, 1895 to 1960	133
7	Christianity and culture	157
8	Empires and missions under human and divine judgment	175
	Notes	185
	Index	205

13

Table of Maps

Figure 1. The Eastern Cape Frontier in the time of John Philip. — 92

Figure 2. Bechuanaland in the time of John Mackenzie. — 117

Figure 3. Nyasaland (Malawi), 1874 to 1894. — 122

Preface

This book has been a long time in the making. Its central themes first drew my attention in the course of my doctoral research during the late 1970s on the domestic base of the early Victorian missionary movement. Subsequent work on other aspects of the history of British Protestant missions deepened my interest in their relationship to imperial expansion, and reinforced my conviction that a book of this kind was called for. Since the 1960s professional historians have examined numerous individual case studies which have illuminated aspects of the subject for the academic specialist. The impact of their writings has, however, been limited in two respects. Firstly, their work has been inaccessible to non-historians. Secondly, it has lacked overall perspective. Specifically, it has been deficient in that perspective which stems from an understanding of the theology and world-view of missionaries who were for the most part in the evangelical tradition.

This book attempts to begin to remedy these deficiencies. It is written both for Christians who are concerned for the contemporary world mission of the church, and for students of history with a particular interest in missions and imperialism. Some sections may have a more immediate appeal to one category of readers than the other, but it is my hope that all readers will be prepared to treat the book as a unity. Christians without historical expertise are encouraged to persevere with the more technical historical sections, while historians are urged to take the theological sections seriously.

I owe a number of debts to those who made this book possible. I gratefully acknowledge the permission of the following bodies to use and make citations from their archives: the Baptist Missionary Society, the Church Missionary Society, the Council for World Mission, the Methodist Church Overseas Division (Methodist Missionary Society). Their archivists, and the library staff of the School of Oriental and African Studies in the University of London, have been unfailingly helpful. I am grateful to the editor of the *Baptist Quarterly*, Mr J. H. Y. Briggs, for permission to reproduce in parts of chapters 4 and 5 sections of an article published in that journal in January 1987. Most of the research and writing for the book was accomplished during two periods of sabbatical leave generously granted to me by the Principal and Council of Spurgeon's College in 1984 and 1987. The chapters were read in draft by my friends Dr David Bebbington and Dr David Killingray. The book is a much better one as a result of their criticisms; the failings which remain are my own.

My wife, Rosemary, has gently urged me to keep going when it seemed that the book would never be finished. My children, Jonathan and, more recently, Rebecca, have been remarkably patient in enduring the demands which the book has placed on their father's time. My parents have always encouraged me in my life as a Christian and an historian. This book is dedicated to them in gratitude.

Brian Stanley
Spurgeon's College 1989

List of abbreviations

AIM	Africa Inland Mission
BMS	Baptist Missionary Society
CCP	Chinese Communist Party
CIM	China Inland Mission
CMS	Church Missionary Society
CSM	Church of Scotland Mission
FNLA	Frente National de Libertação de Angola
IBEAC	Imperial British East Africa Company
KCA	Kikuyu Central Association
KMT	Kuomintang
LMS	London Missionary Society
MPLA	Movimento Popular de Libertação de Angola
SPCK	Society for Promoting Christian Knowledge
SPG	Society for the Propagation of the Gospel in Foreign Parts
SVMU	Student Volunteer Missionary Union
UMCA	Universities' Mission to Central Africa
WCC	World Council of Churches
WMMS	Wesleyan Methodist Missionary Society
YKA	Young Kikuyu Association
YMCA	Young Men's Christian Association

CHAPTER ONE

Christianity and the anti-colonial reaction

'Hand in hand with the colonial powers'

'It has been alleged with truth that the trader and the settler followed the missionary, who was the agent of European imperialism, working hand in hand with the colonial powers for the subjugation of the black people and the territorial extension of the imperialist power.'[1] This damning verdict on the Western missionary movement was passed at the beginning of the 1970s by a South African black theologian writing with the tragic history of his own country primarily in mind. But his statement is a characteristic expression of a theme which can now be heard not only throughout the developing nations of the 'Third World' but also in the West itself. Delegates to the Fifth Assembly of the World Council of Churches in Nairobi in 1975 were told in the Assembly newspaper that the missionaries came to Africa with 'the Bible in one hand and the gun in the other'. The newspaper article was summarizing the message of a play entitled 'Muntu' ('Man' in many African languages) which was performed at the Assembly. 'Muntu', written by a Canadian, was a ruthless portrayal of the exploitation of Africa by outsiders: Arab slave-traders, European colonialists and Christian missionaries were all tarred with the same brush – they were all part of a common programme of imperial aggression.[2]

Although the most vehement contemporary denunciations of the missionary movement for complicity in the processes of colonial exploitation tend to issue from the continent of Africa, voices from Asia and Latin America are not wanting from the anti-colonial chorus. According to the Asian theologian Tissa Balasuriya, it is not merely Western missionaries but Western theology itself which has been

> a handmaid of Western expansion; an ally, at least, in the centennial exploitation of the peoples of other continents by the North Americans. The combination of the 'sacred' duty of civilizing, baptizing, and saving the pagans with the military, economic, political, and cultural domination by Europe over our countries has been disastrous for Christianity itself.[3]

The modern missionary movement, insists the radical Latin American evangelical, Orlando Costas, was a 'product of mercantile expansion', 'part and parcel of the colonial or neo-colonial system', with the sad consequence that Christ himself 'has been thought of either as a white saviour, the great European conquistador, the justifier of the rich and powerful, or the soother of the guilt-ridden conscience of oppressors'.[4]

Formulations of the case that the Western missionary movement was an integral part of the broader process of Western imperial expansion vary greatly in their degree of sophistication. Very few treatments of the subject by professional historians, even those of avowedly Marxist sympathies, present the relationship in terms of the crude conspiracy which seems to be implied by comments of the kind just cited. It is, however, the less sophisticated presentations of the theme by theologians, church leaders and journalists which are the more influential in shaping popular understanding of the past. The belief that 'the Bible and the flag' went hand in hand in the history of Western imperial expansion is fast becoming established as one of the unquestioned orthodoxies of general historical knowledge, and no amount of specialized historical monographs by academic historians is likely to affect substantially the received views of those unfamiliar with the world of historical scholarship.

The aim of this book is to submit the theme of 'the Bible and the flag' to detailed historical investigation. No one book could hope to deal adequately with the whole subject of the relationship between the Christian religion and imperial expansion from Roman times to the twentieth century. The focus of this study will be almost entirely on the British empire of the nineteenth and twentieth centuries, and on the role played within the changing patterns of British imperialism by British Protestant missions. These limitations, although they will not be adhered to with absolute consistency (this opening chapter in particular will set the debate in a broader context), need to be clearly understood at the outset: no attempt will be made, for example, to present a detailed assessment of the role of Roman Catholic missions in the massive colonial empires of Spain and Portugal. It ought also to be emphasized that it is no part of the intention of this book to exonerate Christian missionaries from all the charges which have been levelled against them. In some cases, indeed, I shall argue that they ought to be exonerated; in others it will become apparent that the evidence is sufficient to secure a 'conviction'. But this book is not primarily an exercise in moral judgment so much as an attempt to convey an informed historical understanding of the issues involved. The themes expounded and the evidence presented will invariably be complex in nature and frequently ambiguous in their wider significance. Different readers will no doubt arrive at markedly different answers to the questions which this subject raises, questions which ultimately pass out of the sphere of history into that of theology. Readers who do not themselves possess a strong religious commitment are likely to find alien and unattractive the confidence in their own rectitude displayed by most of the missionaries who will be discussed. Some committed Christian readers, on the other hand, may feel that even to make the suggestion that missionaries may have collaborated in the exploitation of human beings is to impugn the spiritual integrity of those who ought to be honoured as men and women of God. Others, who by conviction and personal experience find themselves in very considerable sympathy with the passionate indignation at colonial oppression currently moulding opinion in the Third World, may deplore this book as a qualified apology for colonialism. Such wide divergences of response are only to be expected. Christians – not to speak of others – are unlikely to arrive overnight at a common evaluation of one of the most controversial themes in modern Christian history. What is, however, of supreme importance is that their several assessments should be based as far as possible on truth and not mythology, on evidence rather than propaganda. The truth about the past can never be recovered in its entirety, but that is no argument for not pursuing it with all the industry and accuracy that can be mustered.

The argument in historical context

The remainder of this opening chapter will be concerned to establish the historical context in which current views of the relationship between missions and imperialism have arisen and developed. It might be supposed that current interpretations of the relationship are essentially no different from what opponents of the Protestant missionary movement have consistently alleged from its beginning. Stephen Neill, whose book *Colonialism and Christian Missions* (1966) remains one of the most perceptive and comprehensive appraisals of the subject, indeed claimed that condemnation of Christian missions for their close alliance with the physical power of Western colonial nations 'has been the standing argument of the critics and opponents of missions for more than a century'.[5] Where a non-Western society has had the opportunity and cultural resources for considered reflection on the nature and composition of the Western impact, it has certainly tended to make the understandable connection between the white man's religions and his guns or goods. However, the fact that 'imperialism' is itself a comparatively new political concept, and more recent still in its current meaning (see chapter 2), must throw into question any assumption that present-day formulations of the Christianity and imperialism issue represent no more than long-established arguments in modern dress. It is surely significant that one of the most influential (and in evangelical circles, notorious) reappraisals of the missionary task to be written in the first half of the twentieth century, the

American report *Re-thinking Missions* (1932), had nothing to say about missions and imperialism. The report's brief paragraph on missions and politics made no reference to questions of Western impact and influence on non-Christian societies, whilst the section on economics, though warning that missions 'should not lay themselves open to the criticism that they are acquiescent to the evils of the present capitalistic regime', actually thought it would be 'a splendid thing' for Western businessmen trading overseas to be associated as trustees in the management of mission hospitals and schools.[6] No missionary commission convened in the years after 1960 could have expressed 'deep regret' that 'there seems to be a great gulf fixed between most European and American business men and the missionaries, especially in the largest cities'.[7] Although the contention that Christian missions have been the ideological aspect or ally of Western political expansion cannot be portrayed as a novelty invented by the anti-colonial reaction of the second half of the twentieth century, it is nonetheless profoundly true that the current attack on missions for complicity in colonial oppression derives its shape, colour, and specific ideological content from the dominant intellectual currents of that reaction.

China, Communism and Christianity

The earliest significant example in modern times of an indigenous society developing an articulated case against Christian missions in terms of their relationship to Western expansion is provided by China in the 1860s. The rapid influx of both Catholic and Protestant missionaries into inland China after its opening to Western penetration in 1858 called forth a spate of tracts written by Chinese intellectuals attacking Christianity as a foreign religion and missionaries as agents of the Western powers which had foisted opium and then gunboats upon China. This anti-missionary literature itself drew upon a tradition of rooted hostility to all foreign and heterodox ideological influences, which characterized Chinese culture from Confucian times onwards and determined Chinese responses to Christianity from its first significant impact on China in the late sixteenth century.[8] The invective of the Chinese intelligentsia against Christianity and missionaries continued unabated into the twentieth century, but increasingly borrowed arguments derived from secular elements within the European intellectual tradition. It thus became a dominant theme in the 1920s that Christianity was a superstitious and anachronistic survival in an age of modern science. Alongside this theme, and eventually superseding it, appeared another: no longer were missionaries vilified in the language of classical Chinese culture for being agents of a particular foreign power and alien ideology; they were now more frequently condemned in the language of Marxist-Leninism as agents of Western capitalism and imperialism as a politico-economic system.[9] This line of argument was characteristic of the propaganda of the Anti-Christian Student Federation, formed in Shanghai in 1922 (see chapter 6). It was the association of Western missionaries with the theory of capitalist imperialism as expounded by Lenin (see chapter 2) which became the characteristic device of the Chinese Communist attack on Christian missions, and provided the rationale for the virtual expulsion of most missionaries from China between the inauguration of the Chinese People's Republic in October 1949 and the end of 1952.[10]

There were parallels in other contexts to the Chinese Communist critique of Christian missions, notably in India, where Christians in the years before independence in 1947 were regularly accused of being 'running-dogs of imperialism'.[11] There can be little doubt, however, that until the 1960s the portrayal of Christian missions as an essentially imperialistic agency was generally associated in the Western mind with Chinese Communist propaganda. This was true even of missionary commentators who were anxious that the churches should respond to the challenge posed by the Communist revolution in a constructive and self-critical fashion. David M. Paton's *Christian Missions and the Judgment of God* (1953) conceded that many of the Communist strictures on the missionary enterprise in China were fundamentally justified, and interpreted the Communist take-over in China as an act of divine judgment upon the Western churches for their cultural imperialism and reluctance to grant autonomy to the mission-founded churches. Yet Paton could write of 'the Communist case that missionaries are the secret agents of imperialism' in a way that would have sounded quite incongruous from a liberal Christian twenty years later.[12] In 1961 the American evangelicals, Eric Fife and Arthur Glasser, could still be equally specific in describing the association of Christian missions with Western imperialism as 'a diabolically clever stroke' of Chinese Communist propaganda, although they too wished to interpret the Communist revolution as an instrument of God's judgment and a call for humble self-analysis by missionary agencies.[13]

It was, therefore, the Communist revolution in China, by its grafting of the 'Leninist' concept of imperialism onto the long-standing Chinese cultural tradition of anti-foreignism, which made common currency of the theory that Christian missions were in essence the ideological arm of Western imperial aggression. Events in China had irrevocably placed the issue of missions and imperialism on the agenda of both historical scholarship and missionary thinking. It was not surprising that some historians unsympathetic to Christianity concluded prematurely that the end of the imperial era in Asian history also marked the collapse of the Christian attempt to convert Asia. Such was the conclusion of the Indian historian K. M. Panikkar, in his book *Asia and Western Dominance* (1953). Panikkar, although devoting only one chapter to Christian missions (and that was concerned primarily with early Roman Catholic missions in Asia), argued that Christianity had become fatally identified with Western imperialism in Asia; imperialism in China had now been destroyed, and 'the Church could not escape the fate of its patron and ally'.[14]

Nationalism and decolonization in Africa

Until about 1960 discussion of the issue of missions and imperialism focused primarily on Asia. Since that date the centre of the controversy has shifted to the continent of Africa. The change is explicable in terms of the substantial difference in the timetable of nationalism and decolonization between the two continents. In India nationalist politics emerged as early as the 1880s and independence was achieved by 1947. China, although never a formal colony of a Western power, can be said to have moved into the era of modern nationalist politics with the fall of the Manchu dynasty and the Republican Revolution of 1911; by 1949 the early pro-Christian phase of Chinese nationalism represented by Sun Yat-sen was already past history, swept aside by the more militant forces of Communism. By the end of 1954 the French had followed the British in withdrawing from colonial rule in Asia. In Africa nationalist politics arrived on the scene much later than in Asia, and the pace of their development and the rate of decolonization were correspondingly more rapid.

The formation in 1949 of Kwame Nkrumah's Convention People's Party in the Gold Coast (modern Ghana) was a landmark in the emergence of mass nationalist political parties in post-war Africa. In the course of the next decade Nkrumah secured for himself symbolic status throughout the continent as the trail-blazer of African nationalist politics and subsequently of political independence from British colonial rule: Ghana's independence in March 1957 marked the beginning of the end of British colonialism in Africa. This first phase of the nationalist revolution in Africa was generally sympathetic to Christianity and the missionary presence. In December 1957 Nkrumah, addressing the Ghana assembly of the International Missionary Council, paid tribute to 'the great work of missionaries in West Africa', saluted in particular those who had given their lives 'for the enlightenment and welfare of this land', and insisted that 'the need for devoted service such as they gave is as great as ever'.[15] Many of the first generation of African nationalist leaders were products of Catholic or Protestant mission schools and theological colleges. In Anglophone Africa a small number of high-quality Protestant schools made a disproportionate contribution to early nationalist political leadership: in Kenya, ten of the seventeen members of Jomo Kenyatta's first cabinet were old boys of the interdenominational Alliance High School in Kikuyuland; in Nyasaland (now Malawi), the Livingstonia

16

Mission, founded by the Free Church of Scotland in the last century, exercised an equally great influence in shaping the country's first post-colonial political elite; in South Africa the leading voice in the African National Congress in the 1950s was the sincerely Christian Zulu, Albert Luthuli. Relations between this generation of African politicians and their former missionary friends were certainly not all sweetness and light – some, such as Zambia's Kenneth Kaunda, toyed for a while with Africanist or 'independent' alternatives to mission Christianity – but by and large this generation of nationalist leaders remained broadly sympathetic to Christian principles, while being severely critical of many aspects of missionary paternalism.[16]

In January 1960 the British Prime Minister Harold Macmillan made his famous speech to the South African parliament, commenting on the awakening of national consciousness in Africa: 'Fifteen years ago this movement spread through Asia. ... Today the same thing is happening in Africa. ... The wind of change is blowing through this continent.'[17] Over the next five years the wind blew strongly. In Ghana's wake the British colonial territories achieved independence in rapid succession: Nigeria and Somaliland in 1960, Tanzania and Sierra Leone in 1961, Uganda in 1962, Kenya in 1963, Malawi and Zambia in 1964, the Gambia in 1965. Only the protectorates of Botswana (1966), Lesotho (1966) and Swaziland (1968) were still to come to complete the process. By the middle of the decade the British empire in Africa was all but dismantled and Africa north of the Zambezi river was in the hands of black nationalist governments. South of the Zambezi, however, white supremacy in the settler republics of South Africa and Rhodesia (after Ian Smith's Unilateral Declaration of Independence from Britain in November 1965) and in the Portuguese colonies of Angola and Mozambique was still strongly entrenched.[18]

The view from the mid-1960s

Decolonization in Africa had been achieved with astonishing rapidity and, with the notable exceptions of the Belgian territories of the Congo (Zaire) and Rwanda, with a relative absence of bloodshed. Missionary strategists were compelled speedily to come to terms with the end of colonial paternalism and the fact that missionaries would henceforth have to operate in a far more bracing political climate. The 1960s accordingly saw a number of historical assessments of the relationship of Christian missions to Western colonialism by influential missionary statesmen. In 1962 Colin Morris, a Methodist missionary in Northern Rhodesia (Zambia) and personal friend of Kenneth Kaunda, published a booklet entitled *The End of the Missionary?*, reviewing the history of the missionary-colonial connection in Northern Rhodesia, and asking whether the imminent end of the colonial era also spelt the end of European missionary service in Africa. It is significant that Morris, one of the most politically radical of all British missionary spokesmen in the 1960s, gave the unequivocal answer that the role of the European missionary in Africa was far from finished: there was certainly no more room for missionary paternalism, but, given the right attitudes of humility and service, there was every reason to expect that 'a new era of opportunity' was dawning for Western missionary service in Africa.[19]

In the autumn terms of 1964 and 1965 Canon Max Warren, recently retired from a twenty-one-year term of office as General Secretary of the CMS, delivered two series of lectures in the University of Cambridge on the history of the missionary movement. Warren, whose position in the CMS had given him a unique perspective on the role of missions in British Africa, devoted much of his lectures to themes arising out of the imperial context of the Protestant missionary movement. Like Morris, Warren insisted that the contemporary nationalist revolution in Asia and Africa demanded an end to racially superior attitudes amongst Western missionaries, and called for a sympathetic Christian response: 'After all', observed Warren in a memorable sentence, 'the nationalism of Africa is the deposit left by the receding tide of western imperialism'.[20] But Warren was even more insistent that the changed political climate in fact offered exciting new possibilities for foreign missionary service.[21] Warren ended one of his lectures in 1965 by citing with approval the prophecy of a Nigerian politician in 1947 that, 'When African historians come to write their own account of the adventure of Africa with imperialism, they will write of the missionaries as the greatest friends the African had.'[22] A decade later, Warren's endorsement of such a prophecy would have been unthinkable.

In 1966 Stephen Neill's *Colonialism and Christian Missions* struck a very similar note of self-critical but even-handed appraisal of the missionary relationship to colonialism. Neill, writing with the benefit of twenty years' missionary experience in India, stressed that the wounds inflicted by the colonial era were very deep, yet declined to align himself with those who were already condemning the colonial enterprise without qualification, and arguing that Christian missions had been fatally compromised by their association with an essentially exploitative movement. Neill shared with Warren a conviction that what was needed was a 'theology of imperialism' which could give equal weight to the workings of human evil and to the undeniable fact that during the colonial period the Christian faith had spread to every corner of the globe.[23]

Measured and dispassionate assessments of the missions and imperialism issue such as those of Warren and Neill were representative of the mood of the early and mid-1960s: the tide had turned decisively against attitudes of white superiority, but a clear conceptual distinction was generally maintained between the discredited colonial imperative and the ongoing missionary obligation. From about 1966 onwards, however, discussion of the question has taken place in an increasingly polarized and highly charged ideological context. In these years the anti-colonial reaction entered its second and more militant phase, and appraisals of the missionary movement soon reflected the change in climate. For the purposes of the present study, five constituent elements of this second phase of the anti-colonial reaction need to be identified. Two of the five relate specifically to Africa, which is very near the centre of the anti-colonial stage throughout this period, and three are of more general reference.

a. Conflicts between church and state in Africa

The majority of the newly independent states of black Africa moved fairly rapidly away from the Western models of constitutional democracy inherited from their former colonial masters towards authoritarian one-party state systems. Many of the new African states were artificial constructs of the colonial era, and multi-party democracy too often appeared to threaten a fragmentation of the state on tribal or religious lines. As African governments moved in a dictatorial direction they endeavoured to gain absolute control of the press and national education, encouraged national youth movements with a strongly ideological flavour, and often promoted the personal glorification of the country's leader on quasi-religious lines. It was inevitable that such tendencies should bring about serious confrontations with the churches. Ghana, the pioneer of independence, also led the way in this less happy respect. As early as 1962 the churches were objecting to aspects of the 'cult' of President Nkrumah, and were then in their turn labelled by the government as disruptive and 'counter-revolutionary' elements.[24] Over the next decade similar crises in church-state relations ensued in a considerable number of African states. By and large government hostility was directed less frequently to the mainstream Protestant churches than to either the Catholic Church or unorthodox sects such as the Jehovah's Witnesses. In Zaire, where Catholicism was extremely strong, President Mobutu launched a campaign in October 1971 to curb the autonomous power of the Catholic Church and promote 'cultural liberation' and 'authenticity'. The dependence of the Catholic Church in Africa on large numbers of expatriate missionary priests and its subjection to external authority in Rome made it an obvious target in authoritarian campaigns of national unification. Jehovah's Witnesses suffered especially under the dictatorial regime of Dr Hastings Banda in Malawi, owing to their refusal to participate in any form of political life.[25] Although the Protestant mission churches suffered less than other religious groups from the rise of dictatorial politics, the church-state confrontations of the late 1960s and

1970s had the effect of identifying all forms of Christianity in the eyes of nationalist governments as at least potential sources of political opposition and instruments of neo-colonial dependence. When national unity was at a premium, external religious links became increasingly suspect.

b. *Marxist influence in Africa*

The period from 1966 onwards was also characterized by an increasing commitment in sub-Saharan Africa to socialist models of economic development and to Marxian ideological constructs. Julius Nyerere's Arusha Declaration of February 1967 launched Tanzania on a radical economic programme of rural 'Ujamaa' socialism, but it also marked Nyerere's assumption of Nkrumah's mantle as the recognized spokesman for black Africa and announced the coming of the second, more explicitly Marxist phase of the anti-colonial reaction in Africa.[26] Nyerere's brand of socialism was not markedly anti-Christian – on the contrary, it was influenced substantially by his own Catholic background – but developments elsewhere on the continent presaged the emergence of a more revolutionary strain of Marxism. In the Portuguese colonies of Angola, Mozambique and Guinea-Bissau liberation movements had arisen in the early 1960s which became more pronounced in their Marxist alignment as the struggle against Portuguese rule proceeded. In Angola one of the liberation movements, the FNLA, drew many of its leaders from the Baptist churches founded by the Baptist Missionary Society, but the victor in the civil war which grew out of the independence struggle, the MPLA, was primarily Marxist in orientation, and once independence had been achieved in 1975, increasingly dependent on Russian and Cuban backing against its rivals.[27] The first president of the FRELIMO liberation movement formed in Mozambique in 1962, Eduardo Mondlane, came from a Swiss Reformed missionary background, and met his American wife, Janet, at a Christian camp for young people in Wisconsin in the summer of 1951. By the 1960s, however, Mondlane's Christian faith had well-nigh evaporated under the impact of a strengthening conviction that socialism of the Marxist-Leninist variety offered the only hope for true liberation in Mozambique.[28] After Mondlane's assassination in 1969 the leadership of FRELIMO passed to a seemingly more doctrinaire Marxist, Samora Machel, who possessed none of Mondlane's residual respect for the churches and attacked the Catholic Church in particular as an instrument of Portuguese colonial oppression; it was only later that Machel emerged as a pragmatist ready to court Western favour.[29]

The leading historian of modern African Christianity, Adrian Hastings, makes the significant observation that the liberation movements of Portuguese Africa were, 'at the level of their leadership, bitterly critical of the part played by Christianity, Catholicism above all, in the history of colonialism. They had swallowed whole the simplest Marxist critique of the role of religion and admittedly in the Portuguese system that role had often seemed verified well enough.'[30] Church and state were as closely connected in Portugal's African colonies as they had been in the Hispanic empires established in South America in the sixteenth century. The plausibility of the Marxist case that Christianity in Africa was the tool of white colonial oppression, was further enhanced by the unsuccessful attempt of Ian Smith's Rhodesia to stave off black majority rule in the name of white Christian civilization, and by the continuing existence of an apartheid regime in South Africa which was openly buttressed by the ideological support of the Dutch Reformed Church. Between them, the differing colonial experiences of the Portuguese colonies and of the white settler republics of Rhodesia and South Africa fulfilled much the same role in determining the attitudes of the post-colonial African intelligentsia towards Christian missions as the Chinese example had played in Asia: although the relationships between the dominant churches and European supremacy in Portuguese Africa and the Republic of South Africa were far from typical of the experience of colonial Africa as a whole. It was very largely these relationships which provided the immediate legitimacy for a Marxist critique of Christian missions that gained widespread acceptance throughout the continent and beyond in the years after 1966.

To suggest that in Africa, as elsewhere, Marxian ideologies were adopted as the most appropriate vehicle for the expression of the nationalist reaction against colonialism, should not be taken to imply a facile conspiracy-theory view of modern Third World politics. There was no monolithic 'Communist plot' pulling the strings of the African puppet-theatre. Marxian political analysis was compelling because it provided plausible answers to the questions which the colonial legacy had posed. Why Christian missions had apparently played such a prominent part in the colonial process was one such question. Another of greater immediacy to most Third World leaders was the question of why the differential in terms of economic growth between the Western nations and their former colonies was maintained and even augmented in the post-colonial era. Issues of world economic development were firmly at the head of the political agenda in the aftermath of decolonization.

c. Dependency and neo-colonialism

In the immediate post-war period most thinking about the economic development of the tropical world had followed the confident assumptions of the Western liberal tradition. Non-Western societies were held to be backward and non-rational; they needed to be 'modernized' to discover the golden pathway towards economic growth which the Western nations had pioneered before them. Western societies had themselves progressed from a feudal, agrarian past through several stages of economic growth towards the point of industrial 'take-off', at which growth becomes self-generating. This view, conventionally labelled 'modernization theory', was most fully expressed by W. W. Rostow's *The Stages of Economic Growth*, published in 1960 and significantly sub-titled 'A Non-Communist Manifesto.'[31] Until the mid-1960s modernization theory retained its status as liberal economic orthodoxy, but it was a self-confident, comfortable theory for the West to adopt; as such it had little chance of surviving the turbulent decade of the 1960s intact.

Even in the 1950s, dissident economic voices had articulated pessimistic alternatives to modernization theory. Left-ward inclined economists such as Ragnar Nurkse, Gunnar Myrdal and Paul Baran had argued that underdeveloped countries were caught in a vicious circle of poverty, for which the capitalist West was largely responsible.[32] During the 1960s their arguments were amplified and extended into a range of alternatives to modernization theory, most of which can be described as variants of 'dependency theory'. The architects of dependency theory, many of them based in Latin America, held that the global economy was an integrated system operated by the capitalist powers in their own interests. By careful manipulation of the terms of international trade, the capitalist West has ensured that it has grown rich at the expense of the Third World. The poverty of the underdeveloped world is actually caused and continually reinforced by the growing affluence of the industrialized West. Although advocated by Marxist economists, dependency theory marked a radical departure from the teachings of Marx himself, who assumed that a society must reach the stage of industrialization before the revolutionary class – the industrial proletariat – could be formed, and the socialist revolution become a possibility.

Dependency theory found a close ally in the concept of 'neo-colonialism', developed by Marxist thinkers in the late 1950s to describe the alleged strategy whereby the Western nations were employing economic devices to maintain their former colonies in essentially the same dependent relationship as obtained during the era of formal colonial rule. Although coined by Soviet political scientists as a refinement of the Leninist theory of imperialism (see chapter 2), the concept of neo-colonialism soon acquired widespread currency among Third World nationalist leaders and Western commentators on Third World economic development. In Africa it was popularized chiefly by a book published in 1965 under the name of Kwame Nkrumah (though in reality not his own work): *Neo-colonialism: The Last Stage of Imperialism.*[33]

Dependency theory yoked to the concept of neo-colonialism formed a powerful ideological partnership which appeared to explain the continued impoverishment of the underdeveloped world. Since the late 1960s the arguments of dependency theory have been fiercely challenged – initially by pro-capitalist economists such as P. T. Bauer – and more recently by Marxist writers concerned to reinstate Marx's belief that capitalist development was indispensable if peasant societies were to be set on the road towards class formation.[34] The validity or otherwise of dependency theory is not our immediate concern. Its significance for our purposes is, firstly, that by providing a common theoretical approach to problems of economic development it helped to cement the ideological unity of the nations comprising the 'Third World' (itself a new term, coined in France in 1952, but only widely adopted during the 1960s). These were, of course, the countries to which Western missionary enterprise had been directed. More significantly still, dependency theory then created amongst the politically conscious groups in these countries (which naturally included the higher echelons of church leadership) a strong predisposition to view with grave suspicion any survival into the post-colonial era of close connections between Third World societies and Western funding, manpower and ideology. Traditional, 'Western' theology and ultimately Western missions themselves were too obviously symbols of continuing dependence on the influence of the neo-colonial powers to escape the reverberations of the new ideological mood.

d. The rise of Third World theologies

The fourth major development to have affected substantially perspectives on the missions and imperialism issue from the late 1960s onwards has been the emergence of indigenous African, Asian and Latin American theologies in self-conscious reaction against the hegemony of the Western intellectual tradition in theology: dependency was as unacceptable a reality in theology as in economics. The timetable of this theological reaction has been remarkably similar in all three continents.

In Africa the convening in 1965 of a consultation on biblical revelation and African beliefs at the University of Ibadan could be held to mark the genesis of 'African theology', a movement which has attempted to portray Christianity as standing in essential continuity with African traditional religion and culture.[35] It has been associated with such names as Bolaji Idowu and Harry Sawyerr in West Africa and John Mbiti in East Africa. Although African theology has been severely critical of Western missions for their repudiation of African religious ideas and cultural values, the movement can be plausibly interpreted as an extension of an existing liberal tradition of missionary thinking (represented by such writers as Edwin Smith and Geoffrey Parrinder) and a close parallel to simultaneous attempts by Western theologians such as John Hick to reformulate understandings of the relationship between Christianity and other religions.[36] More politically aggressive and racially polemical has been the variant of African theology known as 'black theology' which surfaced in South Africa in the early 1970s. Black theology was in fact even less indigenous to Africa than African theology, for the term and its theoretical framework were borrowed from the USA, where black theology was the theological counterpart to the secular Black Power movement which arose in 1966. James Cone, the most radical exponent of American black theology, was an indirect participant (by means of a taped address) in one of the first South African seminars on black theology held at Roodeport near Johannesburg in March 1971.[37] Nonetheless, the appeal of black theology in Africa has derived from its close identification with the reality of racial oppression in South Africa: it is a self-conscious theology of 'praxis' which takes the dehumanization and exploitation of the black population of South Africa as its starting-point. Black theology has been consistent in its unqualified condemnation of Western missionaries for having been in the vanguard of colonial oppression (the quotation with which this chapter began is a typical example). It has directed its most withering fire against the 'cultural imperialism' of white missionaries: missionaries brought to Africa 'a cold and cruel religion' which taught its converts to despise indigenous cultural values; missionary Christianity destroyed the psychological and cultural defences of the African and thus played an essential role in the ideological thrust of Western colonial aggression.[38]

1965 was also a land-mark in the emergence of Asian theology as a distinctive and autonomous theological movement. In that year M. M. Thomas, the Indian theologian whose writings in the 1950s and 1960s foreshadowed some of the themes of the new Third World theologies of the 1970s, delivered a series of lectures in Edinburgh and Glasgow on 'The Christian Response to the Asian Revolution.' Thomas believed that behind the current ferment of Asian nationalism lay a spiritual quest which Christianity alone could ultimately fulfil. The challenge confronting the Asian churches was to discover 'a new self-hood' and develop 'their own confessions to Christ in their own historical situations' so that the aspirations of Asian humanity might find their fulfilment in Christ.[39] The answer to Thomas' call was not slow in coming. 1965 also saw the appearance of the Japanese theologian Kazoh Kitamori's *Theology of the Pain of God*, which was a powerful restatement of Luther's 'theology of the Cross' from a specifically Asian perspective. Other Asian theologians followed in Kitamori's wake, developing a theological tradition focused on the themes of suffering, struggle and hope; by the 1980s its exponents – theologians such as Kosuke Koyama (a pupil of Kitamori's), Raymond Fung and Choan-Seng Song – had established themselves in the first rank of academic theologians.[40] Asian theology, as much as its African counterpart, professes to liberate Christian theology from its paralysing captivity to Western cultural norms, and associates the missionary movement with the history of colonial oppression in Asia.

Most significant and influential of all the Third World theologies is Latin American 'liberation theology'. Even more than African or Asian theology, liberation theology claims to be a 'theology of praxis', formed inductively from the realities of poverty and oppression rather than deductively from abstract theorizing. The roots of the new social radicalism in Latin American Catholicism can indeed be traced back to the mid-1950s, when Dom Helder Camara led a number of bishops and priests in the north-east of Brazil in responding to the extreme poverty of that region (and arguably also to the challenge to the church's influence posed by rural unionization and left-wing politics) by promoting radical programmes of change.[41] The formation of a coherent theology of liberation did not, however, take place until after 1965, when the Catholic Gustavo Gutiérrez and the Protestant Rubem Alves initiated the transposition into a theological key of the classic statements of the theme of liberation from colonialism by the popular Marxist theorists of the 1960s – the philosopher Herbert Marcuse and the psychiatrist Frantz Fanon, self-proclaimed champion of the victims of colonialism as 'the wretched of the earth'.[42] In 1968 the theology of liberation acquired semi-official status in the Latin American Catholic Church at the Second General Conference of Latin American bishops held at Medellín in Colombia; the documents of the conference were unequivocal in their condemnation of colonialism, neo-colonialism and multinational capitalism.[43] In its bitter opposition to colonialism, liberation theology was necessarily also adopting an antagonistic attitude to the history of Christian missions in Latin America, for in Latin America as nowhere else Christian missions had provided the unacceptable Christian face of European colonialism. In both Spanish and Portuguese America the Catholic Church had been almost completely subordinated to the power of the Crown and closely identified with the landowning elite throughout the colonial period. Liberation theology is, in part, an exercise in repentance and judgment, seeking the liberation of the church itself from its historical complicity in colonial and capitalist oppression.

With differences of emphasis and cultural perspective, the new indigenous theologies of Africa, Asia and Latin America all focus on the themes of liberating Christianity from its dependence on the 'cultural imperialism' of Western theology and from its compromising association with Western political expansion. These governing motifs of the Third World theologies derive from the wider political context of the reaction against all forms of colonial dependency and the accompanying surge of revolutionary Marxism in both the West and the Third World in the late 1960s. 1968 – the year in which liberation theology achieved its initial breakthrough in the Latin American Church – was also the heyday of radical student protest in the USA, France, Britain and elsewhere.[44] From such a perspective the historical missionary movement stood almost inevitably condemned. Even if not directly associated at a political level with the colonial power it had consistently disseminated a culturally alien theology and destroyed indigenous cultural values, leaving the colonized peoples with no ideological resources to resist the imposition of Western rule.[45]

e. *The ecumenical movement and the call for a 'missionary moratorium'*

The successful propagation and interpenetration of the new indigenous theologies owed a great deal to the role of the World Council of Churches as a global forum for theological exchange. The twentieth-century ecumenical movement was, of course, the historical offspring of the Protestant missionary movement initiated in the nineteenth century, and support for Western missionary activity was a major ecumenical preoccupation throughout the life of the International Missionary Council (1921–1961). Until the mid-1960s the controlling influences in the World Council of Churches (formed 1948) were Western Christians of liberal evangelical or neo-orthodox theological persuasion, and questions of Christian unity and mission generally took precedence over social and political concerns. Attitudes in the ecumenical movement to colonialism were mixed – the Commission of the Churches on International Affairs (formed in 1946) did not adopt an anti-colonialist stance until 1960 – and the New Delhi Assembly of the World Council in 1961 was still remarkably conciliatory towards the white churches of South Africa.[46] Between 1963 and 1968, however, a tangible shift in the centre of gravity of ecumenical interest took place. The older generation of ecumenical leadership passed away, to be replaced by more radical voices from the younger churches or by Western Christians who were active in the human rights movements of the 1960s.[47] Changes in personnel were reflected in changes in priority: the pursuit of structural unity between churches now took second place to relating the churches to the questions which the world was asking. The first significant public indication of the new orientation of the World Council was the 1966 Geneva Conference on Church and Society, convened to consider the appropriate Christian responses to 'the technical and social revolutions of our time'. Participants included the FRELIMO leader, Eduardo Mondlane, advocating a revolutionary alignment of the churches with 'a home-grown style of self-determination free of both colonialist rule and post-colonialist paternalism or exploitation'.[48] The Fourth Assembly of the World Council of Churches in Uppsala in 1968 set the seal on the radical re-orientation of the ecumenical movement towards the achievement of liberation and humanization in the world. In the words of the veteran ecumenist and former missionary, Norman Goodall, Uppsala 'signified much more than another shift of balance in the direction of a social gospel' – it was a theological re-evaluation of a more fundamental kind.[49]

The increasingly overt political alignment of the World Council, symbolized most controversially in the Programme to Combat Racism (instituted in 1969) and in the grants made from its Special Fund to liberation movements in southern Africa, attracted widespread criticism. Evangelicals deplored in particular the Council's apparent neglect of the evangelistic commission of the church and tendency to redefine mission in terms of salvation from this-worldly oppression.[50] Even ecumenical statesmen of an earlier generation such as Norman Goodall or the former WCC General Secretary, W. A. Visser't Hooft, expressed their reservations about the change of direction taken by the Council in the late 1960s.[51] The subsequent assemblies in Nairobi (1975) and Vancouver (1983) qualified but did not wholly reverse the trend set at Uppsala. The Vancouver assembly in particular was welcomed by a group of 200 evangelical delegates as marking a return to more biblical emphases by the WCC. However, other evangelicals, led by Professor Peter Beyerhaus of Tubingen, insisted that the post-Uppsala ecumenical leopard had not changed its spots.[52]

More relevant to our theme is the extent to which the radicalization of the World Council in the late 1960s and 1970s aligned the official ecumenical movement with the anti-colonial reaction and hence also with the anti-colonial case against the missionary movement. In his plea before the 1966 Geneva conference for 'self-determination' and freedom from 'post-colonialist paternalism', Eduardo Mondlane was giving typical expression to the Marxist understanding of neo-colonialism and articulating a plea for an end to ecclesiastical forms of international dependency. Attacks on missions intensified rather than weakened after decolonization, simply because they represented an obvious and uncomfortable expression of continuing Third World dependence on the West. The Christian parallel to the post-colonial propaganda battle against neo-colonial dependency was the campaign in the 1970s for a 'moratorium' on Western missionary activity.

The call for a moratorium on the sending of missionaries from the West to the Third World was first made explicit at a mission festival held at Milwaukee in the United States in 1971.[53] The originator of the call was a Kenyan Presbyterian with an evangelical background in the East African Revival movement, the Rev. John Gatu. Gatu began by asserting that the only way for the younger churches to liberate themselves from 'the bondage of western dependency' was for missionaries to be withdrawn for a period of at least five years, but subsequently amended his proposal to the suggestion that they should be 'withdrawn, period'. Gatu insisted in language surely derived from Panikkar's *Asia and Western Dominance* that it was time for the 'Vasco da Gama era' of the church to be brought to an end, time for the Third World churches to discover their 'selfhood'. Gatu's call, which had been made with primary reference to Africa, was given a more explicitly global connotation in January 1973 at the Bangkok conference on 'Salvation Today' organized by the World Council's Commission on World Mission and Evangelism. At Bangkok the call for a moratorium was integrated into the redefined theology of mission promulgated at Uppsala in 1968. The concept of a moratorium on both funds and personnel was now presented as the means of terminating the historical missionary movement, with its irredeemably colonialistic associations, in order to release resources for the liberating task of 'new mission'. The mood of Bangkok was summed up in the comment of Emilio Castro (shortly to become the director of the Commission on World Mission and Evangelism, and later WCC General Secretary) that 'the missionary era has ended and the era of world mission has just begun'. Castro, it must be said, insisted that the moratorium call in no sense represented an abandonment of the missionary mandate, but many delegates at Bangkok undoubtedly believed that the curtain had fallen on Western understandings of mission as evangelization.[54]

The campaign for a moratorium received a further impetus at the third assembly of the All Africa Conference of Churches at Lusaka in May 1974. Discussion of the issue was coloured by the assembly's support for liberation movements in neighbouring Rhodesia (Zimbabwe), and by recent events in the Portuguese colonies (notorious massacres perpetrated by Portuguese troops) and Portugal itself (the right-wing Caetano government fell in April 1974). It was surely no accident that the same assembly which denounced the agreements of 1940 and 1941 between Portugal and the Vatican regarding church-state relations in the Portuguese colonies for having turned Christian mission into 'an accomplice of a system which contributes to the [sic] cultural genocide', should also pass by an overwhelming majority the resolution:

> to enable the African Church to achieve the power of becoming a true instrument of liberating and reconciling the African people, as well as finding solutions to economic and social dependency, our option as a matter of policy has to be a Moratorium on external assistance in money and personnel. We recommend this option as the only potent means of becoming truly and authentically ourselves while remaining a respected and respons-ible part of the Universal Church.[55]

Hastings comments that few of the church leaders present at Lusaka can have seriously entertained a complete cessation of external support for their churches.[56] The call for a moratorium had become a rhetorical device for focusing the frustration of many African church leaders at the continuance of a massive missionary presence (and in particular a massive American missionary presence) into the post-colonial era. The subsequent history of the moratorium debate confirms that its significance was largely symbolic.

At the Lausanne Congress on World Evangelization in July 1974 pressure from John Gatu and other radical evangelicals ensured that the moratorium issue was debated, but the weight of conservative opinion in the Congress guaranteed that the 'Lausanne Covenant' made only a severely limited concession to the concept of a moratorium by acknowledging that 'a reduction of foreign missionaries and money in an evangelised country may sometimes be necessary to facilitate the national church's growth in self-reliance and to release resources for unevangelised areas'.[57] Within official ecumenical circles, the issue continued to be actively canvassed during the early months of 1975 – notably at a special consultation in Geneva in January 1975 – but the campaign appeared to run out of steam in the course of the year. Radicals must have been disappointed at the failure of the Fifth Assembly of the WCC at Nairobi in November-December to do more than urge the churches to study the reasons for and aspects of the moratorium call and recommend a temporary moratorium in situations of dependence which threatened 'the integrity of a church's witness in its own culture'.[58] The issue received little prominence at the 1980 Melbourne conference of the Commission on World Mission and Evangelism,[59] and the Vancouver Assembly of the WCC in 1983 appears to have ignored the issue altogether: the section of the Assembly's report entitled 'Witnessing in a divided world', though stating that the Western missionary era had often gone 'hand in hand with Western colonial expansion', was moderate in tone, having been revised to accommodate criticisms that it was originally too negative towards missionary work and insufficiently scriptural in approach.[60]

By 1983 the specific issue of a moratorium on Western missionary funds and personnel had blown itself out. Its significance for our subject lies in its role in further popularizing a simplistic interpretation of the relationship of the missionary movement to Western colonialism and in its adaptation of such an interpretation to accommodate the altered circumstances of the 'neo-colonial' era, in which the leading neo-colonial power, the USA, has also been the dominant force in Protestant world missions. More specifically, the debate focused attention on the concepts of the selfhood and authenticity of the younger churches, and thereby brought into new prominence recurrent questions about the interplay between Christianity and culture which will be discussed in chapter 7.

Propaganda and history in assessing the missionary movement

The combined effect of these five aspects of the anti-colonial reaction has been the establishment and widespread acceptance of a more systematic and sophisticated version of the old Chinese Communist accusation that the Western missionary movement was the ideological expression of the total imperialist aggression of the West. The pervasiveness of this view is evidenced by the fact that even a professed evangelical writer such as Orlando Costas can insist that the missionary movement was a product of the expansionist impulse of Western capitalism and hence functioned as an instrument of 'domestication' instead of the liberation which Christian mission ought to represent.[61] Most recent Christian discussion of the issue has been conducted by those who are not professional historians and has consequently paid comparatively little attention to specific historical examples. The period of the anti-colonial reaction has, however, happily also witnessed a remarkable spate of historical writing on the overseas missionary movement as a whole and on particular instances of the missionary-imperial relationship. The growth in critical historical study of the missionary movement was, indeed, to some extent a by-product of the reaction against the colonial past and against all narrowly 'Euro-centric' views of history.

Until the 1960s the majority of historical writing on Christian missions took the form of enthusiastic Christian biographies of missionary heroes or of encyclopedic official histories of the different missionary societies. Neither genre was well suited to answering the questions of critical historical interpretation which have been raised by the anti-colonial reaction. During the last three decades the previously meagre state of historical scholarship on the missionary movement has been transformed. The study of imperial and extra-European history has achieved an established and respected status in the history faculties of Western universities. A steady stream of doctoral theses and published monographs has issued from the rich archival resources of the missionary societies; and, especially in West and East Africa, Third World historians have begun to write missionary history from distinctively non-European perspectives. Some of the most respected of the new generation of non-European historians, such as the Nigerians J. F. A. Ajayi and E. A. Ayandele, have written in an empiricist historiographical tradition and have produced non-partisan and judicious assessments of the missionary role; more recently, however, Africanist historiography has taken an explicitly Marxist turn with the emergence of a school of historians, associated particularly with the University of Dar es Salaam, who have proclaimed the bankruptcy of the empirical method and advocate a 'materialist' perspective as the only way forward.[62] Although inevitably diverse in approach and quality, the new historiography has made possible a more detailed and informed appraisal of the connections of Protestant missions with British imperialism than could have been attempted in the 1960s.

The time is thus ripe for a survey and assessment of the theme of 'the Bible and the flag' founded on the evidence of history rather than the assertions of propaganda. The next chapter will discuss the shifting meanings of the terms 'imperialism' and 'colonialism', and will suggest that a moral evaluation of British colonialism may not be quite as straightforward an exercise as current orthodoxy tends to imply. Chapter 3 will attempt a brief survey of the origins and growth of the Protestant missionary movement, and discuss the extent of the correlation between its development and the rise and fall of colonialism. This discussion will be set in the context of the perspective on the world which British Christians in the nineteenth century came increasingly to share, a perspective which had far-reaching implications for imperial attitudes. The heart of the book, chapters 4, 5 and 6, presents a series of studies of the missionary-imperial relationship in three different periods of British imperial history. Chapter 7 discusses the conceptually distinct but supremely relevant issue of the interaction between Christianity and culture. The final chapter summarizes the conclusions of the book, and suggests for the benefit of Christian readers some provisional theological answers to the problems which this important subject poses for today.

CHAPTER TWO

What is imperialism?

The missionary movement stands accused of having been in consistent liaison with an unholy historical partner described interchangeably as imperialism or colonialism. The intention of this chapter is to submit this secular party in the relationship to closer examination. Current discussion of the missions and imperialism issue makes a number of historical assumptions about the nature of imperialism which ought not to be allowed to influence the tone of the debate until they have been carefully tested. It is presupposed, most fundamentally, that the term 'imperialism' has a readily identifiable meaning and that a confident appeal can be made to a clear consensus of opinion about what it was, and is. A second assumption discernible in contemporary discussion is that we may safely talk in terms of an imperial or colonial period in world history, commencing at some point variously located between the Spanish discovery of the New World in the early sixteenth century and the emergence of Britain as the first industrial nation at the beginning of the nineteenth century, and drawing to a close in the 1950s and 1960s. The third and most controversial assumption to merit closer scrutiny is the insistence that imperialism was and is inherently exploitative both in intention and in effect, and therefore deserves unequivocal moral censure. The first of these assumptions will be examined by means of a survey of the changing meaning of the word 'imperialism' and of the ongoing academic debate about the source and nature of imperialism. Although it will become clear that there is still profound disagreement on these issues, an attempt will then be made to identify some kind of scholarly consensus about how the British empire of the nineteenth and twentieth centuries came into being, how it worked, and why it came to an end. This provisional model of British imperialism will enable us to evaluate the second and third assumptions and will also shed further light on the first. The intricate and technical arguments of political and economic history which will be the concern of this chapter may strike some readers as unnecessarily complex and confusing, but they are an essential prerequisite to an informed understanding of the historical context of the British missionary movement.

Definitions

'Imperialism', writes Professor D. K. Fieldhouse, 'is an umbrella word', a slippery term which 'has meant all things to all men'.[1] Dictionary definitions of the word vary according to the date of compilation of the dictionary and the ideological sympathies of its compilers. The *Oxford English Dictionary*, published in 1933, significantly lists as the first meaning of 'imperialism': 'An imperial system of government; the rule of an emperor, especially when despotic or arbitrary.' The *Dictionary* admittedly goes on to present less archaic definitions of the word relating to the pursuit of global expansion in recent British or American politics, but noticeably absent is any concept of imperialism as a generalized tendency of advanced capitalist societies such as would be used by those of Marxist sympathies today. More helpful is W. L. Langer's definition of imperialism as 'the rule or control, political or economic, direct or indirect, of one state, nation or people over other similar groups, or perhaps one might better say the disposition, urge or striving to establish such rule or control'.[2] Langer's concluding emphasis on imperialism as an act of will by the expanding power is, however, one which much recent scholarship would dispute, and his definition would be more acceptable to some with its second half omitted. The essence of imperialism is control by an alien national or racial group; such control may be primarily political or primarily economic, and need not imply formal territorial rule; it may also be contrary to the original intentions of the imperial power, or only indirectly related to those intentions.

From the sixteenth to the mid-nineteenth centuries European imperialism most frequently took the form of colonization, the movement to establish white settler communities in the non-European world. In British history this process led to the growth of the 'first' British empire in North America and subsequently to the colonization of Australasia. The white settler colonies will not figure largely in this book, partly because they were only tangentially related to the mainstream of the missionary movement, and partly because the nations to which they gave rise are in the twentieth century cultural and ideological members of the Western bloc rather than of the Third World. The alternative (and largely subsequent) expression of imperialism known as 'colonialism' is distinguished from colonization by the fact that the alien dominant group remains non-resident in the imperialized territory. Colonialism, therefore, may be defined as that form of imperialism in which the imperial power imposes governmental control on a territory without resort to large-scale human settlement.[3] The distinction between colonization and colonialism cannot, however, be treated as an absolute one: there were territories annexed by Britain in the colonialist second phase of British imperial expansion – such as Kenya or Southern Rhodesia (Zimbabwe) – which became colonies of substantial European settlement not entirely dissimilar to the settler colonies of the first British empire.

Colonialism in most current scholarly usage is also characterized by the existence of formal territorial control: legal sovereignty has been ceded to or usurped by the imperial power. A third form of imperialism may therefore be identified, namely that of informal imperial control, in which the imperial power wields predominant influence in a territory without resort to either human settlement or formal political rule. This variant of imperialism is arguably as important as formal colonialism in the history of British expansion. It is also a prominent contemporary theme, since modern Marxist theory, as was explained in chapter 1, alleges the continuation of imperialism into the post-colonial period by the forces of 'neo-colonialism', among which the United States of America is reckoned to be chief.[4]

It is important that these distinctions should be clearly established at the outset of this chapter, even though the currency of imperialism and colonialism as virtually equivalent terms of Marxist propaganda renders such differentiation a largely academic exercise. An accurate assessment of the relationship of missions to the different forms of European expansion does demand greater precision in terminology than current popular usage will admit. It must also be conceded, and indeed emphasized, that the suggested meanings of the terms 'imperialism' and 'colonialism' cannot claim the support of consistent historical usage. For the duration of the nineteenth century 'colonialism' was the term applied to describe the network of increasingly informal ties binding Britain to the white settler colonies, and was not normally employed in relation to India or Africa. Not until the 1950s did the proposed meaning of colonialism as the formal governmental expression of imperialism become established in scholarly practice.[5] Far more tortuous, and more revealing, is the history of the changing meaning and interpretation of imperialism itself, to which we must now turn.

'Imperialism': its history and interpretation

The word 'imperialism' has undergone twelve distinct changes in meaning since its origins in the 1840s, according to a major study by R. Koebner and H. D. Schmidt.[6] The section which follows will identify only the main trends in the evolution of the concept. The term originated in the 1840s in France, where it denoted the desire to restore to France the glories of national greatness which were hers under the Emperor Napoleon Bonaparte. This revival of romantic nationalism was championed by Napoleon's nephew Louis Napoleon, who by the end of 1852 had styled himself as the Emperor Napoleon III. From 1852 to 1870, therefore, the term 'imperialism' signified to any Englishman, not his own country's overseas possessions, but a style of domestic politics in France characterized by militarism, bombast, and scant respect for constitutional liberties. As such, imperialism was a tendency to be deplored and scorned.[7] Imperialism remained a term of heavily negative connotations in Britain at least until the 1880 general election; between 1872 and 1880 it was used as a pejorative slogan to describe another quest for national glory and 'imperial' grandeur – Disraeli's policy of using Britain's overseas possessions, and above all India, to enhance British power and prestige in the world. Imperialism thus became linked with foreign and colonial rather than domestic policy, but it referred not to the possession of colonial territories as such but to a policy of national self-aggrandizement, military power and financial extravagance. Imperialism was the antithesis of Gladstonian liberalism.[8] It was not long, however, before distinctions began to be drawn between a false imperialism modelled on continental despotism and a true imperialism based on principles of morality, civilization and colonial self-government. This positive concept of imperialism gathered strength in the 1880s and early 1890s, when the term came to be used to describe the aspirations of those who wished to unite the white colonies in an imperial federation that would guarantee Britain's pre-eminence as a world power. Imperialism was being severed from its despotic connotations and proclaimed by some as the fulfilment of liberal idealism. In the 1895 general election campaign Lord Rosebery, one of the leading imperialist federationists, declared himself a 'liberal Imperialist' and defined his creed as follows:

> Liberal Imperialism implies, first, the maintenance of the Empire; secondly, the opening of new areas for our surplus population; thirdly, the suppression of the slave trade; fourthly, the development of missionary enterprise; and fifthly, the development of our commerce, which so often needs it.[9]

Rosebery's conjunction of humanitarian and economic imperatives was typical of the mounting imperial fervour of the 1890s. As imperialism became 'High Imperialism' it also became broader, incorporating enthusiasm for tropical Africa as well as India and the older imperial territories, and combining calculated national self-interest and lofty philanthropic idealism without awareness of incongruity. Ideas of trusteeship, nurtured by a century of evangelical missionary activity and theory, were the most important ideological ingredient in the new imperial recipe, although they were blended with cruder elements derived from Disraeli's rhetoric and theories of Anglo-Saxon racial superiority. By its peak in 1897–98 late Victorian 'High Imperialism' had divested itself of its lexicographical history to become a proud ideology of national idealism. Imperialism now meant, in the words of Kipling's famous poem of 1899, the willing assumption of 'the white Man's burden' to conquer and civilize 'the dark peoples of the world' for their own good.[10]

The second South African or Anglo-Boer War of 1899 to 1902 has often been seen as the high-water-mark of British imperialism. In public sentiment the war could be portrayed as a struggle between the mission of the British empire and the Boers (Afrikaners), the traditional enemies of humanitarianism in South Africa. Yet to many minds, including Christian minds, the war also revealed the ugly reality concealed by the moral vocabulary of imperialism: it was a war fought in defence of the private interests and ambitions of Cecil Rhodes and other capitalists. Even more significant than the effect of the war in bringing the concept of imperialism into renewed discredit was its contribution to the genesis of a theory of imperialism which would in time dominate twentieth-century thinking. The lure of Witwatersrand gold ensured that the nexus between imperialism and capitalism was more blatant in the case of British imperialism in South Africa than in any other instance of European expansion in the era of global partition from 1880 to 1900. The nature of the linkage became particularly clear to a radical journalist with the *Manchester Guardian*, J. A. Hobson, whose personal experience of the war convinced him that the sectional interests of parasitic capitalists were the 'economic taproot' of imperialism. Hobson's book, *Imperialism* (1902) explained imperialism as a device of capitalists for solving a fundamental malaise of industrial capitalism, which Hobson had diagnosed as early as 1889: the problem of under-consumption within capital in the British economy. According to Hobson, investment flowed abroad because of the lack of sufficiently profitable outlets at home. Imperial annexations took place when capitalists succeeded in persuading governments of the necessity of political intervention to safeguard their private investment interests in overseas territories. Hobson's theory of imperialism, which had primary reference to Britain, recognized that most of Britain's new tropical colonies were of only marginal importance to the nation's trade: they were economically necessary only to certain 'parasitic' capitalist elements.[11]

At the same time as Hobson was developing his theory of capitalist imperialism, a number of European socialist theorists were observing the increasingly militaristic and expansionist tone of European politics, above all in Germany, and drawing the conclusion that militaristic expansionism was a tendency inherent within capitalist societies. This conclusion was developed by the Austrian Marxist, Rudolf Hilferding, in his work *Das Finanzkapital* (1910), into a theory which interpreted imperialism as the political and ideological product of 'monopoly' or 'finance' capitalism. Hilferding followed Marx in believing that the tendency of capitalism was to concentrate ownership of the means of production in ever fewer hands, and argued that this process reached its end-point in the ownership of industrial enterprise by a small number of all-powerful bankers – the 'finance capitalists'. It was, according to Hilferding, the bankers, the monopoly men of the Western world, who were the motive power behind 'imperialism' – a concept which had as much reference to Europe as to the tropics.[12]

Hobson and Hilferding offered two similar but distinct versions of a theory of capitalist imperialism. In 1916 their arguments were conflated and taken up into the most famous and influential of all interpretations of imperialism, V. I. Lenin's *Imperialism the Highest Stage of Capitalism*. Lenin defined imperialism as the hall-mark of capitalism in its final, monopolistic stage:

> Imperialism is capitalism at that stage of development at which the dominance of monopolies and finance capital is established; in which the export of capital has acquired importance; in which the division of the world among the international trusts has begun, in which the division of all the territories of the globe among the bigger capitalist powers has been completed.[13]

Lenin believed that 'free competition' or 'pre-monopoly' capitalism attained its peak in the 1860s and 1870s, observed that 'it is *precisely after* that period that the tremendous "boom" in colonial conquests begins', and concluded that there could be no doubt that the transition of capitalism from its competitive to its monopolistic phase '*is connected* with the intensification of the struggle for the partitioning of the world'.[14] Nonetheless, Lenin insisted that monopoly capitalism in its fullness did not emerge until the turn of the century, subsequent to the partitioning of the tropical world. Lenin's primary interest was in the struggle between the capitalist powers to partition Europe, especially Eastern Europe, rather than in European possessions in the tropics. For Lenin, the supreme example of an 'imperialist' nation was not Britain or the USA, but Russia before the Revolution; the supreme manifestation of imperialism was not the partition of Africa but the First World War.[15]

Lenin's formulation of the theory of capitalist imperialism has been remembered with no more than selective accuracy. In the new configuration of European politics that resulted from the Bolshevik Revolution and the First World War, Lenin's location of the 'storm centre' of imperialism in Eastern Europe seems to have been largely forgotten, while his more speculative connection of late nineteenth-century colonialism with structural changes in capitalism became an increasingly dominant motif in European socialist thought, which was in any case more directly influenced by Hobson's version of the theory.

Between the World Wars 'imperialism' acquired a more exclusively tropical frame of reference in Western parlance than at any previous period in its history. Strict Marxist orthodoxy, however, continued to focus on the confrontation between capitalism and the proletarian revolution in Europe itself. It was the achievement of Mao-Tse-tung and the Chinese revolution to identify the Third World as the chief theatre of the battle against imperialism.[16] Mao, and in his wake Fidel Castro, Che Guevara and Frantz

Fanon, completed the growing equation of imperialism with Western colonialism in the Third World, thus ensuring that the theory of capitalist imperialism became the dominant orthodoxy for explaining the origins and objectives of Western colonial possessions. Grossly simplified versions of what is conventionally (but not wholly accurately) termed the 'Leninist' theory of economic imperialism have entered the currency of popular politics and opinion, especially in the developing world. According to this popularized orthodoxy, all forms of Western imperial expansion were the product of the capitalist pursuit of easy profits overseas, which was the brutal reality beneath the veneer of imperialist philanthropic sentiment. In collaborating with 'imperialism', therefore, Christian missions were promoting the exploitative designs of Western capitalism.

Was capitalism the source of imperialism?

Although the theory of capitalist imperialism has wielded such an immense influence on conventional understanding of imperialism, it can no longer claim many supporters amongst professional historians. Since 1945 the Marxist-Leninist view of imperialism has come under growing attack from a series of historians who have questioned each of its principal assumptions. It will be helpful to summarize the main features of their critique under four headings.

1. If imperialism was the consequence of the evolution of capitalism towards its final, monopolistic stage, in which large-scale financial interests sought to carve up the globe into units of monopolistic control, then such advanced 'finance' capitalism ought to have been an increasingly prominent feature of the nations involved in the colonial partition of 1880 to 1900. In fact, only two of the partitioning states – Germany and the USA – exhibited in 1900 the degree of economic control by large banking trusts which the model of 'finance capitalism' requires. Indeed, none of the other colonial states, with the possible exception of Belgium, conformed to the characteristics of finance capitalism by 1914, by which date capitalism was, according to Lenin, well into its final stage. Tropical imperialism cannot be convincingly related to structural changes in the capitalist economies.[17]

2. Many of the states prominent in late nineteenth-century imperial expansion, far from being advanced industrial economies with a surplus of capital for export, were either recently industrialized or at a very early stage of industrialization, and hence suffered from a shortage of capital rather than the reverse. This was true of Russia, Japan, Italy, and Portugal.[18]

3. The advanced industrial economies which *did* export capital in large quantities – chiefly Britain, France, Germany and the USA – exported remarkably little of their capital to the new tropical territories annexed

during the last two decades of the nineteenth century. Britain was the only one of these four powers to have invested substantially in her colonies by 1914, and the vast majority of this investment was not in the new tropical colonies but in Canada, Australia, New Zealand, India and South Africa. Beyond the boundaries of the British empire the United States and the Argentine were immensely more important as fields of British investment than any of the territories which were the object of late Victorian imperialism.[19] The marginality of Africa to the British economy at the end of the nineteenth century is shown by the fact that in the 1890s Britain did more trade with Belgium than with the whole of the African continent.[20]

4. There is no evidence that investment in new colonial possessions produced a higher return on capital than domestic investment. As far as British colonies are concerned, the reverse is true. The Imperial British East Africa Company, the chartered company which represented British economic imperialism in East Africa from 1888 to 1895, never paid out a penny of dividend to its investors. Cecil Rhodes's British South Africa Company, operating in a part of Africa which excited greater business enthusiasm than most, took years to return a profit. Even the Rand gold mines, the choicest of all Africa's economic pickings, produced during their first forty-five years of effective exploitation an estimated mean annual yield of capital of only 4.1%.[21]

These four findings of recent scholarship have reduced the classic formulations of the theory of capitalist imperialism to tatters. This is not to say that all attempts to explain imperialism primarily in terms of economic forces have been discredited. Some recent scholarship has made much of the distinction between economic aspirations and economic reality in analysing the partition of Africa in the 1880s and 1890s: Britain's new African territories may have turned out to be economic white elephants, but that fact should not be allowed to obscure the strength of their beckoning attraction for British businessmen harrassed by economic depression, stiffening competition from German, French and American industry, and the return of protective tariffs.[22] Even if this account of the partition of Africa eventually proves inadequate, there is still room for plausible broader theories of imperialism which accord ultimate primacy to national economic self-interest as the engine which drove the diverse forces of imperial expansion. It will become apparent in the next section that the concentration of so much scholarly argument about British imperialism on the reasons for the late Victorian scramble for colonies is beginning to appear as wasted effort, for it is seeking to explain only one manifestation, albeit the most dramatic, of British imperialism.

For our present purposes, the most important conclusions to be drawn from this aerial survey of the shifting meaning and interpretation of 'imperialism' are simply these:

1. Although there has been majority agreement throughout the history

of the term that imperialism is bad, there has been no historically consistent understanding about what it is.

2. The establishment in the twentieth century of a more stable meaning and interpretation of imperialism derives from the influence of a tendentious historical theory, now academically discredited.

3. Agreement on the causes and nature of European imperialism continues to elude professional historians, but all except the most partisan Marxists now accept that the simplistic attribution of imperialism to the conspiratorial designs of capitalist interests simply will not do.

The theory of capitalist imperialism has met the academic fate of all monocausal explanations of imperialism, and deserves to be buried once and for all. 'All theories to explain the growth of imperialism', said the late Jack Gallagher with characteristic wit, 'have been failures. Here and there on the mountain of truth lie the frozen bodies of theorists, some still clutching their ice-picks, others gripping their hammers and sickles. All perished; and most of them because they believed they could find some single cause or factor which could satisfactorily explain imperialism's efflorescence in the later nineteenth century.'[23] Christians, whose determination to scale the mountain of historical truth should be second to none, would do well to heed the warning of one of the canniest mountaineers of imperial historiography. The remainder of this chapter will endeavour to explain the rise and fall of the British empire with due regard for the complexities and crevasses which lie round every corner of the terrain.

A provisional model of British imperialism

Although academic debate about the nature of British imperialism continues to be fast and furious, sufficient common ground does now exist, at least among non-Marxist historians, to enable us to delineate the principal features of a provisional model of the workings of British imperial expansion in the nineteenth and twentieth centuries. The model will be presented in the form of a series of seven statements which would now command widespread but not universal scholarly consent.

1. The continuities in the aims of British imperial policy were more important than the discontinuities.

Until the 1950s the historiography of British imperialism posited a fundamental disjunction between the period up to 1870, which was said to be characterized by 'indifference to empire', and the period from 1870 to 1914 or beyond, which was defined as an era of 'high imperialism'. In 1953 this categorization was challenged by an article on 'The Imperialism of Free Trade' by two Cambridge historians, Ronald Robinson and Jack

Gallagher.[24] Robinson and Gallagher argued that the contrast between the two epochs of British imperial history was more apparent than real, and suggested that a single motto held true for British expansion throughout the nineteenth century: 'Trade with informal control if possible; trade with rule when necessary.'[25] The difference between the mid- and late-Victorian years was simply that in the latter the necessity to impose formal control became more frequent and more pressing. This thesis, which was developed in subsequent writings by the two historians,[26] has had to weather a formidable battery of academic gunfire, but it is probably fair to say that its central contention – that the new tropical empire of the post-1870 period reflected not so much a change in the aims of British expansion as a change in the conditions in which it operated – remains unvanquished. Later work by Gallagher in particular has extended the applicability of their motto to the whole colonial period up to 1950, so that by 1974 Gallagher could assert: 'The history of British imperialism between 1850 and 1950 can be summarized as a system predominantly of influence turning into a system predominantly of rule and then trying, unsuccessfully, to return to influence.'[27] Although very different from the Marxist view of imperialism, the 'Robinson and Gallagher thesis' ultimately explains the aims of British expansion in terms of economics: as 'the first industrial nation' and 'the workshop of the world', Britain needed secure access to sources of raw materials (especially cotton) and guaranteed markets for her products. For the first seventy years of the nineteenth century, in which Britain's economic pre-eminence was unchallenged, these objectives were secured with relative ease; in the late Victorian period Britain discovered that her position of global commercial supremacy was harder to defend than to acquire, and could be maintained only by increasing resort to methods of rule instead of methods of mere influence.

An enduring concern to protect British global economic interests dictated an equivalent continuity in Britain's strategic priorities. A recurrent theme in British imperial policy was the anxiety to forestall anticipated threats to British interests in a region, either by rival European powers or by disruptive political forces on the spot. After the abolition of the British slave trade in 1807, Britain's chief commercial interests lay increasingly in the Eastern rather than the Western hemisphere, and crucial to the defence of those Eastern interests was the developing British position in India. India was important to Britain, not initially for her own economic sake, but more as the centre of a web of British trading activity throughout the Asian seas.[28] India's importance also rapidly acquired a military dimension: the Indian army was employed as an 'imperial fire service', the means of damping down threatening conflagrations in the Far East, East Africa and the Middle East, and in the twentieth century was an indispensable element in Britain's military strategy during the two World Wars.[29] The defence of India thus became a prime strategic objective in its own right, a priority which in time had far-reaching 'knock-on' effects in terms of British policy in Africa and the Middle East.

A third element of continuity in British imperial strategy, less potent and less consistent than the other two but still significant, must now be mentioned. Commitment to humanitarian objectives was always a powerful current in British public opinion on imperial questions and was not infrequently a principle shared by individuals within government. The potential leverage of humanitarian opinion, which was often represented to government by the missionary societies, increased as the parliamentary franchise broadened. Although benevolent considerations were rarely, if ever, decisive on their own for British policy making, the strength of the humanitarian lobby was a dimension to imperial questions which no government could afford to ignore. Humanitarian objectives for the empire were made up of three inter-woven strands. The most politically influential was the anti-slavery imperative, which not only achieved the signal victories of slave trade abolition in 1807 and West Indian emancipation in 1833, but also shaped British policy in West and East Africa for most of the nineteenth century. The campaign against the slave trade soon redirected its focus from the West Indies and the Atlantic passage to the source of the trade in Africa itself, with the inevitable corollary of escalating British involvement in the continent.[30] A second strand was concern for 'native' interests, particularly in colonies of substantial European settlement, such as the Cape Colony or New Zealand in the nineteenth century or Kenya in the twentieth. Although missionary endeavours to protect native interests against white settler power were only moderately successful, humanitarian pressure did ensure that the Colonial Office acted as a broker striking bargains between the mutually contradictory demands of the missionary and settler lobbies.[31] The third strand within humanitarian thinking was the concern of both Anglican and Nonconformist opinion to see fair play for Protestant missionary activity within the empire. Although Nonconformists were committed by their principles to refusing direct government aid or protection for their missions, Nonconformists as much as Anglicans protested and agitated whenever government attempted to curtail freedom of missionary action or appeared to encourage Roman Catholic or non-Christian systems in competition with the gospel. Subsequent chapters will return to this theme at greater length.

In all three spheres, economic, strategic and humanitarian, the continuities of theme in British imperial policy between 1800 and 1950 were ultimately of greater weight than the admitted discontinuities. All three spheres, however, intersected with a fourth sphere of continuity, which will be discussed in section 6 below, but must be mentioned at this point: the consistent fiscal objective of British imperial policy was that the empire should impose the minimum of burden on the domestic tax-payer, and hence should as far as possible be self-financing. This goal operated as a constant restraint on all other lines of policy, and was in the long run decisive in determining the future of the empire.

2. There was no direct correlation between British economic expansion and British territorial control.

One of the most significant emphases of the Robinson and Gallagher approach to British imperial history was its high-lighting of the 'remarkable asymmetry' between the two patterns of economic and territorial expansion in the nineteenth century.[32] For a century after the American Revolution of 1776 the boundaries of British formal empire in the white colonies progressively contracted, as the ideal of responsible self-government for these colonies came to fulfilment. At the same time, however, these territories saw a steady expansion in British commerce and investment. Roughly the reverse was true in Asia and later in Africa: the boundaries of formal control were pushed ever outwards, but relatively little trade or investment either preceded the British flag or followed it. To what extent India constitutes a weighty exception to this generalization remains a bone of contention: Robinson insists that its economic significance was a product and not a cause of its annexation, but it is tempting to see some connection between the 'free trade imperialism' of Manchester cotton interests in the mid-nineteenth century and the formidable series of British annexations in India between 1843 and 1856.[33] In Africa, however, the asymmetry is undeniable. Britain acquired her tropical African empire at a time when its economic value was minimal, and abandoned it in the wake of the first concerted effort to drive the African economy hard in British interests. The 1940s and 1950s saw European settlement and investment pour into Africa on a quite unprecedented scale, yet this 'second colonial occupation' was the immediate prelude to decolonization.[34] No simple relationship can be established between British imperial annexations and the desire to extend British economic interests into new areas of the globe.

3. British formal control was less a reflection of strength than an acknowledgment of failure or weakness.

The reasons for the multifarious British annexations of tropical territories in the nineteenth century can only be understood by reference to the consistent aims of British world policy described above. In the economic sphere, the imposition of formal control was usually a reflection of the collapse of informal techniques of preserving freedom for existing British commercial activity. European trade often undermined indigenous political structures, precipitating crises of political order that could be resolved only by the establishment of formal colonial rule. In some cases the nature of the threat posed by these crises to British interests was primarily economic, but it has been cogently argued by Professor Fieldhouse that such break-downs engendered by commercial activity led to annexation only when they raised some broader political or strategic problem: even economic problems had to be 'politicised' before they led to formal empire.[35] In the sphere of wider strategic objectives, British annexations took place when Britain's European rivals *appeared* to be about to establish monopolistic control over tropical territories: Britain acted to pre-empt anticipated expansion by other powers which threatened British strategic interests or implied the bolting of the door to British business. This was very largely the story of the European partition of Africa initiated in the 1880s. Neither Gladstone nor Bismarck wanted African colonies, 'but neither of them knew the other did not want them'.[36] There was little evidence that tropical Africa had much to offer the businessman, but in an age of fierce industrial competition and protective tariffs it was too risky to permit a European rival to peg out a claim for potential future rewards.[37] A similar argument relating British annexations to relative British weakness can be constructed in the sphere of humanitarian objectives. Where these played a part in the decision to establish formal control, such action reflected the failure of earlier British efforts to eliminate slave trading activity or secure native interests by less formal and expensive means. Because formal rule was invariably more expensive than informal influence, colonialism 'was not a preference but a last resort'.[38] The massive expansion of the British empire at the close of the nineteenth century indicated, not the growth of British world power, but its waning.[39]

4. The growth of the British empire was apparently random but reflected an underlying unity of purpose.

Sir J. R. Seeley's Cambridge lectures on 'The Expansion of England', published in 1883, contained the famous statement: 'We seem, as it were, to have conquered and peopled half the world in a fit of absence of mind.'[40] Seeley was referring to British expansion in the eighteenth century, but his remark seemed even more relevant to his own day. The characterization of British imperialism as 'reluctant', although interpreted by Marxist historians as a cynical rationalization of the lust for power and profit, did in fact frequently correspond to political reality. Gladstone's second ministry of 1880–85, returned to power on a platform of opposition to Disraeli's 'imperialism', played a greater part in the creation of Britain's African empire than any other Victorian government. The British occupation of Egypt in 1882, according to Robinson and Gallagher the spark that ignited the conflagration of African partition, seemed to fly in the face of all the high moral principles of Gladstonian liberalism.[41] It was no wonder that the *Manchester Guardian* drew the conclusion in April 1884 that 'the conquests which we make are forced upon us'.[42] This theme has immense significance for Christian attitudes to the empire, as we shall see in the next chapter, but it is sufficient at this point to emphasize that the empire grew by a series of unpremeditated and apparently random responses to particular crises of stability in Asia, Africa and the Pacific. The haphazard nature of European colonial expansion in the late nineteenth century is so marked that Professor Fieldhouse can even insist that 'colonialism was not a rational or planned condition' but 'rather the product of a unique set of circumstances before and during the later nineteenth century that resulted unpredictably in the formal partition of much of the world between the great powers'.[43] However, to imply, as Fieldhouse does, that late nineteenth-century colonialism simply 'happened' because of a 'general crisis' in the relations between Europe and the underdeveloped world, comes perilously close to abandoning any attempt at explanation.[44] Behind and beneath the randomness of British colonial expansion in the nineteenth century were the consistent principles of global policy outlined in section 1 above. It was, strictly speaking, British colonialism which was reluctant; British imperialism, in the sense of a determination to maintain and extend Britain's strategic and commercial pre-eminence in the world, was not. The Victorians discerned purpose as well as randomness in the growth of their empire, and historians ought to do the same.

5. The existence of an 'ideology of empire' cannot explain the growth of the British empire, but it significantly affected the conduct of the empire.

The emphasis of recent scholarship on the fortuitousness of late Victorian expansion would seem to imply the fundamental irrelevance of ideology to the process of annexation. 'People do not become imperialists as a matter of ideology', asserted Gallagher; 'they do so as a matter of necessity'.[45] If colonial rule was, in Fieldhouse's words, 'a complex improvization', then it appears logical to conclude that 'an ideology of empire was evolved to justify what it was found necessary to do'.[46] It is certainly true that popular imperialism, in the sense of a general hunger for new colonial acquisitions, was both a late development and, in its crudest 'jingoistic' form, a relatively short-lived one. There is little evidence of popular imperialism in this sense in Britain before 1894, more than a decade after the scramble for Africa had begun, and by 1903 enthusiasm for new colonies was on the wane.[47] Nevertheless, popular imperialism was an increasingly powerful reality in Britain in the half-century that followed the scramble for Africa. Study of the vehicles of popular culture – such as the cinema, the radio, school textbooks and juvenile literature – suggests that popular devotion to the ideals, symbols and heroes of 'Empire' reached its peak as late as the 1920s.[48] British missionaries from the 1880s through to the 1950s were undoubtedly moulded by a public mood that accorded the values and institutions of the British empire a high degree of respect.

Equal stress needs to be given to the weakness in Britain of any tradition of principled opposition to imperial possessions. Richard Cobden, leader of the 'Manchester school' of free traders in the mid-nineteenth century, firmly believed that the British attempt to rule India was impracticable and contrary to God's 'visible natural laws', yet by the 1860s his opposition to all colonial possessions was shared by few even of his own supporters. Many of them were Nonconformists, whose attitudes to imperial matters began to correspond more closely to those of W. E. Gladstone.[49] Gladstone abominated Disraeli's 'imperialism' of national self-aggrandizement, but himself subscribed to an elevated moral conception of the empire as a sacred trust. Gladstonian Liberalism was anti-imperialist but not anti-imperial, a tradition that was inherited by the Radical critics of empire in the period between 1900 and 1914: they wanted to reform the British empire, not dismantle it. The tradition was carried on after the First World War by the Labour Party, which stood for imperial retrenchment but never adopted a moral opposition to empire as party policy. It was, after all, a Labour Government which after 1945 made the last big push for the economic development of Africa in the interests of the British economy.[50]

Mid-way between the two poles of the crude but sporadic jingoism which wanted empire for empire's sake and the extremely weak opposition to the principle of empire, thus lay a sizeable and influential body of British opinion which may be termed imperial idealism. It conceived of the existence of the empire as a national responsibility or mission, and insisted that colonial rule was to be exercised in a moral fashion for the benefit of the subject peoples. Imperial idealists believed that a moral and benevolent empire was in fact the only one which would benefit Britain and endure, at least till its work was done. Duty and self-interest were ultimately as one.[51] This 'trusteeship' concept of empire, whose origins and nature will be discussed more fully in the next chapter, was an ever-present theme in British imperial history, ensuring that the essentially self-interested orientation of the empire as a system was continually qualified and softened by philanthropic and paternalistic imperatives. There were undeniable elements of rationalization concealed within the ideology of imperial idealism, but it was far more than pure rationalization – it was a potent ideology, affecting both metropolitan policy-making and its implementation in the colonial territories.

6. The empire was worthwhile only if it could be had on the cheap.

Reference has already been made to the consistent objective of British imperial policy that the empire should be run at the minimum of cost to the domestic tax-payer. The financial resources for the maintenance of the empire were to be drawn as far as possible either from within the colonized territories or from independent agencies. To this end the revenues of India were maximized in order to finance both the administration of India itself and the wider role of the Indian army in the preservation of British interests throughout the East.[52] For the same reason Britain in Africa initially resorted to devices of formal 'paper' partition designed to secure British interests in a territory without incurring the costs of full colonial administration: the concept of a 'protectorate' denoted a primarily negative sphere of influence, intended to exclude other powers from interference, without saddling Britain with the burden of yet another colony; chartered commercial companies were also used as convenient means of maintaining British paramountcy by proxy.[53] Neither device was ultimately successful: with the passage of time protectorates grew more and more like colonies; whilst the frequently irresponsible activities of chartered companies led inexorably to direct governmental control in either the short or the long term. More successful, and of primary relevance to our subject, was the policy of employing Christian missions to 'service' the structure of colonial rule by the provision of medicine and supremely of education. Mission hospitals and schools enabled British colonialism to satisfy humanitarian obligations at minimum cost, and placed a premium on the maintenance of a co-operative relationship between the missionary societies and the Colonial Office. The final implication of the concern to minimize the costs of empire was the dependence of colonial rule on existing networks of indigenous rulers, known as 'collaborators' in scholarly parlance. Because large political units comparable to European nation-states were extremely rare, the collaborators were usually local, small-scale traditional rulers of generally conservative inclination: the maintenance of their authority and the continuance of their co-operation were essential to the stability of the empire. The degree of dependence on indigenous authorities varied – from the system of 'Indirect Rule' typified by northern Nigeria under Lord Lugard, where African political structures were maintained to the maximum extent – to the Indian pattern of 'Direct Rule' by a European civil service. The distinction was, however, one of degree and not of substance: in India, as much as in Nigeria, British colonial rule depended on a small number of Europeans eliciting and sustaining the co-operation of a much larger number of indigenous authorities. If control was to be cheap, it was necessarily fragile.[54]

7. *The empire contained the seeds of its own destruction.*

Because formal colonial rule was always a last resort, and because it had to be cheap, minimum intervention in a newly annexed territory was almost invariably the initial goal of British administration. The central contradiction of British colonialism was the seemingly inescapable process whereby this goal was progressively undermined as Britain was sucked into the vortex of deeper and deeper involvement in her colonies.[55] It has already been observed that devices of paper partition or 'imperialism by proxy' were of strictly limited success – notional responsibilities had a disconcerting habit of evolving into real ones. A disturbing paradox was also raised by the primacy of fiscal considerations. If revenue was to be raised from within the colonies by taxation, administrative machinery was required to collect it. The greater the revenue required, the more elaborate the machinery had to be, and the greater the risk of social unrest, necessitating higher expenditure on police and other mechanisms of control. In the long term, therefore, the effect of the constant pressure for immediate revenue was an escalation in both the risks and the costs of colonial rule. Financial stringency was the chief reason for the growing weight of British intervention in late nineteenth-century India. In mid-twentieth-century Africa the same effect was achieved by the attempt to develop the continent's mineral and agricultural resources in order to rescue Britain's ailing war-time and post-war economy.[56] Throughout the tropical empire the prescription of minimum involvement was further diluted by the solvent of humanitarian and idealist principles. As more and more of those who ruled and administered the empire came to accept that imperial rule could be justified only in terms of its contribution to social reform, educational progress and the advance of Christianity, the diffusion of Christian, liberal and democratic values became an increasingly prominent goal. The professed British commitment to prepare all her colonial possessions for eventual representative self-government (along the same lines as the white colonies in the nineteenth century) implied the grooming for power of a new educated elite capable of exercising political leadership on a 'national' scale according to Western democratic ideals.[57]

It was this unplanned but relentless progression from minimum to maximum involvement which eventually destroyed the delicate equilibrium of British colonial rule. The small-scale traditional collaborators lost their hold on their popular base to the new urban and educated elites produced by mission and government schools. These new political leaders were propelled by the increasingly heavy hand of colonial intervention in their societies into operating on a larger political scale than the old traditional rulers. Education and urbanization brought local spokesmen together, and indigenous politics moved, in Gallagher's phrase, from locality to province to nation.[58] The 'nationalists' (for so they had become) were able to exploit the fiscal and economic grievances inflicted by interventionist colonial policies to call the bluff of imperial idealism, and demand national independence as an immediate goal rather than a long-term profession.

This process first came to a head in India in the 1940s. By 1945 Britain was committed to bringing India to speedy independence after the war, but until 1947 the plan was for a kind of United States of South Asia which would preserve British paramountcy and a role for the Indian army in defending British interests throughout the East. These hopes dissolved into thin air with the partition of the sub-continent into India and Pakistan. In retrospect it is easy to see Indian independence in 1947 as the beginning of the end of the British empire, but at the time the Attlee Government thought very differently: a revitalized Africa was being prepared to take India's place.[59] What Britain failed to foresee was that her tardy embarkation on a programme of full-blooded imperial intervention in Africa would have precisely the same effect as it had a generation earlier in India: the combination of economic exploitation, Western education and Christian idealism proved just the right mixture to bring the developing embryo of nationalist politics to birth. African nationalism raised the hazards and costs of colonial rule to the point where they surpassed its usefulness to a British global system of influence that was now but a shadow of its former self. When that point was reached, in the late 1950s, the dignified British exodus from West Africa (planned as early as 1951) was extended with unseemly haste to East and Central Africa, areas which had been assumed to be decades away from the political maturity appropriate to independence.[60] The empire had reaped what it had sown. The imperial idealists could still claim with some plausibility that its great work had been done: new nations had been born and sent on their way with democratic constitutions and flourishing Christian traditions. Not until the post-colonial era would some aspects, at least, of that idealism prove to have been misplaced.

An evaluation of British imperialism

Our model of the rise and fall of the British empire has been necessarily simplified and generalized, but it will serve to set the more detailed analyses of missionary-imperial relationships in subsequent chapters in context. In conclusion, we must return to the three assumptions about imperialism with which this chapter opened.

The first half of the chapter has sought to demonstrate that 'imperialism' is a problematic concept, whose meaning has rarely been stable or crystal clear since its origins in the 1840s. It may be objected that the semantic debate about the term 'imperialism' is irrelevant to the historical fact of aggressive Western expansion, which is the reality with which both Christian missions and the colonized peoples have had to deal. The semantic history of the concept of imperialism is certainly of lesser importance than the history of what actually happened in European expansion, but it is not unimportant. Current understandings of what imperialism is have been shaped as much by theory as by practice, and the continued existence of competing theories of imperialism is sure evidence that the 'facts' of imperial history are too complex to allow any one monolithic interpretation to gain universal academic acceptance. Argument about the meaning of imperialism has reflected argument about its interpretation, and argument about its interpretation has reflected argument about its practice. It is imperative that evaluation of its practice should eschew the facile generalizations of propaganda, and recognize the extraordinary complexity of the phenomenon which produced the subjugation of so much of the globe to the European powers in the nineteenth and twentieth centuries.

The second common assumption identified at the beginning of the chapter – that the period from the sixteenth to the twentieth centuries, or possibly from the eighteenth to the twentieth centuries (there is considerable imprecision about when it began), may be characterized as the 'colonial' period in world history – cannot be addressed directly in a book which is concerned almost exclusively with British imperial history. It ought, however, to be stressed in passing that the assumption is highly questionable. On the one hand, it must be said that Western European enthusiasm for the acquisition of colonies has been extremely intermittent in modern history, and most European expansion in Asia was a weak and tentative affair until the eighteenth century. In comparison with the great empires of the Moghuls in India or the Ch'ing dynasty in China, European power was genuinely insignificant until the European industrial revolutions began to swing the balance in favour of the West. It should also be pointed out that the conventional assumption that the colonial era came to an end in the 1960s is equally questionable: the vast Russian empire in Asia, built up from the fifteenth century onwards and inherited by the Soviet Union at the end of the Tsarist era, remains intact, although not without its problems caused by the stirrings of nationalist feeling. The truth of the matter is that there have been imperial states in all periods of history; what distinguished the nineteenth and twentieth centuries was that Asian and African empires were increasingly replaced by European ones, as the West established an undisputed lead in terms of economic and military power. It is historically accurate to describe the period from the eighteenth century onwards as one of European expansion, and from the mid-nineteenth century we may fairly speak of European pre-eminence. Within this framework, it is perfectly valid to characterize British history from about 1750 to 1950 as a period of British expansion and cumulative global power, provided it is recognized that both before and after 1870 this expansion was not necessarily colonial in intent and nature. The increasing British resort to formal colonial rule after 1870 was in fact an indication that British power was already in decline.

The third and final assumption – that imperialism was and is inherently exploitative both in intention and in effect – defies a simple answer even more obstinately than the other two. The British empire, no less than any other empire, was the product of the pursuit of national self-interest, whether directly economic or strategic. British colonies were intended to be run on the cheap, and were expected to yield economic or strategic rewards which more than compensated for the expense of their administration:

whether, in actuality, the rewards of empire outweighed the costs remains a matter of some contention.[61] Nonetheless, in terms of policy objectives, the equation between empire and exploitation appears an entirely reasonable one. Our model of the workings of the British empire has, however, suggested three very substantial qualifications which need to be added to the equation.

In the first place, the role of economic motivation in the acquisition of colonial possessions was almost invariably indirect rather than direct: Britain annexed territories not because she wanted new sources of profit but because she appeared to have no alternative if her existing network of interests (interests which were, in the final analysis, economic) were to be maintained.

Secondly, it has been argued that British colonialism was uneven in both the depth and the nature of its impact on the colonized societies. The original British aim of minimal intervention could mean abandonment of a territory to the exploitative whims of a commercial company, or it could mean the virtual maintenance of the *status quo* of an underdeveloped agrarian economy. With the passing of time, the progressively deeper involvement of colonial rule in the host economies brought greater injuries for some and greater benefits for others. Sooner or later, the British integrated their possessions into the global economy, and hence introduced them to the rewards and perils of dependence on the world market.[62] Although Britain consistently operated the engine of economic modernization in her own interests, it is surely romantic nostalgia to insist that the pre-colonial subsistence economies offered a higher standard of living for the majority of the population than the modernizing economies of the colonial era.

The third and most fundamental qualification of the equation of British imperialism with exploitation relates to the prominence of humanitarian idealism in the vocabulary and self-consciousness of the British empire. The concept of empire as a sacred trust was shared even by many of the politicians whose imperial policies appeared to reflect the priority of national interest, and the pressure of missionaries and Christian public opinion ensured that such profession was more than empty homage. In the long term, the commitment of many imperialists to refashion colonial societies by the diffusion of Christianity and Western education did much to bring about the substitution of nationalist for traditional politics. Cultural imperialism, the most hated of all forms of imperialism, in fact did more than any other to bring the empire to an end.

Even if we leave out of account the contribution of the empire to the spread of the Christian gospel, it should by now be apparent that neither unequivocal moral censure nor unqualified praise can do justice to the tangled web of exploitation and service which was the British empire. If we are forced to choose between an ultimately negative and an ultimately positive evaluation, the choice is likely to be determined by the answers we give to fundamental questions about the validity and purpose of the structures of human political and economic power. For the Christian, these questions become theological ones, and we shall return to them in the final chapter.

CHAPTER THREE

The gospel for the globe

1. The missionary awakening in Britain

Until the 1790s the concern of British Protestants for the spiritual condition of the non-European world was sporadic and geographically limited. What missionary interest there was focused on the North American colonies or on India, which were the only areas of substantial British penetration until the end of the eighteenth century. The Puritan settlement of New England in the mid-seventeenth century resulted in some evangelistic work amongst the North American Indians, a sphere of activity which contained the seeds of a much broader missionary awareness among both British and American Christians. The diary of David Brainerd, appointed to work amongst the Indians by the Scottish Society for the Propagation of Christian Knowledge (founded in 1710), became a classic of Protestant literature which made a deep impression on men such as John Wesley, William Carey and Henry Martyn. The revival of Anglican piety at the close of the seventeenth century bore fruit in the formation of two societies dedicated to the diffusion of Christianity at home or overseas. The Society for Promoting Christian Knowledge (1699) included missionary concern for the American planta-tions in its original objects, and in 1728 assumed responsibility for the mission founded by Danish pietists at Tranquebar in South India. The Society for the Propagation of the Gospel in Foreign Parts (1701) was commissioned by the terms of its royal charter to provide Anglican clergy for British subjects settled in 'our Plantacons (*sic*), Colonies and Factories beyond the Seas', but also to make such other provision as might be necessary 'for the Propagation of the Gospel in those parts'.[1] In practice, however, the role of the Society was confined to the provision of colonial clergy until it took over the Indian missions of the SPCK in 1825. Neither the Church of England nor English Dissent in the eighteenth century was so absolutely indifferent to overseas concerns as is frequently imagined. Isaac Watts's explicitly universal hymn, 'Jesus shall reign where'er the sun', was published as early as 1719, and Philip Doddridge's evangelistic concern had a distinctly global flavour.[2] Nevertheless, in the period before the Evangel-ical Revival there was no consistent acceptance of the missionary obligation by either Anglicanism or Dissent.

The missionary awakening in Britain is conventionally dated from the publication in 1792 of William Carey's *An Enquiry into the Obligations of Christians, to Use Means for the Conversion of the Heathens*, and the consequent formation of the 'Particular-Baptist Society for Propagating the Gospel among the Heathen' (the Baptist Missionary Society) at Kettering in October 1792. Carey's initiative was significant because it led to the formation of the first of the evangelical missionary societies, but his was not the only voice calling for missionary action. John Wesley's lieutenant, Dr Thomas Coke, had published his *Plan of the Society for the Establishment of Missions among the Heathens* as early as 1783, and had issued a further appeal for Methodist missionary organization in 1786. Between Christmas 1786 and February 1787 Coke planted the first Methodist missionaries in the West Indies; by 1793 Methodist membership in the islands had grown to 6,570.[3] However, financial support of the Methodist missions was almost entirely dependent on Coke's personal fund-raising efforts, and no formal structure of Methodist missionary organization existed until 1813, when the Leeds District of Methodist societies formed the first Wesleyan Methodist Missionary Society. Other districts followed the Leeds example, and the various district missionary societies were united in the national Wesleyan Methodist Missionary Society in 1818.[4]

At the same time as Baptists and Methodists in England were being awakened to missionary responsibility, appeals for missionary endeavour were issuing from English clergy working as chaplains in India or Sierra Leone. In 1787 the East India Company chaplain David Brown and the leading Company official Charles Grant issued *A Proposal for Establishing a Protestant Mission in Bengal and Bihar*, and sent copies home from Calcutta to leading churchmen and evangelicals in Britain.[5] Melvill Horne, one of the first two chaplains employed by the Sierra Leone Company in its colony for emancipated Negro slaves at Freetown, wrote, during his stay in Sierra Leone, a series of letters urging the missionary obligation on the Protestant ministers of the British churches. Horne's *Letters on Missions*, published in 1784, appealed to 'liberal Churchmen and conscientious Dissenters, pious Calvinists and pious Arminians' to 'embrace with fraternal arms' and join in promoting an interdenominational missionary society.[6] Horne's book was warmly reviewed by Thomas Haweis, former chaplain to the Countess of Huntingdon, in the *Evangelical Magazine* for November 1794, and his vision of a truly ecumenical evangelical missionary society was the most important of a number of influences which contributed to the formation of the London Missionary Society in September 1795.[7] The London Missionary Society (LMS), originally entitled simply 'The Missionary Society', professed to unite churchmen and dissenters, Calvinists and Arminians, Baptists and paedobaptists, but gradually lost its ecumenical comprehensiveness; by the 1820s it had assumed its historical identity as the missionary organ of the

Congregational denomination. Even in its earliest years, the LMS failed to attract the support of significant numbers of the Evangelical Anglican clergy. From 1799 Evangelical Anglicans had their own society, the 'Society for Missions to Africa and the East', known from 1812 onwards as the Church Missionary Society (CMS). The CMS owed its origins to a series of discussions in the Eclectic Society, formed by a group of Evangelical clergy and laymen in 1783. At meetings held in 1786, 1789 and 1791 the Society discussed what would be the best method of propagating the gospel in Botany Bay (newly designated by the British government as a penal settlement), the East Indies (*i.e.* India) and Africa respectively. In 1796 Charles Simeon raised the more specific question 'With what propriety, and in what mode, can a Mission be attempted to the Heathen from the Established Church?', but received only a hesitant response. Finally, in 1799 John Venn, Rector of Clapham, introduced the topic which led directly to the formation of the CMS: 'What methods can we use more effectually to promote the knowledge of the Gospel among the Heathen?'[8]

The missionary awakening in England found more than an echo north of the border. In February 1796 the Glasgow Missionary Society was founded, shortly followed by the Scottish Missionary Society, founded in Edinburgh, and by a number of local missionary societies throughout Scotland, most of which initially sent their contributions to the LMS in London.[9] In May 1796 the Evangelical Dr John Erskine failed to persuade the General Assembly of the Church of Scotland to establish its own foreign missions scheme, primarily because the opposing 'Moderate' party in the Church of Scotland succeeded in labelling the promoters of overseas missions as political radicals. The Church of Scotland did not engage in foreign missions on its own account until 1824, but this omission was partially compensated for by the continuance of strong links between Scotland and the LMS: of the 475 missionaries appointed by the LMS between 1795 and 1845, eighty-one came from Scotland, including such notable names as John Philip, Robert Moffat and David Livingstone.[10]

The evangelical world in Britain at the turn of the eighteenth and nineteenth centuries was, despite its denominational and political divisions, a cultural and ideological unity, in which ideas and movements spread from one section to another with remarkable rapidity.[11] Between the early 1780s and the second decade of the nineteenth century the obligation to bring the Christian gospel to the 'heathen' world seized the conscience and imagination of evangelicals in all parts of the church. Traditional High Church Anglicans and the rationalistic Unitarians of 'Old' Dissent were the only significant Protestant groups to be almost entirely untouched by the new missionary fervour. The rash of Protestant missionary societies soon spread to America, where societies for the evangelization of the North American Indians were formed from 1796 onwards, followed in 1810 by the first organization committed exclusively to overseas mission, the American

Board of Commissioners for Foreign Missions. On the continent of Europe the pioneering societies were the Basel Mission of 1815 and the Berlin Society of 1824. Similar societies followed in France and Scandinavia.

2. What was the relationship of the missionary awakening to British expansion?

The missionary awakening in Britain came about at the end of a century during which European knowledge of and interest in the non-European world had increased enormously. British horizons in the second half of the eighteenth century were dominated by the expansion of East India Company rule in India. By the end of the century, 'Asia', which to most Englishmen in the seventeenth century had retained its biblical location in the Near East, had become almost a synonym for India.[12] Indian affairs were the subject of extended parliamentary enquiry and public debate in 1767, 1772–73, 1781–83, and supremely during the trial of Warren Hastings from 1787 to 1795. The demands in Parliament by Edmund Burke and others that British power in India should be exercised in a moral fashion for the benefit of the native population, found their Christian reflection in the plans of Evangelicals such as Charles Grant, David Brown and Claudius Buchanan for missionary work in India. Less politically sensitive but more romantically alluring than the expansion of British control in India was the opening up of Australasia and the South Pacific to European exploration. The published accounts of Captain James Cook's three voyages to the South Seas between 1768 and 1780 created intense public interest in the 'primitive' peoples of the area. William Carey later acknowledged that 'reading Cook's voyages was the first thing that engaged my mind to think of missions'.[13] Cook's *Voyages* had a similar effect on Thomas Haweis: Haweis referred in his inaugural sermon preached before the LMS in September 1795 to the new world recently uncovered in the South Pacific, and his persuasion of the missionary prospects of the South Seas was decisive in determining the destination of the first missionary party sent out by the LMS in 1796.[14] The selection of India and the South Seas as two of the earliest fields of British missionary activity was undoubtedly the result of their prominence in contemporary secular argument and interest, and a similar connection can legitimately be drawn between the importance of West Africa in early missionary strategy and the beginnings of European exploration of the West African interior.

In this general and quite unremarkable sense the British missionary awakening had undeniable connections with British expansion, if we extend that term to include geographical exploration as well as the growth of British power. The breadth of the Christian conscience is inevitably related to the scope of secular general knowledge; the church has only rarely been concerned about those of whom it has virtually heard nothing. To acknowledge such a truism is not to lend support to the contention that the processes of British secular expansion in some way 'explain' the origins of the missionary movement. It is well-nigh impossible to establish any plausible connection between the revival of the Protestant missionary conscience and either trends in British colonial policy or the expanding needs of British industrial capitalism. The loss of the North American colonies between 1776 and 1783 in fact implanted in British governments a marked antipathy to the acquisition of new colonial responsibilities which took a very long time to evaporate. Even if the missionary movement is regarded as no more than a by-product of the anti-slavery movement (which it was not), it can no longer be maintained that evangelical humanitarianism functioned as a class ideology legitimating the transfer of economic interest from the pre-capitalist structures of West Indian plantation slavery to the free market offered by new trading opportunities in the East. Recent writing by Roger Anstey and Seymour Drescher has established that Britain abolished the slave trade in 1807 at a time when the West Indian slave economy, far from being on its last legs, was in fact extremely healthy: abolition flew in the face of perceived British national interests.[15] The missionary movement was, in any case, more than a mere spin-off from British abolitionism: the abolitionist connections of the Clapham-Sect-inspired CMS were responsible for the Society's early emphasis on West Africa, but in the Nonconformist societies the anti-slavery theme was considerably less dominant in their early years.

The only adequate explanation of the origins of the missionary societies is in terms of theological changes which were quite autonomous of developments in imperial history, and these must now be briefly considered. Most important of all was the Evangelical Revival itself, a multi-faceted movement which gave birth to the Evangelical party in the Church of England and transformed the ethos of Calvinistic Dissent, as well as spawning the new denominations of Wesleyan and Calvinistic Methodism. The Revival generated an absorbing passion for the spread of the gospel of the atoning death of Christ, a passion which found institutional embodiment in the welter of societies, both denominational and interdenominational, dedicated to domestic evangelism and foreign mission. Amongst Particular (Calvinistic) Baptists and Independents (Congregationalists) the crucial theological precondition for the rise of missionary concern was the weakening of the rationalistic hyper-Calvinism which had caused some mid-eighteenth century Dissenters to distrust the use of any human means of urging men and women to repent and believe. One of the most powerful solvents of such attitudes was the Baptist Andrew Fuller's *The Gospel Worthy of all Acceptation* (1785), which applied the moderate Calvinism of Jonathan Edwards to argue that divine sovereignty in the spread of the gospel operated through the channel of human responsibility. William Carey's *Enquiry* of 1792 did no more than harness Fuller's theology to the cause of overseas missions, insisting that the Great Commission was binding on all Christians for all history, and arguing that providence had furnished British Christians with all the means that were necessary for the missionary obligation to be discharged.[16]

Evangelical confidence in the efficacy of the preaching of the gospel to achieve God's sovereign purposes for the world was balanced by the conviction that evangelistic endeavour would be crowned with success only in proportion to the measure of the outpouring of the Holy Spirit in response to the fervent prayers of God's people. The origins of both the BMS and the LMS can be traced to the issue of a call to prayer by the Northamptonshire Association of Baptist churches in 1784. The Prayer Call was itself modelled on Jonathan Edwards' proposal of a period of 'extraordinary united prayer' made in a pamphlet published in 1748 or 1749, *An Humble Attempt to Promote Explicit Agreement and Visible Union of God's People in Extraordinary Prayer*. The 1784 Prayer Call followed Edwards in appealing to Christians to unite in prayer for the outpouring of the Holy Spirit on ministers and churches and for 'the spread of the Gospel to the most distant parts of the habitable globe'. As a result of the Prayer Call, monthly Monday-evening prayer meetings for the revival of evangelical religion and the extension of the kingdom of Christ in the world were instituted in Baptist churches, both within the area covered by the Northamptonshire Association (the East Midlands) and beyond it, and also in Independent churches.[17] Monthly missionary prayer meetings on this pattern remained a regular feature of congregational life in many Nonconformist and some Anglican churches well into the nineteenth century.

Even before the formation of the BMS, William Carey believed that he could see 'some tokens for good' granted by God in initial response to the prayer movement.[18] Those who do not share Carey's confidence in the efficacy of prayer as an historical agent will nevertheless perceive the significance of the fact that regular prayer meetings for the missionary cause anticipated the inception of missionary organization in England by eight years. The prayer movement provides further evidence that the theological roots of the missionary awakening were embedded in the piety of Jonathan Edwards and the 'Great Awakening' in New England in the 1740s. Edwards' burgeoning missionary enthusiasm was related to his growing belief that the Awakening signified that the last days of human history were at hand; the fullness of the last days would be brought in by the universal spread of the gospel. The great majority of the pioneers of the British missionary movement shared Edwards' confidence that the propagation of the gospel throughout the globe in partnership with the earnest and united prayers of the church would usher in the last age of history.[19] If any one circumstance can be held responsible for the transformation of the embryonic missionary stirrings of the 1780s into the institutional action of the 1790s, it was the unfolding of portentous political events on the continent of Europe. As early as 1790 Melvill Horne could infer from the signs of the times that the 'latter ends of the world are fallen upon us', challenging Christians to 'more than apostolick labours' to bring the gospel to the world.[20] By 1792 it seemed even more likely that the course of the Revolution in France would result in the overthrow of the Roman Catholic Church, which most Protestants identified with Antichrist. 'The present age', reflected Baptist minister John Ryland in May 1792, 'seems pregnant with great events.'[21] By 1798 French armies had set up a republic in Rome itself, dragged Pope Pius VI into exile, and Bonaparte was in Egypt threatening the Ottoman hold on Palestine; evangelicals speculated that the restoration of the Jews to their homeland might be imminent.[22] The missionary awakening had relatively little to do with the expansion of British imperial power, but it had everything to do with the shaking of the foundations of the old order in Europe caused by the French Revolution. The Europe which gave birth to the missionary movement was neither self-confident nor generally expansionist: rather it was a continent in the throes of political upheaval and anguish. British overseas interests merely shaped British missionary priorities: they cannot account for the birth of the missionary movement itself.

3. Gospel perspectives

a. Evangelicalism and the Enlightenment

The Protestant missionary movement was in its origins an exclusively evangelical phenomenon. High Churchmen did not jump onto the missionary bandwagon until the 1830s, when the SPG underwent a remarkable transformation from a colonial church society financed by parliamentary grants and royal letters (directives inviting collections in parish churches) to a missionary society prepared to press its claims on the voluntary support of the Anglican public. Later still, the formation in 1859 of the Universities' Mission to Central Africa brought to the mission fields of East and Central Africa the new and aggressive Anglo-Catholicism nurtured by the Oxford Movement. However, the SPG and the UMCA remained strange children in a movement whose attitudes and assumptions remained essentially evangelical throughout most, if not all, of the nineteenth century. In certain societies, as we shall see, some of the distinctive tenets of evangelical belief had been substantially diluted before the end of the century, whilst in the twentieth century the division between theological liberals and conservatives becomes a determinative category. Nonetheless, the thought-forms of nineteenth-century evangelicalism remain the key to evaluating the most characteristic features of the ideology of the missionary movement, and these 'gospel perspectives' will occupy our attention for most of the remainder of this chapter.

Evangelicalism was distinguished from other forms of Protestantism in the early nineteenth century supremely by its total absorption with the message of the cross of Christ. The doyen of early nineteenth-century Anglican Evangelicals, Charles Simeon, left provision in his will for copies of a university sermon entitled 'Evangelical Religion Described' to be distributed after his death to his Cambridge parishioners; the sermon was on the text, 'I determined not to know anything among you, save Jesus Christ, and him crucified.'[23] Evangelicals preached other doctrines than the atoning death of Christ, but the cross was the very heart and essence of their message. Missionaries went out to the field convinced that the preaching of the cross was both what the 'heathen' needed to hear and also the only agent capable of effecting regeneration in individuals and society. John Angell James's annual sermon preached before the LMS in May 1819, entitled 'The Attraction of the Cross', illustrates this confidence admirably:

> If then you would arrest the savage of the desert; if you would detain him from the chase; if you would rivet him to the spot, and hold him in the power of a spell that is altogether new to him, do not begin with cold abstraction of moral duties, or theological truths; but tell him of Christ crucified, and you shall see his once vacant countenance enlivened by the feelings of a new and deep interest.[24]

James's characteristic expectation that the 'heathen' would respond with immediate interest to the message of the cross did not correspond to the realities of the field. Also worthy of comment is his repudiation of the 'cold abstraction of moral duties' and of 'theological truths'. Evangelicals abhorred abstraction, whether it came in the form of the moralism of eighteenth-century rational religion or in the shape of argument about the finer points of systematic theology or denominational polity. The message of the cross was more than an arid 'theological truth' – it was a living truth of power and experience.

In their hostility to any form of religion which was merely moralistic, rational or abstract, evangelicals were consciously reacting against the religious temper of the Enlightenment. The fact that evangelicalism was and is a religion of enthusiasm, experience and activism has long been a truism of historical scholarship. It is only more recently that historians have come to recognize that evangelicalism, even as it reacted against the Enlightenment, also borrowed a great deal from it. This interpretation was pioneered by a remarkable essay written at Cambridge in 1962 by Haddon Willmer, and is now becoming a prominent theme in published work on nineteenth-century evangelicalism on both sides of the Atlantic.[25] The nature of the impact of the philosophy of the Enlightenment on evangelical thought can be summarized under two headings. In the first place, evangelicals, though they denied the all-sufficiency of reason, placed a very high value on it. Man had been created as an essentially rational being, and there was no incompatibility between reason and biblical faith. Natural theology – the deduction of the existence and nature of God from the structure of his created work – had a valuable role in supporting the claims of biblical revelation. Reason declared to be probable what revelation declared to be true. Secondly, evangelicals, under the influence of a world-view which derived ultimately from the physics of Isaac Newton, believed the universe to be a self-consistent and harmonious system which operated according to the natural laws which God had imposed upon it. These laws were moral as well as physical, dictating the course of history as well as shaping the natural world. Divine providence, always an important concept within the Calvinist theological tradition, now acquired pre-eminent status as an intellectual device determining an evangelical's responses both to events in his own life and to the unfolding of history.

The thought-world of evangelical missionaries and missionary supporters was a strange amalgam of distinctively biblical preoccupations and other assumptions which owed more to Enlightenment philosophy than to Christian theology. On certain issues the blend was achieved with a minimum of difficulty. For example, both Protestant biblicism and respect for rational knowledge implied that teaching the 'heathen' to read ought to be given a high priority in missionary strategy. But the union of the two was not always so smoothly accomplished, and different evangelicals resolved the tension within their intellectual inheritance in different ways. Christian attitudes to imperialism in its political, economic and cultural forms were fashioned within this ideological matrix. As the nineteenth century proceeded, of course, the matrix itself changed shape: the cultural and philosophical emphases of European Romanticism began to weaken Christian confidence in reason, order and mechanism, so that by the end of the century the evangelical consensus had begun to lose its ascendancy and cohesion.[26]

b. A crusade against idolatry

Evangelicals understood the objective of the missionary enterprise to be the restoration of mankind to a right relationship to its creator, a restoration that would be achieved through the realization of the lordship of Christ over the kingdoms of this world. Through the instrumentality of Christian missions the messianic promise of Psalm 2:8 – 'Ask of me, and I shall give thee the heathen for thine inheritance, and the uttermost parts of the earth for thy possession' (King James Version) – would be brought to fulfilment in the vision of Revelation 11:15 – 'The kingdoms of this world are become the kingdoms of our Lord, and of his Christ' (King James Version). The dynamic of the missionary movement was supplied by the acute awareness of Christians that much of humanity, far from recognizing the governance of God and the lordship of Christ, was in overt rebellion against them. The visible manifestation and proof of that rebellion was heathen idolatry. All religions apart from Protestant Christianity were classified as idolatrous: they worshipped other gods and thus transgressed the first of the Ten Commandments.[27] The absolute Old Testament condemnations of the idolatry which threatened Hebrew monotheism were taken to be directly applicable to Christian attitudes to other world religions. Christian interpretation of the biblical evidence on the human alternatives to revealed religion was refracted through a particular theory of the historical development of religion which became established in the eighteenth century. The book of Genesis appeared to teach that all people derived from a common created origin, but after the tower of Babel were scattered over the face of the earth.[28] As different human groups migrated further and further from Babel, their religion became increasingly corrupt, degenerating into idolatry. The various world religions, therefore, were believed to represent different stages and directions of degeneration from the original biblical state of pure revealed religion.[29] Moreover, Romans 1:18-32 implied that increasing recourse to idolatry had brought about cumulative moral deterioration, as God gave people up to the consequences of their own rejection of him.

This corpus of belief explains the extreme negativism which characterized the missionary approach to other religions for most of the nineteenth century. Idolatry was 'the master-sin of Heathenism'.[30] 'Other sins transgress God's law', the Rev. Peter McOwan told the anniversary meeting of the WMMS in 1856, 'but idolatry strikes at His existence. It substitutes another in His stead.'[31] Here was the highest of all motives to the missionary enterprise, claimed the *Wesleyan Methodist Magazine* in 1858:

> The most serious controversy that ever rose between God and man is represented in the system of idolatry. In every idol we see God's rival. In every idolater we see a man who takes against God, and supports a system which involves the rankest injustice toward God.[32]

If alien religious systems were thus an affront to the sovereignty and glory of God, it followed that the Christian should oppose them as he opposed sin. Missionaries were engaged in a spiritual battle with the satanic forces of heathendom, and missionary literature made frequent use of strident military imagery. 'The gospel of love', comments one historian, 'was inextricably tied to a propaganda system which used the militant language of war.'[33]

It will become apparent in subsequent chapters that the conception of the missionary enterprise as a crusade against idolatry contained the seeds of attitudes and responses which can legitimately be construed as imperialistic. In situations where British troops were ranged against Hindu or Islamic armies, some missionaries and missionary supporters proved unable to resist the temptation to identify the former with the cause of God. In the late Victorian period especially, excessive emphasis on the darkness and degradation of idolatrous peoples could lead some missionaries into statements which teetered on the brink of racialism. Most widespread and most significant of all was the assumption that the baneful influence of idolatry extended to all aspects of a people's culture and society, as we shall see in chapter 7.

c. 'The perishing heathen'

For probably the majority of Protestant missionaries throughout the nineteenth century the grave moral seriousness of idolatry seemed to allow only one conclusion with regard to the eternal destiny of the 'heathen': unless they believed in Christ they must be presumed lost for all eternity. Specific biblical support for this sombre conclusion was found in Paul's teaching in 1 Corinthians 6:9-10 that no idolater would inherit the kingdom of God. All would have agreed with the speaker at the BMS anniversary meeting in 1849 that the starting-point of the gospel was the stark epigram that 'Man is lost wherever man is found.'[34] Many Christians were haunted by an acutely arithmetical vision of the vast numbers of those who were being lost. Robert Moffat, the pioneering LMS missionary in Southern Africa, when preaching to a congregation at the Barbican Chapel in January 1843, put the searching question:

> Who can look to the East Indies now, and to China now; who can look to those interesting portions of the globe, because the most populous, the most dense, without yearning with compassion over the teeming millions that are there moving onward every day like some vast funeral procession; onward and downward, sadly and slowly, but certainly to the regions of woe? 'Oh, you are a hard man,' some might say; 'do you think they will go to hell?' Where do they go to? Do they go to heaven? All idolaters, we are told, have their portion in the lake that burneth with fire and brimstone. I wish that someone would enlighten my mind, if it wants light on this subject, and tell me whether or not all the heathen have perished, all idolaters have perished. But we know that nothing that is unclean, or that loveth and maketh a lie, can enter the holy place. Where do they go to?[35]

On this issue, perhaps more than any other, the tension between evangelical fidelity to the Bible and the claims of reason was acute. Even Moffat, who had no doubts on the subject, was in effect admitting that he wished he could find his way to some other conclusion. Moffat's son-in-law, David Livingstone, held the same view in the early stages of his missionary career, but was profoundly affected in July 1851 by the death of the Makololo chief, Sebituane: 'The deep dark question of what is to become of such as he, must, however, be left where we find it, believing that, assuredly, the "Judge of all the earth will do right".'[36] Henry Venn, the most influential British missionary theorist of the nineteenth century, declared himself in 1850 unable to come to 'any firm conclusion in my own judgment either from scripture or reason' as to the final state of the 'heathen'. Venn professed to follow 'all enlightened writers upon the question' in believing that 'the heathen dying without the offer of Gospel (*sic*) will not be punished with the same punishment as those who hear and reject it. Now the Scripture sufficiently informs us of what that punishment will be; but it does not enable me to pronounce upon degrees, or differences of kind, in eternal torments.' Venn insisted that the CMS took no official party line on the question, and observed that CMS annual sermons and platform speeches showed a considerable diversity of view, although with the majority admittedly on the side of the eternal perdition of the 'heathen'.[37] The very first CMS annual sermon, by Thomas Scott in 1801, had indeed declined to pronounce on the eternal perdition of the 'heathen', but had nevertheless insisted that Christian love demanded that the church should act on the assumption that they *were* lost.[38]

It is certainly an oversimplification to imply that British Protestantism moved in the course of the nineteenth century from an unquestioned belief that all the 'heathen' were destined for hell to a more agnostic or optimistic view. In the first half of the century, evangelicals felt that biblical teaching required them to proceed on the assumption that those who had never heard the gospel would be lost, even though rational arguments gave some of them a residual hope that this might not be so. Later in the century, as attacks on the orthodox doctrine of eternal punishment gathered strength, some sections of British Protestantism, notably Congregationalism and those parts of the Church of England influenced by the quasi-universalism of F. D. Maurice, veered towards a total repudiation of belief in the perdition of the 'heathen'.[39] A comparison of the doctrinal papers submitted by LMS candidates between 1845 and 1858 with those submitted between 1876 and 1888 has revealed that in the later period 'candidates were not only less inclined to state a belief in the doctrine of everlasting punishment, but in a number of cases questioned its validity'.[40] Probably the majority of Congregational ministers and missionaries had abandoned the traditional eschatology by the end of the 1880s.[41] Amongst Methodists and Baptists the same process had begun but was less far advanced – Baptist denials of the doctrine of eternal punishment were one of C. H. Spurgeon's items of complaint in his 'Downgrade' controversy with the Baptist Union in 1887–88. The majority of candidates for the CMS in the 1870s and 1880s (and some in the 1890s) appear to have retained an unequivocal belief in the eternal perdition of the heathen.[42] The considerable numbers of CMS missionaries in the late Victorian period who adhered to a premillennial eschatology (see pp. 76–77 below) almost certainly exhibited a more absolute insistence on the fate of the 'heathen' than had most of the more rational evangelicals of the Simeon or Venn eras. In this, as in other respects, they were influenced by the stance of James Hudson Taylor and the China Inland Mission. Hudson Taylor's burning vision of the 'million a month' in China 'dying without God' was the stimulus behind his formation of the Mission in 1865, and Taylor inserted into a new basis of faith for the CIM, adopted in January 1884, a clause requiring assent to the doctrine of the everlasting punishment of the lost. It is noteworthy, however, that by 1903 Taylor was expressing regret at this step and was far less certain about the fate of those who had never heard.[43]

The significance of this problematic theological issue for our subject is two-fold. On the one hand, it must be emphasized that belief in the eternal perdition of the 'heathen' imparted a sense of absolute urgency and priority to the missionary imperative, besides which political considerations appeared ultimately secondary. Since British evangelical missionaries predominated in Protestant missions in the last century and American conservative evangelical missionaries have been equally predominant in the twentieth century, it can be asserted that the greater number of Protestant missionaries have been concerned more than anything else with the business of saving souls: their relationship to political forces has been to them a matter of subordinate importance. This rather obvious point needs to be balanced by a more subtle one. By the First World War it was fairly widely held in the older denominational societies that the relationship between Christianity and other religions ought to be seen as one of fulfilment rather than one of judgment and discontinuity. This approach became characteristic of liberal Protestant missiology in the twentieth century, although it was trenchantly criticized by neo-orthodox voices such as Hendrik Kraemer.[44] Chapters 6 and 7 will show how, in the period of 'high' imperialism (c. 1880–1920), those who wished to ground the missionary obligation in something other than soteriological necessity tended to find their alternative rationale in the dissemination of the benefits of Western civilization. A missionary theology whose dynamic rested on this life rather than the next was, if anything, *more* open than traditional theology to the dangers of uncritical cultural imperialism.

d. Providence and responsibility

Evangelical understanding of the doctrine of divine providence provides the most telling illustration of the confluence of biblical and Enlightenment influences in fashioning the evangelical world-view in the nineteenth century. The biblical revelation of God as the sovereign Lord of history was married to the Newtonian concept of God as the supreme governor of the universe, so that human history was regarded as an ordered process, moving according to fixed rules of operation towards the fulfilment of the purposes of the divine architect. The Bible's insistence on the consistent moral character of God's sovereignty was viewed through the philosophical spectacles of Bishop Butler's *Analogy of Religion*, producing a perspective on history which expected to find rewards following virtue, and punishments following vice with almost inevitable regularity.[45] Evangelicals, however, were not content with the eighteenth-century understanding of God's working in history as being of an essentially moral intent: they readily accepted that God's government was of a discernibly moral character, but God's *primary* purpose in history, they argued, was not the reinforcement of virtue but the forwarding of his plan of salvation. All the operations of divine providence were directed to the supreme end that the earth should be full of the knowledge of the Lord. Human history was the story of the divine preoccupation with the furtherance of the gospel of salvation. God directed all human affairs with this end in view.

Divine purpose was thus written large over the face of history, just as it was over the face of nature. The master of teleological argument, the eighteenth-century Anglican divine, William Paley, had founded his natural theology upon the assertion that evidence of contrivance and design in any set of natural circumstances indicated that those circumstances had been so ordered by providence with a specific purpose in mind.[46] Natural theology dictated that order implied purpose, and furthermore that the purpose behind any display of order must needs be commensurate with the evident grandeur of the design. Paley's logic of natural history was equally applicable to human history. Nineteenth-century Christians reflected on the sheer immensity of the power and territorial possessions granted to Britain, and concluded that it was inconsistent with any 'rational idea of a superintending and benevolent Providence' that their country should be thus exalted among the nations merely in order to satisfy carnal motives of national pride and self-aggrandizement.[47] The purpose behind the bestowal of such signal privilege and influence could be no other than that Britain had been uniquely commissioned by God to bring the gospel to the world. A double responsibility lay heavily on the nation's shoulders. Since the Protestant Reformation, Britain had enjoyed to a unique degree the blessings of true evangelical religion and the civil liberties which it was believed to bestow. Now she had been given the further privilege of world power. The two together constituted 'a high trust to be turned to God's glory'.[48] Formulated in this way, Christian belief in divine providence led by logical steps to the concept of Britain's imperial role as a sacred trust to be used in the interests of the gospel.

Imperial historians have conventionally traced the origins of the 'trusteeship' theory of the British empire to the arguments of Edmund Burke and others during the debates on Indian affairs in the 1770s and 1780s that East India Company power could not be justified unless it were exercised with morality and subjected to parliamentary control.[49] The specifically evangelical conception of empire as a trust given for missionary purposes originated a little later but may have been more influential in the long term. Initially this view was confined to the missionary societies and their constituency of public support. After the Indian mutiny of 1857 the notion of the empire as a God-given trust became increasingly accepted among a wider circle of opinion which took the liberty of re-interpreting the terms of the trust; by the late 1890s the nature of 'the white man's burden' was frequently defined more broadly as the dissemination of a package of Christian civilization and liberal government in which Christianity itself was only one ingredient. In the twentieth century the language and ideology of trusteeship were shared even by the many imperial administrators and propagandists whose Christian commitment was minimal or non-existent. It should be noted in passing that a similar ideology of national mission entered the currency of American Protestantism in the 1880s and 1890s. Its most notable advocate was Josiah Strong, secretary of the Evangelical Alliance for the USA and a pioneer of the 'Social Gospel', who believed that America was called by providence to join Britain in spreading Christianity and Anglo-Saxon civilization throughout the globe.[50]

It will be emphasized in the next three chapters that this ideology of 'imperial idealism', although very widely diffused through all sections of Christian opinion, proved capable on occasion of accommodating a considerable range of missionary and Christian responses to particular issues and crises in imperial history. It was possible to be a persistent critic of many of the policy decisions which governed the growth and operation of the empire while at the same time retaining a profound theoretical conviction that the empire had a God-given destiny to fulfil. The apparently random and irrational nature of much British imperial expansion in the nineteenth century was as evident to contemporaries as it is to many modern historians, and Christian observers could rarely resist the inference that divine over-ruling was the hidden engine driving the process. Divine purpose seemed all the clearer when the purposes of human policy were either confused or professedly hostile to new colonial possessions. It was in India above all that British sovereignty appeared, in the words of Bishop Samuel Wilberforce, 'to have been put into our hands in a great measure against our will'; territorial expansion had been effected by those who 'not only did not seek after, but really did not wish to possess' territory which was 'as it were, thrust into their hands'.[51]

It is easy to fault this ideology of providence as being dangerously open to callous rationalization, but it should be perceived that nineteenth-century Christians were providing an interpretation, consonant with their own understanding of the world, of the series of crises at the periphery of

European expansion which play so large a part in the 'Robinson and Gallagher' thesis of imperialism. The LMS missionary William Clarkson observed in his book *India and the Gospel* that British conquests in India had not issued from forethought, purpose and plan, but had indeed been 'frequently in the absence of advices from home, and even counter to the deliberate commands of the chief authorities'. Doubts about the morality of the British conquest of India could not do away with the fact of British rule: 'The consequent obligation', remarked Clarkson, 'is not removed by any dubiousness as to the righteousness of the conquest itself. Nay, if there be any dubiousness, it becomes the more incumbent on us to furnish the best reparation for all the wrongs that may have been inflicted.'[52] Christian belief in divine providence goes a long way towards explaining why most missionaries and their supporters accepted imperialism as a general historical process, but the converse of their belief in providence was their unrelenting insistence on moral and spiritual responsibility – an insistence which again and again led missionaries to challenge and criticize the reality of imperial policy on the field.

e. Commerce and Christianity

The distinctive philosophical shape which the doctrine of divine providence assumed in the thought of nineteenth-century evangelicalism may provide the key to understanding one of the most controversial themes in the history of the missionary relationship to imperialism. Probably the best-known instance of the theme is the concluding section of David Livingstone's public address delivered in the Senate House of the University of Cambridge on 4 December 1857:

> ... I beg to direct your attention to Africa; – I know that in a few years I shall be cut off in that country, which is now open; do not let it be shut again! I go back to Africa to try to make an open path for commerce and Christianity; do you carry out the work which I have begun. I LEAVE IT WITH YOU![53]

Here in a nutshell, it might be supposed, was the fatal ambiguity vitiating the Victorian sense of mission – the propagation of the gospel had been coupled quite unashamedly with the pursuit of British commercial expansion.

Livingstone's immense impact on the Victorian popular imagination ensured that the slogan of 'commerce and Christianity' passed into history in close association with his own name. In fact neither the slogan itself nor the ideology which lay behind it were original to Livingstone. Livingstone hoped to accomplish the civilization of central Africa by a partnership of missionary work and 'legitimate' trade. The promotion of cotton cultivation in the Zambezi region would drive out the slave trade and at the same time benefit the English cotton industry, which was dangerously (and, in the eyes of many Christians, immorally) dependent on supplies of slave-grown cotton from the southern United States. This scheme for Africa's spiritual and commercial regeneration was merely the most highly developed expression of a Christian ideology whose essential components are identifiable from the very beginning of the British missionary movement.[54] 'Commerce and Christianity' was an anti-slavery ideology. As early as 1789 William Wilberforce had advocated legitimate commerce as the best way to cut off the slave trade at its source within Africa. Like Livingstone after him, Wilberforce believed that providence had so arranged things that a humanitarian option on Britain's part for righteous, as opposed to unrighteous, trade would redound to Britain's own advantage: 'we shall soon find the rectitude of our conduct rewarded, by the benefits of a regular and a growing commerce.'[55] This confidence in the restorative properties of legitimate trade was embodied in the Clapham-Sect-sponsored Sierra Leone Company, formed in 1790. Thomas Clarkson described the Company as the first ever formed for 'the abolition of the slave trade, the civilization of Africa and the introduction of the Gospel there', and Melvill Horne went out as a Company chaplain with firm intentions of fulfilling a missionary role.[56] These expectations of the colony's function were not confined to the Evangelical Anglicans of the Clapham Sect. William Carey, believing that one of the distinctive features of the latter-day glory of the church would be that 'commerce shall subserve the spread of the gospel', expressed the hope that the Sierra Leone colony would not only 'open a way for honourable commerce' with Africa, and promote its civilization, but also 'prove the happy mean' of introducing amongst its inhabitants 'the gospel of our Lord Jesus Christ'.[57] The BMS sent two missionaries to Sierra Leone in 1795, and the LMS followed two years later.

When evangelicals gave voice to their faith in the regenerative role of lawful commerce within the providential order, they were revealing themselves to be true children of the Enlightenment. The assumption that there could be no essential contradiction between the spheres of economics, politics and theology was inherited from the social philosophers of the eighteenth century who had pioneered the study of economics, such as Adam Smith, author of *The Wealth of Nations* (1776), and the Anglican cleric, Joseph Tucker. Universal commerce, good government and true religion were, in Tucker's words, 'so many Parts of one general Plan'; the unity of God's providential rule implied that no final contradiction between the several interests of the different spheres was conceivable; the Creator had so constituted the world that morality and policy, duty and interest were in fundamental harmony one with another.[58]

Theoretical confidence in commerce as an instrument of God's providential rule of human affairs was a major determinant of missionary attitudes to British commercial expansion in the nineteenth century. Yet missionaries were consistently critical of the deleterious effect of ungodly traders on the morals of the 'heathen', and the missionary societies usually took a dim view of any personal participation in trading activity by their missionaries. The BMS wrote Carey a letter 'full of serious and affectionate caution' when the Society learnt that he had accepted a post as manager of an indigo factory in order to provide himself with some regular means of support.[59] The LMS administered similar rebukes to its early missionaries in the South Seas when they too responded to inadequate financial supplies from England by engaging in trade.[60]

The apparent contradiction between the role often allocated to commerce in missionary theory and missionary distrust of the exploitative reality of European trading activity could be seen as a logical development of an ambiguity within the tradition of political economy which evangelicalism inherited. Adam Smith himself had a more realistic view of the social and moral effects of the unbridled pursuit of commercial selfishness than is conventionally imagined: economic progress was a necessary but in no sense a sufficient condition for the creation of liberty.[61] For evangelicals, however, moral reservations about the impact of autonomous commerce sprang in the first instance from their vivid awareness of the natural sinfulness of the human heart. The slave trade itself was the supreme example of the moral iniquity worked by those whose only god was profit. Later in the nineteenth century other trades – notably the opium trade with China and the firearms and spirits trades in Nigeria – received equally unequivocal condemnation from missionaries and Christian public opinion. Illegitimate commerce of this kind stood in clear antagonism to the interests of the gospel. Even legitimate commerce was unwelcome if it was not accompanied by the diffusion of Christianity or subject to appropriate control. Charles Grant and other advocates of the introduction of missions to British India opposed the opening of India to free trade: India had received more than its fair share of exploitative autonomous commerce in the eighteenth century; what it needed at the beginning of the nineteenth century was not uncontrolled commerce but Christian preaching and education.[62] The three missionary society secretaries who testified before a parliamentary select committee in 1836–37 on the condition of the aboriginal inhabitants of the British colonies all agreed that the contact of European settlers and traders with the natives had a uniformly adverse effect on their morals if missionary activity had not first been introduced. Indeed, they argued that such unholy external contact positively inhibited the growth of Christianity, civilization and wholesome commerce amongst the native population. The correct order was rather to introduce Christianity first: the gospel would of itself begin to civilize the natives, and advancing civilization would then promote healthy commercial activity of mutual benefit to the native population and to Britain.[63]

Missionary attitudes to commerce were thus the result of an interplay between the Enlightenment conviction that sound commerce would promote liberty and even religion, and the distinctively evangelical emphasis that Christianity alone was the key to health and happiness in society. Sir Thomas Fowell Buxton's Niger Expedition of 1841 is remembered as an ill-fated attempt to extinguish the slave trade in West Africa by means of legitimate commerce. In fact Buxton believed that lawful commerce alone would be inadequate to counteract the slave trade – it would require both government naval intervention against the slave traders and the only lasting solution of Christianity itself.[64]

Buxton's remedy of Christianity and commerce for the ills of West Africa was taken up by Henry Venn, who assumed office in the CMS in the same year that the Niger Expedition sailed. Venn encouraged cotton cultivation at Abeokuta in Nigeria in the belief that the development of a major cash crop for export to Britain offered the most viable economic alternative to the slave trade. However, Venn's faith in commerce was no utopian vision which blinded him to the realities of European commercial exploitation. Venn complained that the object of European traders in Africa had always been 'to obtain the produces of Africa for the least possible consideration, at the cheapest rate. ... Everywhere the white trader has degraded the Native and kept him down.' The commerce which Venn wished to see was commerce in the hands of an educated and Christian African middle class; there would be no quick and easy profits for European traders, although in the long term Britain as a nation would benefit from a reciprocal trading relationship with a prosperous and peaceful West Africa.[65]

David Livingstone's advocacy of 'commerce and Christianity' as the divine prescription for the regeneration of an East Central Africa ravaged by the Arab slave trade was not essentially different from the earlier remedies of Buxton and Venn for West Africa. Although Livingstone's public speeches in Britain in the autumn of 1857 appeared to idolize commerce as a providential institution for diffusing liberty and the knowledge of Christianity, he was eager in his more reflective moments to concede that commerce by itself was of strictly limited value:

> Commerce has the effect of speedily letting the tribes see their mutual dependence. It breaks up the sullen isolation of heathenism. It is so far good. But Christianity alone reaches the very centre of the wants of Africa and of the world. The Arabs or Moors are great in commerce, but few will say that they are as amiable as the uncivilized negroes in consequence. You will see I appreciate the effects of commerce much, but those of Christianity much more.[66]

Livingstone's faith that legitimate commerce in the hands of Christian men was designed by God to be the perfect partner of missionary activity was expressed in the initial policy of the High Anglican mission founded in 1859 in response to Livingstone's appeals on behalf of Central Africa – the Universities' Mission to Central Africa. However, the disastrous outcome of the Mission's first expedition to the Zambezi under Bishop C. F. Mackenzie in 1860–62 brought in due course an Anglo-Catholic reaction not merely against confidence in commerce but more fundamentally against civilization as a missionary ideal.[67] We shall see that evangelical missionary theory subsequently moved in a similar direction, although some evangelical missions continued to maintain a providentialist doctrine of commerce right into the early years of this century.[68] As evangelicalism moved into the twentieth century, it increasingly conceived of the world not as a harmonious system operating in the missionary interests of the church but as a dark arena of satanic domination in which the lamp of evangelical witness burned in lonely isolation. Christians continued to believe in providence, both in their own personal lives and as a theological interpretation of the fact of the empire, but their understanding of providence had lost much of the mechanistic imprint which the legacy of the Enlightenment had previously stamped upon it.

f. Missions and the future

The missionary movement was born out of a conviction that the church stood on the brink of the last days of history. Christians expected that the work of foreign missions would initiate a turning of the 'heathen' to Christ on such a scale that the kingdoms of this world would become in actuality the kingdom of Christ. The biblical vision of the rule of Christ and his saints over the earth for a thousand years – the millennium – was understood to refer to the era of world-wide gospel triumph which missionary evangelism would inaugurate. In so far as Christians thought at all of the second coming of Christ, they related it to the status of a non-catastrophic event bringing the last days of global Christian victory to their close. Christian hope focused not on the parousia but on the promises apparently given in the Bible that at the end of time the world would turn to God in response to the preaching of the gospel.

This eschatology, known as postmillennialism, was shared by most missionaries and missionary supporters until about the 1880s. Three important consequences followed from such a view of the future. It should be noted, first of all, that postmillennialism was incurably optimistic: evangelism was destined to succeed on an unprecedented scale, and as it did so the world would become a better place. The spirit of buoyant missionary optimism permeated the entire character of Victorian Protestantism and fused quite naturally with the national self-confidence produced by Britain's industrial and commercial pre-eminence. Combined with the providentialist conviction that Britain was uniquely commissioned by God to bring the gospel to the world, postmillennial eschatology constituted an ideology of exceptional self-confidence and power. Missionaries who saw the future in this light were highly motivated.

Postmillennialism not only imparted an optimistic tone to Victorian religion as a whole – it also (secondly) generated remarkable qualities of persistence amongst missionaries who, for most of the century, had to work with very little visible fruit in terms of conversions. Experience of the mission field soon revealed that existing religious systems were far more tenacious than domestic enthusiasm fondly imagined. 'When I first left England', wrote Carey in April 1794, 'my hope of the conversion of the heathen was very strong; but among so many obstacles it would utterly die away, unless upheld by God, having nothing to cherish it.' Faced with such difficulties, Carey turned increasingly to the promises of Scripture: 'Yet this is our encouragement, the power of God is sufficient to accomplish every thing which he has promised, and his promises are exceeding great and precious respecting the conversion of the heathens.'[69] After half a century of disappointing missionary results in India, William Clarkson was no less sanguine that ultimate success was divinely guaranteed:

> ... we only acknowledge a want of *visible* results. All that has been done is treasured up by God ... It is a fundamental principle of God's administration, that 'one soweth and another reapeth'. In the fact of *delayed* success, we find only an illustration of it ... Nothing done or endured in faith can be lost. All shall appear in the great account ... The issues of all that has been done are certain. They are only delayed.[70]

Postmillennialism induced optimism and reinforced missionary stick-ability. It also led missionaries to expect and work for a fundamental transformation of non-Christian societies. The content of their hope was not merely a conglomerate of individual conversions but a comprehensive revolution in 'heathen' society in which every aspect of that society would be prised from the grip of satanic dominion and submitted to the liberating lordship of Christ. Chapter 7 will explore the implications of this expectation for missionary attitudes to culture.

From the 1870s onwards two parallel theological developments progressively undermined this eschatological consensus. Those evangelicals who began to move in a liberal direction in their doctrines of the atonement, the authority of Scripture and eternal punishment retained the postmillennial hope but in an increasingly diluted form. The expectation of social transformation was no longer tied so explicitly to the process of personal conversion, and began to be understood more loosely in terms of the spread of Christian civilization and idealism. The mood of this liberalized postmillennialism is well expressed by those missionary hymns composed at the turn of the century which look forward to a coming age of universal human brotherhood, truth and sweetness, peace and light.[71] Postmillennialism without the cutting edge of Puritan theology degenerated all too easily into a facile creed of liberal imperialism.

Other sections of evangelicalism moved in a contrary theological direction. One of the distinctive tenets espoused by the group of evangelicals who gathered around the Presbyterian Edward Irving in the 1820s was the belief that the Bible taught an imminent and personal return of Christ prior to the establishment of his earthly reign. This alternative Christian view of history posited that the moral and spiritual state of the world would actually get worse before the cataclysmic intervention of the second coming. The mission of the church, therefore, was not to transform human society into the kingdom of God, but to rescue individuals from an increasingly evil world, and hasten the return of Christ by a policy of rapid evangelistic expansion. Christ could not return until every nation had had an opportunity of responding to the gospel.[72] This 'premillennial' eschatology was most widely disseminated by the Brethren movement, and was given specific application to missionary strategy by two men who were strongly influenced by Brethren ideas – the Quaker missionary philanthropist Robert Arthington (1823–1900), and James Hudson Taylor, who came from a Methodist background. The impact of their views on the older missionary societies was initially limited. However, from the late 1870s Arthington began to exercise a substantial influence on the policy-making of the BMS (and to a lesser extent of the LMS).[73] Similar ideas become influential within the CMS after the introduction in 1887 of missionary meetings to the programme of the annual holiness conventions held at Keswick from 1875.[74] From 1887 Keswick becomes a major theme in the history of the CMS and of the interdenominational 'faith missions' which sprang up in the wake of Hudson Taylor's China Inland Mission. The Nonconformist societies were less affected by the Keswick movement, but to differing degrees were subsequently brought into the sphere of holiness and premillennial influences by the student volunteer movement, formed in the United States in 1886 and introduced to Britain as the Student Volunteer Missionary Union in 1892. The SVMU encouraged university students to sign pledges declaring 'It is my purpose, if God permit, to become a foreign missionary', and at its first conference in 1896 adopted the famous American watchword (attributed by John Mott to A. T. Pierson) of 'the evangelization of the world in this generation'.[75] The movement embraced postmillennialists and premillennialists, liberals and conservatives, but to premillennialists such as Pierson the watchword summed up their conviction that missionary policy ought to be shaped by the overriding priority of rapid evangelization.[76]

Chapters 6 and 7 will indicate that there is some evidence that missionaries holding this theological position differed significantly in their political and cultural attitudes from missionaries in the postmillennial tradition. At this point it will be sufficient to emphasize the radical novelty which premillennial theology must have possessed for Christians accustomed to thinking on the basis of the reasoned and measured assumptions of 'Enlightenment evangelicalism'. With a few early exceptions, missionaries had not placed any confidence in the ability of civilization in itself to reform the 'heathen'. But they had hitherto been quite sure that the gospel would bring civilization in its train and shatter the evil hold of Satan on 'heathen' society. Now these cherished convictions were being challenged, not by liberals but by the most theologically conservative elements within the evangelical camp. Graham Wilmot Brooke, subsequently joint leader of the CMS Sudan Mission party of 1890, gave this new radical conservatism forcible expression when he confessed in 1886:

> I see no hope given in the Bible that wickedness in this world will be subdued by civilization or preaching of the gospel – until the Messiah the Prince come. And to hasten that time is, I believe, the function of foreign missions, 'for the gospel must first be preached for a witness, unto all nations and then shall the end come'. I therefore should be inclined to frame any missionary plans with a view to giving the simple gospel message to the greatest number possible of ignorant heathen in the shortest possible time.[77]

Statements such as Wilmot Brooke's seemed to undermine the most foundational assumptions of nineteenth-century evangelicalism. Believing as they did that they lived in a world of order, regularity and proportion, evangelicals had always supposed that the conversion of the world would be progressively achieved in proportion to the means which the church devoted to that end. As early as 1842 one perceptive missionary theorist had warned that premillennialism threatened to open a great gulf in the divine economy between means and ends, implying that the church was commanded to do what could in fact be achieved only by the 'stupendous miracle' of the parousia.[78] That criticism may itself have been theologically suspect, but the historical point not to be missed is that by the end of the nineteenth century evangelicalism, and with it the missionary movement, no longer possessed a single world-view common to all its adherents. The marriage of the Evangelical Revival and the Enlightenment was falling apart, and evangelicals began to split into liberal and conservative groupings. The 'liberals' were, in philosophical terms, the true conservatives, for they retained a belief in the ability of the church to bring the kingdom of God to fulfilment in human history. On the mission field in the twentieth century such a stance implied an emphasis on the service ministries of medicine and education, an acceptance of the concept of Christian civilization, and a greater openness in theory to a providential understanding of imperialism. The conservatives were in fact philosophical radicals – having absorbed the Romantic Movement's preference for immediacy, passion and conflict.[79]

Their individualist and other-worldly theology was intrinsically more likely to be anti-imperialist, or at least indifferent to imperialism. In practice, however, twentieth-century missionaries cannot be neatly accommodated within such an ideal philosophical categorization. It is as well to conclude this survey of the ideological framework of the missionary movement with a reminder that the ideas which missionaries took with them to the field were constantly refashioned in response to the immense variety of circumstances which confronted them in their work. Ideas are extremely important in understanding the responses of the missionary movement to the imperial process, but they cannot always explain the actions of individual missionaries.

4. The course of British missionary enthusiasm

It was suggested in the second section of this chapter that the origins of the missionary movement in Britain cannot be explained by reference to the course of British overseas expansion. We shall conclude this chapter with a brief survey of the progress of missionary enthusiasm in Britain and a discussion of how far changes in the scale of the British missionary movement can be related to trends in the history of British imperialism. More detailed analyses of individual episodes in British missionary history will follow in the next three chapters.

Until the mid-1830s the income of the English missionary societies remained at a relatively low level and the flow of candidates was at best intermittent. Lack of candidates from Britain compelled the CMS in its early years to rely on recruits from Germany. In the late 1830s the income of all the societies increased sharply in real terms, and candidates became much more plentiful. At a single meeting in October 1837 the LMS commissioned thirty-five missionaries to their work, the great majority of whom were new recruits. Over the three years 1838 to 1840, fifty-eight new LMS missionaries sailed for the field; in the CMS the corresponding total was thirty-five.[80] The burgeoning missionary enthusiasm of these years was prompted by a variety of influences. Missionary interest was still linked very closely to the anti-slavery campaign, and undoubtedly benefited from the achievement of emancipation in the British West Indies in 1834, the ending of the apprenticeship system for former slaves in 1838, and T. F. Buxton's cultivation of public support for his Niger Expedition. The LMS was able to make capital out of the interest aroused by the visits to Britain of two of the best-known missionaries of the day: John Williams from the South Seas in 1836 and 1837, and Robert Moffat from South Africa from 1839 to 1843. The news of Williams' martyrdom in November 1839 established the type of the missionary hero in popular mythology, and contributed greatly to the sales of Williams' *A Narrative of Missionary Enterprises in the South Sea Islands.*

At the close of this period of exciting missionary developments came the dramatic news of the first opening of China to Western missionaries through the Treaty of Nanking signed in August 1842: as we shall see in chapter 4, China dominated the horizons of the missionary movement in late 1842 and 1843.

The missionary upsurge of 1837 to 1843 came to an abrupt halt amidst the harsh economic conditions of the 'hungry forties'. From about 1844 to 1857 the missionary cause remained at a consistently low ebb. Between 1857 and 1860 enthusiasm for foreign missions attained a new peak in response to Livingstone's appeals for Central Africa, the impact of the Indian mutiny which broke out in May 1857, and the opening of inland China to missionary penetration in 1858. Missionary giving reached an exceptionally high level in 1858, and remained well above average until 1861. Buoyant giving was matched by rising recruitment. The LMS noted in April 1858 that 'an unusually large number of suitable men had within the last few weeks offered themselves for Missionary Service'.[81] The CMS received seventy-eight applications from British candidates in 1858, more than in any other year between 1850 and 1875.[82]

It will be suggested in the next chapter that the peaks of missionary enthusiasm in 1843 and 1857 to 1860 bore some relationship to the intentions of British informal 'free trade' imperialism in China and India. The second peak came to an end as abruptly as the first. In the 1860s the income of the societies increased only marginally in real terms, and numbers of candidates dwindled. Henry Venn lamented to the Islington Clerical Meeting in 1865 that despite the progress of the Evangelical party in the Church of England, missionary zeal had distinctly 'retrograded'.[83] In 1870 R. W. Dale expressed his firm conviction that missionary interest was not what it had been.[84] The missionary movement appeared to need a new challenge and a new opportunity. The challenge was provided by the death of David Livingstone at Ilala in Central Africa in 1873. The new opportunity was opened up by British economic expansion: the Suez Canal had been opened in 1869, making East Africa readily accessible to missionary penetration for the first time.

The Scottish churches were, appropriately enough, the first to respond to the challenge to launch new missionary initiatives in East and Central Africa to 'carry out the work' which Livingstone had begun. In May 1874 the Free Church of Scotland and the Church of Scotland approved plans for the missions which became the famous Livingstonia and Blantyre missions of Nyasaland (see chapter 5, section 3, page 123). In November 1875 a letter appeared in the *Daily Telegraph* from H. M. Stanley, the journalist-turned-explorer who had 'found' Livingstone in 1871, appealing to the English missionary societies to respond to the openness to Christianity which Stanley believed he had found at the court of Kabaka Mutesa I of Buganda. Within two days an anonymous supporter had offered the CMS £5,000 to undertake a Nyanza mission in response to Stanley's appeal; by July 1877 the first CMS missionaries had arrived in what is now Uganda (see chapter 5, section 4, page 127). Two new missions by the LMS and the BMS completed the new Christian thrust into the heart of Africa. Both were inspired by Robert Arthington's vision of a chain of mission stations crossing Central Africa from East to West. In March 1876 the LMS accepted £5,000 from Arthington to commence a mission on the shores of Lake Tanganyika, and the first party left early in 1877. The BMS decided in July 1877 to accept Arthington's offer of £1,000 for a mission on the Congo, and proceeded to raise support for the new mission under the stirring slogan of 'Africa for Christ'.[85]

The CMS received applications from 118 British candidates in 1876, more than in any other year of the nineteenth century except 1896.[86] It is tempting to interpret the events of 1874 to 1877 as the beginning of the late Victorian missionary boom, and to argue that this massive expansion of the British missionary movement in the last twenty-five years of the century was indeed the religious expression of the secular impulse which led the European powers to partition the African continent between 1880 and 1900. There is no denying that from the mid-1870s CMS recruitment began a rise which was sustained (apart from a slight faltering in the early 1880s) until it reached its peak between 1896 and 1900.[87] Between 1880 and 1904 the CMS sent 50% more missionaries to the field than it had done throughout the first eighty years of its history.[88] In the single decade of the 1890s, in which Victorian popular imperialism reached its apogee, the Society sent out only ten fewer missionaries than in the previous forty years from 1850 to 1889 (see Table 1).

Table 1: Decennial totals of CMS recruits and candidates from Great Britain and Ireland, 1800–1900[89]

DECADE	ALL RECRUITS	FEMALE RECRUITS	MALE RECRUITS	MALE CANDIDATES
1800–09	2	0	2	not known
1810–19	28	0	28	,, ,,
1820–29	80	7	73	,, ,,
1830–39	104	7	97	,, ,,
1840–49	76	9	67	,, ,,
1850–59	133	5	128	561 (+)
1860–69	132	6	126	518
1870–79	166	6	160	593
1880–89	250	0	210	606
1890–99	671	315	356	870

Note: Missionary wives are excluded. The figure for male candidates in the 1850s is marginally too low, since it excludes the first three months of 1850, for which no data are available.

The seemingly obvious inference that the golden age of the British missionary movement from 1880 to 1914 can be explained primarily in terms of the high imperialism of these years cannot, however, be regarded as proven. It must be emphasized, in the first place, that the aggregate figures for CMS recruitment are not an accurate index of the level of missionary enthusiasm even within the Evangelical Anglican constituency of the Society. A large proportion of the increased recruitment of the late 1880s and 1890s was due to the Society's recruitment of substantial numbers of single women missionaries who had previously been regarded as unsuitable for most types of missionary employment. The Society's abandonment in 1887 of its policy of discouraging single women candidates soon effected a complete transformation of the sex ratio among CMS recruits (see Table 1 above).[90] Changes in evangelical attitudes towards the role of women may have been important as augmented Christian enthusiasm for imperialism in determining the high level of missionary recruitment at the end of the century. Nevertheless, male recruitment to the CMS still increased very significantly from the mid-1870s, with the most marked rise coming after 1887. It is here that reference must be made to the final column of Table 1, which gives the decennial totals for male candidates from 1850 to 1899. These figures indicate that the level of male application to the Society was on average scarcely higher in the 1880s or 1870s than it had been in the 1850s. They also confirm that applications in the 1890s (more accurately, from 1890 to 1897) were considerably more numerous than in the 1880s, but not to the extent that is implied by the figures for total recruitment taken in isolation. What distinguished the 1880s from the immediately preceding decades was not an increased number of male candidates but the fact that a far higher percentage than before were accepted. The explanation of the change lies in the social and educational background of the candidates. Between 1877 and 1893 the CMS received 140 offers of service from graduates or undergraduates of the University of Cambridge, of which ninety-seven were accepted.[91] It appears to have been very rare for a university-trained man to have been declined on grounds other than poor health. The extraordinary numbers of Cambridge men (and in particular graduates of Ridley Hall, the Evangelical Anglican theological college opened in 1881) volunteering for the CMS was paralleled to a lesser extent by an increase in recruitment from the University of Oxford and from Trinity College, Dublin.[92]

It is fair to assume that this new generation of highly educated missionaries was heavily influenced by ideas of a broadly imperialist nature – for the concepts of England's mission and responsibility to the so-called 'younger' peoples of the world were now deeply ingrained in the Christian idealism of the middle classes – but imperialism in itself cannot explain the missionary fervour which seized Cambridge and other universities in the 1880s and 1890s. The answer lies rather in the emergence of a new brand of evangelical piety which has been touched on in the earlier sections of this chapter – a piety of radical consecration to the ideals of holiness and absolute submission to the will of God, a piety which was distrustful of the old slogans of civilization, commerce and Christianity, and lived in conscious anticipation of the imminence of the second coming. The roots of this new and powerful stream of evangelical spirituality lie in the impact on British Christianity of D. L. Moody's revivalism, the American holiness movement, and supremely the Keswick movement in Britain itself – religious movements which bear no obvious relationship to imperial history. Also of relevance are trends in the educational history of the ancient British universities and the public schools which fed them: from the 1860s Victorian public schools began to cultivate the virtues of 'muscular Christianity' through the introduction of organized and compulsory sport, Rifle Corps and public school missions to the working classes; the new educational ideals of leadership, duty, responsibility and sacrifice soon became part of the distinctive cultural ethos of late Victorian Oxford and Cambridge. These ideals could readily be turned to imperial purpose – and were indeed intended to be – but their origins lie primarily in the growth of new convictions about the essential importance of character formation in the educational process.

Closer analysis of the figures for CMS recruitment in the late Victorian period thus suggests that independent religious and social trends may have been at least as important as specifically imperial developments in producing the massive increase in numbers of missionaries. Statistics for other societies and missions are less readily available, but those which have been compiled tend to reinforce this impression. Recruitment in the WMMS, which was largely untouched by the holiness and student volunteer movements, made a modest advance in the 1880s but fell back in the 1890s to levels little different from those characteristic of the 1860s or 1870s.[93] The decline is significant in view of the greater strength of imperialist sentiment among Wesleyans than other Nonconformists in the 1890s. Nonconformists were, of course, virtually excluded from Oxford and Cambridge until 1871, and even in the 1880s and 1890s were slow to send their sons to the ancient English universities. The Congregationalists opened their own college (Mansfield) in Oxford in 1889, but Mansfield produced only a handful of LMS missionaries in the first twenty years of its history (and none at all till 1897). The LMS had, however, established strong links with the faculties of medicine in the Scottish universities, and sent out substantial numbers of medical missionaries at an earlier date than other societies. Medical students were the largest faculty group in the early years of the SVMU. The influence of the student movement in the Scottish universities, especially Edinburgh, was an important contributor to the rise in LMS recruitment from a total of 128 British missionaries sent out in the 1880s to 194 in the 1890s. The trend of ministerial recruitment to the Society was in fact downward for most of the last thirty years of the century.[94]

In the interdenominational China Inland Mission the pattern of recruitment was different again. A steady flow of recruits was not achieved until D. L. Moody's first visit to Britain in 1873-75, which imparted renewed evangelistic energy to the revivalistic circles where the Mission's support was located. As the holiness movement gathered strength in the 1880s, candidates for the CIM multiplied correspondingly, reaching their peak in the aftermath of the departure of the 'Cambridge Seven' for China in 1885: 102 missionaries left for China in 1887. The success of the CIM in the 1880s was due to the impact of C. T. Studd and his colleagues on the student world, but also to its willingness to recruit single women, who accounted for 45% of all candidates in the decade. However, recruitment declined quite markedly in the 1890s, primarily because the CIM was less adept than the CMS had now become in harnessing the enthusiasm of the student world.[95]

Even in Scotland the period between Livingstone's death and the outbreak of the First World War cannot fairly be described as a golden era of unbroken missionary enthusiasm. Candidates for the Church of Scotland mission at Blantyre were extremely scarce until about 1888, and even thereafter there was no more than 'a steady trickle' of candidates.[96] In Scotland as in England missionary fundraisers continued to complain of the lack of missionary commitment of most church members and of the greater attractiveness of immediate domestic objects in the allocation of Christian giving. Enthusiasm for foreign missions has in reality always been the preserve of a committed minority within the churches. The high imperial period of 1880 to 1914 was less of an exception to this generalization than is often imagined: the size of the minority undoubtedly expanded, and particular social and educational groups were gripped by the missionary vision to an unprecedented extent, but it would be quite false to imply that the Christian public in this period were uniformly and consistently preoccupied with either missionary or secular imperial concerns.

The doyen of missionary historians, the American Kenneth Scott Latourette, in his monumental *History of the Expansion of Christianity*, had some justification for describing the nineteenth century as 'the great century' of missionary expansion, for the period between 1800 and 1914 indeed witnessed an unprecedented geographical advance of Christian influence.[97] Yet the phrase must be used with great caution. For the first eighty years of the 'great century' the numbers of foreign missionaries were extraordinarily few. From about 1880 the scale of the missionary enterprise increased very considerably, but in 1899 the total number of Protestant foreign missionaries in the world was estimated to be only 17,254, of whom 9,014 came from Great Britain and Ireland and 4,159 from the USA.[98] Figures of this order of magnitude need to be compared with the most recent available estimates for the late twentieth century: D. B. Barrett estimates that in 1973 there were 56,623 serving Protestant foreign missionaries in the world, of whom 7,490 came from the United Kingdom and 32,573 from the USA; by 1989, according to Barrett, the global total of missionaries from all denominations had reached 273,700.[99] In terms of global aggregates of missionary numbers, both Protestant and Catholic, the 'great century' has been the twentieth, not the nineteenth. As far as British missions are concerned, we paradoxically know less about the course of recruitment in the years after 1914 than before it. The decline which seems to have affected most of the denominational societies in the inter-war years probably owed more to the combined impact of the depression and of diminishing theological confidence than it did to any waning in Christian enthusiasm for the British empire. To some extent this decline may have been offset by the continuing vitality of the conservative evangelical 'faith missions'. The progressive diminution of the British missionary force since about 1960 may be related to the passing of the imperial era, but it also reflects the growing self-sufficiency of the younger churches and, more recently, a discernible shift in the evangelical world conscience from evangelistic to humanitarian concerns.

In the twentieth century, as in the nineteenth, trends in imperial history have been only one influence, and not necessarily the most important, affecting the state of health of the missionary enterprise. The missionary awakening at the end of the eighteenth century cannot be convincingly explained by reference to developments in British colonial policy or overseas investment. Neither can it be claimed with any degree of certainty that the great upsurge in missionary recruitment between 1880 and 1914 was the simple product of the heightened imperial fervour of these years. Clearly missionary recruits from the 1880s onwards were more likely to adopt political and racial categories drawn from secular imperialism, but the rate of recruitment varied from society to society, and reflected a mix of secular and theological influences. Further research is required, particularly on rates of recruitment after 1914, before any final verdict can be delivered on the connection between the rise and fall of imperialism and the pattern of missionary enthusiasm.

CHAPTER FOUR

The claims of humanity, 1792 to 1860

In chapters 4, 5 and 6 our discussion moves from the generalities of the theology and ideology of the Protestant missionary movement viewed as a whole, to more detailed analyses of how the missionary societies, their missionaries and domestic supporters responded to, and interacted with, the course of British imperialism in particular mission fields. As it would be impossible to cover every field and every major episode with any adequacy, we shall confine our attention to a representative selection of the more significant fields at crucial points in imperial history. The focus of this chapter, which deals with the early period of the British missionary movement up to about 1860, will be on four mission fields which vary widely in their political circumstances. In the British West Indies (notably in Jamaica) missionaries found themselves in a context where British colonial rule and a substantial degree of political autonomy for white planters were well-established facts. In early nineteenth-century South Africa, on the other hand, British sovereignty was comparatively recent, the geographical frontier of colonial rule was extremely unstable, and the position of European setters far more precarious. India was different again. During the period covered by this chapter Britain's involvement in the Indian sub-continent completed its evolution from a purely commercial role to a full-blown imperial one; missionaries had to relate, not primarily to planter or settler power, but to the collective force of government itself in the shape of the East India Company. Finally, we shall turn to the controversial story of the opening of China to Western secular and Christian influence during the era of the opium wars of 1839 to 1860: here the accent will be on the attitudes of Christian opinion, both missionary and domestic, to the employment of British 'informal' imperialism to prise open an empire which had proved singularly resistant to all forms of European penetration.

1. Missions and slavery in the West Indies

In most of the British West Indian colonies the Church of England was the established church – in Jamaica and Barbados this had been so since the imposition of British rule in the seventeenth century. However, the Anglican clergy were closely identified with the plantation owners and virtually ignored the slave population. The SPG had no work in the West Indies prior to 1833 except for its ministry to the slaves on its own Codrington estates on Barbados. The CMS had no official mission in the West Indies until 1823, and made little headway thereafter with a mission on Jamaica which was abandoned in the 1840s. The complicity of the Church of England with the planter community left the field of evangelistic work among the negro population open for the Nonconformist societies. The pioneers were, of course, the Methodists, who by 1823 had fifty missionaries and 26,000 members throughout the West Indies.[1] The BMS mission in Jamaica, opened in 1813, was on a smaller scale but was destined to play an even larger part in influencing the course of West Indian history. Also important was the LMS mission at Demerara on the South American mainland in what is now Guyana, which was opened in 1807.

The issue confronting Christian missionaries in the West Indies was not what attitude to adopt to British colonial rule – which in Jamaica and Barbados had been in existence for 150 years – but rather how they should relate to the distinctive nature of West Indian colonial society. Dissenting missionaries, influenced to a greater or lesser extent by the egalitarian ideals of the Enlightenment and the French Revolution, found themselves at work in a system of slavery, controlled by a planter class which had the approval of the Anglican establishment in the West Indies and the support of a powerful West Indian lobby in Westminster. The missionaries arrived in the islands armed with explicit instructions from their parent societies to avoid all political entanglements. The BMS warned John Rowe on his departure for Jamaica in December 1813 against allowing his feelings for the slaves to lead him into words or actions inconsistent with Christian duty, and reminded him of Paul's teaching that slaves should be obedient to their masters. He was also advised that, although he was going to a British colony,

> if any local regulations should seem not exactly answerable to your expectations, it is not for you to interfere in political matters, but to exemplify that quiet and peaceable conduct, which you will inculcate on your hearers; and to endeavour by a respectful demeanor to recommend yourself and the gospel to the white inhabitants of the Island.[2]

Three years later, the LMS committee emphasized to John Smith in his instructions for the Demerara mission that the 'holy Gospel you preach will render the slaves who receive it the most diligent, faithful, patient, and useful servants' and would thus recommend his ministry even to previously hostile plantation owners.[3] As late as 1824, when some Nonconformists in Britain had espoused the view that slavery ought to be gradually abolished throughout the British colonies, the BMS still held unswervingly to the principle that its missionaries in Jamaica must have 'nothing whatever to do' with civil or political affairs, and reminded William Knibb on his departure for the field that the 'gospel of Christ, you well know, so far from producing or countenancing a spirit of rebellion or insubordination, has a directly opposite tendency'.[4] Whilst none of the evangelical missionary societies was in the delicate position of the SPG in being the owner of a slave plantation, the treasurer of the LMS from 1816 to 1832, W. A. Hankey, had inherited a West Indian estate. Although pressure from LMS auxiliaries compelled Hankey to resign his office in January 1832, the point to be noted is that until 1831 there was no suggestion that Hankey's implication in slavery was in any way inconsistent with his office in the missionary society.[5]

Early evangelical missionaries in the West Indies were thus instructed not to speak out against slavery or the colonial authorities, and the evidence suggests that they dutifully refrained from doing so.[6] There is nothing to support the charge subsequently levelled against John Smith that he incited the Demerara slaves to insurrection, and in 1832 BMS missionaries in Jamaica defended themselves against similar accusations by protesting that they had always urged slaves to be obedient to their masters in accordance with New Testament teaching.[7] There is no doubt, however, that first-hand contact with the realities of plantation slavery created in many missionaries a deep moral abhorrence of slavery and a determination to defend the interests of the slaves in so far as the system allowed. Within seven months of his arrival in Demerara, John Smith was confiding to the privacy of his journal 'O slavery! Thou offspring of the Devil, when wilt thou cease to exist?' Increasingly Smith found himself in conflict with the plantation authorities over such matters as physical maltreatment of the slaves or their being compelled to work on Sundays, and the very act of teaching the slaves to read was accurately regarded by the colonial authorities as having alarming potential for subversion.[8] Smith was hence already a marked man when rumours spread among the slave population of the colony in July to August 1823 that King George in England had decreed their freedom, which was now being withheld by the Governor. The truth behind the rumour was the existence of a dispatch from London containing measures for the amelioration of slave conditions, following T. F. Buxton's assumption in 1823 of the leadership of a parliamentary campaign to press for the 'mitigation and gradual abolition' of slavery throughout the British dominions. Rumour led to insurrection, in which a few of Smith's baptized slaves were involved. Martial law was proclaimed, the rising was brutally suppressed, and Smith was court-martialled for conspiracy to rebellion. Smith was found guilty on the slenderest of evidence, sentenced to death, but died in jail in January 1824 before the news of George IV's commutation of his death sentence could reach him.[9]

The Demerara insurrection was the first in a series of rebellions or conspiracies to rebellion between 1823 and 1832, in which slaves began to demand the emancipation which abolitionists in Britain had now adopted as an eventual goal. Buxton and his fellow 'gradualists' were now pressing for major reforms of slave society, and in response the British government instituted a defensive programme of piecemeal amelioration, one feature of which was the encouragement of religious instruction for the slaves. Missionaries thus became unofficial agents of imperial policy and could now expect some degree of imperial protection. At the same time, however, the gradualist campaign was hardening planter attitudes in defence of the slave system and in opposition to the missionaries. After the Demerara insurrection planter opinion throughout the West Indies became almost uniformly hostile to Nonconformist missions, seeing them as a front for abolitionist intentions. Missionaries began to encounter unprecedented difficulty in obtaining the necessary licenses to preach.[10]

The initial reaction of some missionaries to this deterioration in the political climate for their work was to lean over backwards to prove their loyalty to colonial society. This was notably true of the majority of the Methodists. John Shipman, a WMMS missionary in Jamaica, urged the WMMS to dissociate itself completely from Smith and the LMS, and got up a statement in September 1824 which declared that, far from being instigators of subversion, the Wesleyan missionaries believed that emancipation would be a 'general calamity – injurious to the Slaves, unjust to the proprietors, ruinous to the Colonies, deleterious to Christianity, and tending to the effusion of human blood'.[11] The statement virtually identified its missionary signatories with the political interests of the plantation owners, and was promptly disowned by the WMMS Committee in London.[12] Under the pressure created by the growing strength of gradualism in Britain, Shipman and his Wesleyan colleagues had transgressed the 'no politics' rule in a conservative direction. From late 1828 onwards, however, events combined to propel Methodist as well as Baptist missionaries towards a markedly different political alignment.

Although the legal position of the right of missionaries to preach in Jamaica was significantly strengthened by a test case in October 1828, the dominant feature of the years between 1828 and 1831 was the progression of many Nonconformist missionaries towards a position which demanded immediate abolition on the grounds of religious liberty. Cases such as that of the Baptist slave, Sam Swiney, arrested in April 1830 for illegal preaching (in fact he had taken part in a prayer meeting when Knibb was away ill), were crucial in hardening both missionary and Nonconformist opinion against the continuance of slavery. The BMS publicized the Swiney case and pressed the Colonial Office for an immediate inquiry. The Methodists, for their part, had three cases of imprisonment of their Jamaican missionaries for unlicensed preaching to complain about.[13] By the end of 1830 the sporadic persecution of Methodist and Baptist missionaries and their converts had swung the great majority of missionaries towards a position of overt hostility to the colonial authorities and open sympathy for emancipation. It had also contributed to a growing sentiment among Nonconformist Christians in Britain that without a complete end to slavery in the West Indies there could be no lasting freedom or security for missionary operations. The outbreak in December 1831 of a further slave rebellion – this time in Jamaica – set the seal on this new evangelical radicalism. Once again missionaries – those of the BMS in particular – were accused of having fostered the rebellion by subversive and egalitarian teaching (a claim which had precious little substance). The formerly sporadic persecution now became systematic. During 1832 fourteen Baptist and six Methodist chapels in Jamaica were destroyed by whites organized in Colonial Church Unions, whose object was to resist all progress towards slave emancipation and oppose the work of Nonconformist missions. Thomas Burchell, a BMS missionary cast by the rebels in the role of a Baptist Moses who would lead them out of bondage, was compelled to leave the islands.[14]

By embarking on a campaign of harassment of Nonconformist missions which were at heart soundly conservative, planter society in the West Indies had paradoxically taken the surest possible route towards slave emancipation. The Jamaican Baptists sent their most vociferous missionary, William Knibb, to Britain to seek redress of their wrongs. Knibb arrived home in June 1832 intent on rousing Nonconformist opinion to demand an immediate end to slavery. His first task was to win over the committee and principal supporters of the BMS, who still adhered to the principle that slavery was a political subject which could not be attacked publicly by the Society's agents – a principle which Knibb and Burchell claimed to have observed scrupulously on the field, until the Jamaican insurrection and consequent planters' attacks on the churches made it impossible for them to do so.[15] Now they had found a higher principle of irresistible force. Knibb told the annual public meeting of the BMS on 21 June:

> ... the Society's missionary stations could no longer exist in Jamaica without the entire and immediate abolition of slavery. He had been requested to be moderate, but he could not restrain himself from speaking the truth. ... He could assure the meeting that slaves would never be allowed to worship God till slavery had been abolished. Even if it were at the risk of his connexion with the Society, he would avow this; and if the friends of missions would not hear this, he would turn and tell it to his God; nor would he ever desist till this greatest of curses were removed, and 'glory to God in the highest inscribed on the British flag'.[16]

Armed with such a distinctively evangelical argument, Knibb need not have feared that the friends of missions would decline to hear him. Over the next year Knibb travelled 6,000 miles on behalf of the BMS or the abolitionist Agency Committee, convincing the Nonconformist public that slavery had 'bid defiance to the gospel' and hence could not be suffered to continue.[17] In the campaign for the general election of December 1832, Nonconformists were urged by their ministers and missionary societies to give their votes only to candidates pledged to support immediate emancipation: even the generally conservative Wesleyan Methodist Conference instructed Wesleyans to vote in this way. The return to Parliament of a bloc of up to 200 such pledged candidates laid the foundation for the passing of the Emancipation Act in August 1833.[18] As from 1 August 1834 all slaves in the British West Indies, the Cape of Good Hope, Mauritius and Canada were declared free, although a period of compulsory apprenticeship to their former masters was to ensue.

This overview of missionary responses to West Indian slave society up to 1833 yields four conclusions of specific relevance to the theme of missions and imperialism. The first and most obvious point to be made is that the planters and their political allies perceived evangelical missions to be a threat to their power and to the stability of colonial society. Relations between colonists and missionaries were never cordial and were frequently antagonistic. Missionary Christianity was not a welcome ally for colonial oppression but a disturbing challenge to it. Yet it must be emphasized, in the second place, that neither the missionary societies nor their individual agents set out with the intention of challenging the structures of colonial society. They firmly believed that the spread of Christianity would enhance the stability of West Indian society as of all societies. Radical political change of a manifestly unjust social system occupied no place in their missionary programme, although most were confident that the gospel would so ameliorate the conditions of the slaves that slavery would ultimately wither away.

The course of events in the West Indies between 1823 and 1833 rendered this posture of missionary non-interference in colonial politics increasingly difficult to maintain. The third conclusion to be drawn, therefore, is that the realities of experience on the field broke up the consensus of idealized missionary theory and forced missionaries to adopt a variety of more or less explicitly political stances. The attitudes of individual missionaries were shaped by the immediate context in which they worked but also reflected their respective religious backgrounds. Methodists, with their instinctive sympathy for the established church, were more likely to gravitate in a pro-colonist direction, unless personally affected by persecution. Baptists, and to a lesser extent Congregationalists, who were in the vanguard of the struggle for full religious liberty for Nonconformists in Britain, moved more rapidly to the conclusion that there could be no freedom for the gospel in the West Indies until the slaves were given their political freedom. Some Evangelical

Anglicans who had little first-hand knowledge of West Indies slavery, but an innate suspicion of anything that smelt of political radicalism, stood aloof from the emancipation campaign with its alarming language of 'natural rights' for the slaves.[19] The tendency for the attitudes of missionaries on the spot to diverge from one another and also from the theoretically grandiose but practically cautious maxims of their masters in London continued to be evident after 1833. William Knibb in particular caused periodic embarrassment to the BMS Committee by his open agitation first on behalf of the apprentices and subsequently, once apprenticeship had been terminated in 1838, for the disestablishment of the Anglican Church in Jamaica. Methodist missionaries, on the other hand, criticized Knibb and his BMS colleagues for political meddling and were not uniformly hostile to the apprenticeship system.[20]

The final conclusion to emerge from this case study is the importance of evangelical concern for the advance of the gospel in determining the political responses of individual missionaries and their parent societies. This concern was ever present but it could result in widely differing policies according to the circumstances of the place and hour. Without their initial insistence on mute subservience to the structures of colonial society, the missionary societies would not have gained entry to the plantation colonies in the first place. Those Wesleyan missionaries who publicly repudiated abolitionist ideas in the mid-1820s did so for fear that any more liberal attitude would have brought their work to an end. Knibb and Burchell led the missionary movement in demanding an end to West Indian slavery primarily on the grounds that plantation slavery had shown itself to be an obstacle to missionary progress, even though they personally had for some time held the theoretical position that slavery *per se* was intolerable to Christian principle.[21] Gospel perspectives thus led British missions into an open confrontation with 'colonialism'. However, a professed desire to see 'glory to God in the highest inscribed on the British flag' could under different conditions lead missionaries of like mind with Knibb to espouse ardent imperialism.

2. Missions and the Cape frontier in the 1830s

In 1795 Britain took control of the Cape of Good Hope from the Dutch East India Company in order to pre-empt anticipated annexation by revolutionary France, which would have imperilled the British route to India. By that date the original staging post for Dutch shipping had grown into a colony of substantial Dutch and German settlement. The white settlers controlled a subject population made up of slaves (some of African origin and some Malays) and so-called 'Hottentots' – the original Khoisan inhabitants of the Cape, most of whom were employed by the colonists as farm and domestic

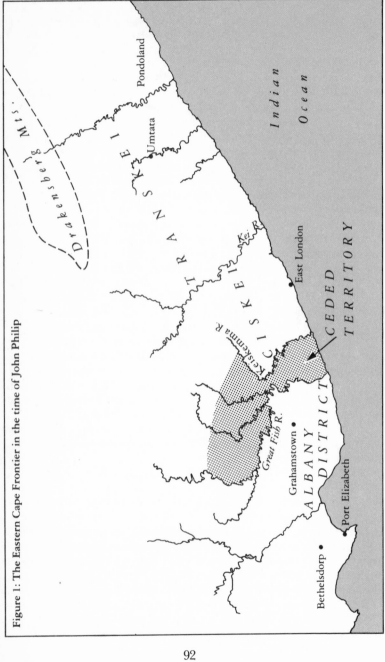

Figure 1: The Eastern Cape Frontier in the time of John Philip

servants. Beyond the Fish River, the colony's eastern boundary, were the Xhosa people, the southernmost of Africa's Bantu-speaking peoples and known to the settlers as 'Kaffirs'. The Xhosa were themselves a conglomerate of different groups, and no one chief exercised undisputed authority. Further north, to the east of the Drakensburg mountains, a remarkable explosion of human forces was under way, known to historians as the 'Mfecane'. Population growth was placing scarce resources of land under great pressure, new and aggressive political units emerged to fight for the pickings, sending other groups scurrying north and south in the search for living space. The southward pressure created by the Mfecane intensified the existing territorial competition between the Xhosa and land-hungry white farmers at the eastern frontier, fixed somewhat arbitrarily at the Fish River. In 1819 the fragility of the border was exposed more brutally than ever before when a force of 10,000 Xhosa attacked Grahamstown and for a time threatened the very existence of the colony. The Governor, Lord Charles Somerset, hastily concluded a dangerously ill-defined oral agreement with Ngcqika, the Xhosa chief whom he fondly imagined to possess paramount authority, whereby the territory between the Fish and Keiskamma rivers was declared to be 'neutral' or 'ceded' territory – a sort of buffer zone beyond the frontier. The issues were clouded still further when Somerset permitted some of the Xhosa back into the territory 'on sufferance' but, as far as they were concerned, as of right. As an additional response to the 1819 war, the British government sponsored the settlement of the territory immediately to the west of the Fish River by 4,000 British settlers, in the hope that they would provide a further line of defence against Xhosa incursions at minimum expense to Britain. The hope proved quite illusory: the presence of a substantial new settler population on the frontier made the frontier less rather than more stable. The whole frontier region continued to be plagued by a reciprocal process in which cattle raiding by the Xhosa sparked off counter-raids by Boer 'commando' groups, and vice-versa. It was in this fraught atmosphere of conflict that Christian missions in the Eastern Cape had to operate.[22]

Apart from some limited work during the eighteenth century by the Moravians, the missionary history of the Cape begins in 1798 with the appointment by the LMS of the Dutchman Johannes van der Kemp to work in the colony. The early activity of the LMS was directed almost exclusively at the Khoisan population within the boundaries of the colony, and the Society's missionaries soon earned the dislike of the Boers for their championship of native interests and tendency to attract the Khoisan away from the Boer farms to Christian villages based on the mission stations. Following repeated complaints to the British government about the conduct of the LMS mission, Dr John Philip arrived in Cape Town in 1819 with a commission from the LMS Directors to set in order the Society's affairs in the colony. In fact the new LMS superintendent in the Cape was destined to make himself more hated among the settler community than any of his predecessors. During the 1820s Philip's chief concern was with the exploited and virtually enslaved condition of the Khoisan. In 1826 he came to England to plead their cause, only to find that many within the LMS and 'a great portion of the religious public thought I had stepped out of my sphere and had committed the deadly sin of having meddled with politics'.[23] However, early in 1827 Philip gained the approval of the LMS Directors for a memorial on the state of the Khoisan to the Colonial Secretary. Equally important was Philip's success in persuading T. F. Buxton to act as parliamentary champion of his cause. Buxton also persuaded Philip to write a book, *Researches in South Africa*, published in 1828, arguing the rights of the Khoisan population to justice and freedom of labour. Philip's representations to the Colonial Office through Buxton, and by personal interview with the Evangelical permanent Under-Secretary, James Stephen, were decisive in securing the British government's endorsement of the Cape government's 50th Ordinance of July 1828, which was a major liberal reform of the legal status of the Khoisan population, and provided the basis for the adoption of a non-racial constitution by the colony in 1853.[24]

Philip returned to the Cape in 1829 to find himself vilified by Boers and British settlers alike as a pernicious humanitarian meddler who had besmirched their reputation in his *Researches*. Many of the accusations made against the colonists in his book have been challenged, but Philip's latest biographer substantially vindicates the accuracy of his central contention that the Khoisan population of the colony were deprived of basic civil rights and treated as a pool of virtual forced labour by the whites.[25] Even before he turned his attention to the Xhosa in 1830, Philip's enduring reputation as the *bête noire* of the white man in South Africa had been firmly established.

The British settlers who arrived in 1820 in the lands immediately to the west of the Fish River – which became known as the Albany district – included a party of Wesleyan Methodists, most of them from Great Queen Street Chapel in London. They were accompanied by the Rev. William Shaw, who was to combine pastoral ministry to the settlers with his role as a WMMS missionary to the Xhosa beyond the frontier. Under Shaw's leadership Wesleyanism became, in the course of the 1820s, the dominant religious influence in the Albany settlement, and the WMMS missionaries became closely identified with the interests of the settler community.[26] Nonetheless, Shaw possessed a strong missionary vision of a chain of WMMS stations beyond the frontier stretching north-eastwards as far as Pondoland. By 1834 the Wesleyans had six stations among the Xhosa, whereas the LMS had only one.[27] The divergence in view between the two missionary groups was already clearly discernible. The LMS under Philip's leadership had assumed the mantle of defender of the Khoisan, and was now turning its attention to the Xhosa: Philip made two journeys beyond the frontier in 1830 and 1832–33 which convinced him that the Xhosa were in dire peril from the cattle raiding of the Boer commandos and the lack of a consistent frontier policy from the British government.[28] Of regular missionary work among the Xhosa, and of the British settlers of the eastern Cape, Philip knew relatively little. The Wesleyan missionaries, on the other hand, had considerable experience of Xhosa resistance to the gospel and a decidedly pro-settler political orientation. The stage was set for one of the most bitter disputes to mar the unity of the early nineteenth-century missionary movement.

In December 1834 the fragile peace of the eastern frontier finally collapsed when the Xhosa chief Maqoma invaded the colony with 12,000 men. Maqoma had been deemed by the Governor to have infringed the terms of his residence 'on sufferance' within the 'ceded territory', and had seen what he regarded as his territory taken away and given to a group of resettled Khoisan. The initial reaction of John Philip and the Wesleyan missionaries to this Sixth Frontier War was remarkably similar: both attributed the war primarily to the vagaries of the colony's frontier policy rather than fixing exclusive blame on either the Xhosa or the settlers. However, attitudes polarized as the war proceeded.[29] Philip reacted to the savage reprisals inflicted on the Xhosa by increasingly portraying the Xhosa as more sinned-against that sinning; they had been provoked by attacks on their cattle and expropriation of their lands, and he implied that the British settlers had been as guilty as the Boers.[30] The Wesleyans, who had suffered the destruction of three of their mission stations by the Xhosa, repeated settler allegations that Philip had incited the Xhosa to rebellion, and denied that the British settlers had been guilty of any injustice towards the Xhosa. This interpretation was accepted by William Shaw, who had returned to England in March 1833 and did not return to the Cape till March 1837. Shaw defended the settlers against what he believed to be the 'unfounded calumny' propagated by Philip and the missionary press in Britain in *A Letter to the Right Hon. the Earl of Aberdeen*, published in 1835. Shaw conceded that British border policy had been 'exceedingly mischievous', fluctuating between extremes of severity and indulgence, but maintained that the 'principal source of the evil' was quite simply 'the moral state and habits of the Caffre tribes'; they shared with all nomadic tribes a natural propensity to robbery, which could be checked only by the benefits of Christianity and a settled existence.[31]

On subsequent reflection Shaw placed increasingly heavy stress on this theological explanation of Xhosa behaviour on the frontier. The Xhosa had endured 'thousands of years' of heathenism, during which 'the light of traditionary knowledge concerning God and moral subjects has been growing more and more dim, till we at length found them in a state of almost total darkness'. The apostle Paul's 'humiliating description of unmitigated ungodliness' in Romans 3:10–18 was '*literally* applicable' to the current state of Xhosa society.[32] The hidden premiss of this ostensibly evangelical argument was the questionable assumption that man's natural sinfulness finds full and free expression in a 'heathen' society but is kept under effectual control by the restraining hand of Christian civilization. The equation of African heathenism with the Pauline account of the moral condition of the Gentile world would have been theologically cogent and practically acceptable if it had been combined with an equal recognition of the continued force of human depravity in the so-called 'Christian' society of the European settlers. The observation of the Wesleyan *Missionary Notices* in December 1835 that 'it would be a mistaken philanthropy, and a palpable contradiction of St Paul's description of the Gentile world, to represent mere Heathen men as combining in their character all that is noble and excellent' would have commanded almost universal assent throughout the nineteenth century as a general missionary principle.[33] Where it became dangerous was in its tacit implication of the virtual moral innocence of the Xhosa's opponents and competitors in the struggle for land. Shaw and the WMMS as a society thus drew heavily on a selective application of the Christian doctrine of total depravity to contradict Philip's humanitarian picture of the Xhosa as victims of European oppression – although in reality Philip did not believe the Xhosa to be the noble innocents supposed by his opponents' caricature of his views.[34]

The response of the Cape government under Sir Benjamin D'Urban to the 'aggression' of the Xhosa was to issue a proclamation in May 1835 sentencing the offending Xhosa groups as 'treacherous and irreclaimable savages' to be expelled for ever from all land west of the Kei River (the Ciskei). To Philip and his LMS colleagues D'Urban's proclamation represented a denial of the power of the gospel as well as of natural justice. Philip immediately made urgent representations to T. F. Buxton and the LMS to demand of the British government that the decree of expulsion should be reversed. However, Philip made it very clear that he was not averse to the extension of the colonial frontier to the Kei River, provided that the land rights of the Xhosa within the Ciskei were fully guaranteed.[35] Buxton and the Rev. William Ellis of the LMS accordingly urged Lord Glenelg, the Colonial Secretary, to 'restore the country to the Caffers, or if it must be part of the Colony, not to give it to the Colonists, but preserve it for the Caffers, bringing them under the laws of the Colony'.[36] During the autumn of 1835 Glenelg changed his mind about the justice and policy of D'Urban's annexation, and at the end of December he ordered D'Urban to prepare to abandon the Ciskei – a decision which Glenelg confirmed in 1836. The decision was greeted with anger and dismay by the British settlers and the Boers; it was the last straw for frontier Boers exasperated by humanitarian interference, and they began the legendary Great Trek northwards to escape British rule. D'Urban and the settlers blamed Philip for Glenelg's decision, but it is far more likely that the Colonial Office was motivated by fear of the additional cost which extension of the frontier would involve. Moreover, Philip did not want abandonment, but a benevolent imperial rule which would give the Xhosa security in their lands and the benefits of British law.[37]

Although increasingly at odds with Philip over the interpretation of the causes of the 1834–35 war, the Wesleyan missionaries took an almost identical view to Philip of the direction which frontier policy now ought to take. William Shaw favoured the incorporation of the 'neutral' territory within the colony but with ample lands reserved for those Xhosa willing to place themselves under British protection.[38] Shaw testified to this effect before the parliamentary select committee on aborigines, appointed in 1835 under Buxton's chairmanship as a direct result of Philip's agitation on behalf of the frontier Xhosa. The committee also heard evidence from the Rev. John Beecham, joint secretary of the WMMS, that William Boyce, a strongly pro-settler Wesleyan missionary, considered D'Urban's policy of expulsion to be unwise and objectionable. Boyce believed, like Philip, that 'if taken under colonial protection and British law ... [the Xhosa] might not only have their active enmity neutralized, but be converted into our good friends'.[39] Although less far apart in their prescriptions for frontier policy after 1834 than they themselves acknowledged, the two groups of missionaries still differed markedly in the extent of their sympathy for settler interests. Relations between Shaw and Philip reached their nadir in 1838–39 in a vituperative exchange of correspondence, subsequently published by Shaw.[40] The seriousness of the strain imposed on the customary amity between the WMMS and the LMS is evidenced by the substantial divergence between the accounts of the episode in their respective society histories.[41]

Britain's abandonment of the Ciskei in 1836–37 was no more than a temporary hiccup in an apparently inevitable process which sucked Britain into deeper and deeper involvement in southern Africa. Within a decade the British had annexed not merely the Ciskei but Natal as well. The small portion of the story which we have examined poses one telling question of importance to the theme of this book. Which of the two opposing groups of missionaries ought to be censured for collaboration with imperialism? John Philip and the LMS showed the same resolution in defending native interests against settler exploitation as Knibb and the BMS had shown on behalf of the West Indian slaves. Philip, like Knibb, had found himself propelled into the political arena by his concern for humanity and the interests of the gospel. Yet Philip was a believer in 'commerce and Christianity' and a disciple of Adam Smith, advocating consumerism as the solution to the economic dependence of Khoisan or Xhosa.[42] More embarrassing to the status of Philip as a liberal hero is his unashamed advocacy of racial segregation, which enables one historian to described him unfairly as 'an advocate of apartheid ahead of his time'.[43] Most incongruous of all to the mind of a modern political liberal is Philip's fervent belief in the benevolent purposes of British imperialism: Britain, like ancient Rome, was called to spread her rule and her institutions among barbarian peoples to protect them from oppression and raise them to civilization.[44] It ought also to be pointed out that Philip's overtly political stance (as well as his dictatorial style) was resented by some of his LMS colleagues – notably by Robert Moffat – and was eventually disowned by his own society.[45]

Shaw and his colleagues in the WMMS, on the other hand, claimed to be non-political, but in practice espoused most of the political and territorial ambitions of the British settler community. William Boyce and the leaders of Grahamstown Wesleyanism even defended the Voortrekkers and deplored 'the loss of so many stalwart Boers from the defensive power of the Colony'.[46] Yet the Wesleyan missionaries were, strictly speaking, far less imperialistic than Philip. They did not share Philip's grandiose imperial dreams, but instead advocated colonial self-government on the West Indian pattern in order to free settler power from humanitarian-inspired control from London.[47] The choice in South Africa in the 1830s was thus between Philip's humanitarian imperialism and the Wesleyans' white colonialism. Much of the subsequent history of southern Africa was to be shaped by the interplay of these two opposing forces. In colonies of substantial white settlement, imperialism and settler colonialism have more often been in conflict than in co-operation. It is hard to resist the conclusion that those missionaries who, when faced with such alternatives, aligned themselves with 'imperialism', were acting in greater consistency with Christian principles, however flawed their attitudes may seem to us to be.

3. Missions in India, 1793–1860

Britain's role in India had its origins in the purely commercial objectives of the East India Company, but in the course of the nineteenth century the weight of domestic public opinion and Britain's own strategic interests in the East both dictated that British policy in India could not be governed by commercial considerations alone. Christian missions played an essential part in the broadening of Britain's imperial objectives in India. Before 1813 the scope for missionary work was limited. Although the East India Company, which ruled British India till 1858, did not prohibit missionary activity, all missionaries (and indeed all European visitors) required a licence from the Company to reside in its territories. The German missionaries who worked in the Madras presidency in South India under the auspices of the SPCK never had any difficulty in obtaining licences and were positively encouraged by the Company's officials.[48] However, the evangelical dissenters sent out by the new missionary societies founded at the turn of the eighteenth and nineteenth centuries were rather a different matter. Not only were the dissenting enthusiasts hostile to the hallowed bond between church and state, but some of them, at least, were known also to be political radicals and republicans who sympathized with the revolution in France. These fears were exaggerated but not wholly without foundation: of the early BMS missionaries in India, John Fountain was acknowledged as harbouring republican views, whilst William Ward had been involved in a corresponding society (devoted to political reform) and radical journalism in Derby and Hull.[49] Knowing that majority opinion on the Court of Directors was hostile, the evangelical societies made the reasonable assumption that no licences would be granted to their missionaries, and consequently never applied for them until 1813. Despite their unlicensed status, however, the early BMS and LMS missionaries in Bengal found that most Company officials were prepared to tolerate or even welcome their presence. Under the Governor-Generalship of Lord Wellesley (1798–1805) the climate for missionary work became positively favourable following Carey's appointment in 1810 as tutor in Indian languages at the Company's college in Fort William. From 1806 relations between missions and the Company were again tense in the wake of a mutiny by sepoys in the Madras presidency, which influential figures, including the chairman of the Court of Directors, attributed to fears of forcible conversion stirred up by missionary evangelism. The Company's religious policy hardened still further in 1811 – probably in tandem with Lord Sidmouth's attempt in Parliament to impose new restrictions on the freedom of Nonconformist ministers to preach in England. An LMS missionary was refused entry to India and sent home. No more unlicensed missionaries were allowed in till after 1813.

In 1793 William Wilberforce had tried and failed to insert in the revised charter of the East India Company a clause specifically requiring the governments of the presidencies to maintain 'a sufficient number of schoolmasters and missionaries in their territories'.[50] The charter was again due for renewal in 1813, and from 1812 Wilberforce led evangelical opinion in demanding the insertion of pro-missionary clauses in the charter. Concerted opposition in the parliamentary committees considering the charter forced Wilberforce to rely more heavily than he would have wished on mechanisms of extra-parliamentary pressure. Between February and June 1813, 908 petitions, containing a total of nearly half a million signatures in favour of the introduction of Christianity to India, were presented to Parliament.[51] Almost all the petitions came from Nonconformists, for whom the campaign was another episode in their struggle for religious liberty. The outcome of the campaign was more of a compromise than is generally believed. The Anglicans secured their objective of a bishop and three archdeacons to be maintained out of Company revenues. The missionary lobby achieved a clause which declared that 'sufficient facilities ought to be afforded by law to persons desirous of going to and remaining in India' for the purpose of disseminating 'useful knowledge' and 'religious and moral improvement' –

but all explicit reference to 'missionaries' had been studiously avoided. Moreover, the requirement for all missionaries to be licensed was retained, although now with provision for the right of appeal beyond the Court of Directors to the supreme Board of Control.[52] The Company continued to exercise a degree of regulation of missionary activity until 1833, when the requirement for a licence was finally withdrawn. Nevertheless, the 1813 changes opened the way for a steady increase in the number of missionaries in British India and gave them for the first time genuine freedom to itinerate and preach in public.

The early relationship between Protestant missions and East India Company rule was thus ambiguous. If it was not characterized by the open conflict which subsequent Christian literature tended to imply, neither can it fairly be described as anything approaching a partnership or conspiracy. The early Serampore missionaries were, on the one hand, united in their confidence that British rule in India constituted 'the greatest temporal benefit that could have been conferred on the inhabitants in general';[53] yet they agitated repeatedly for the reform of the Company's policy on religious and moral issues. They thus set the tone of missionary attitudes in India for the remainder of the nineteenth century: Christians questioned, not the fact of British rule, but the way in which it operated.

Between 1813 and 1857 missionary-imperial relationships in India were focused on two categories of issue – issues of humanity and issues of idolatry. Nineteenth-century Christians would not have perceived any clear distinction between the two categories. Foremost among the issues of humanity until 1829 was the missionary campaign for the prohibition of *sati* – the Hindu practice of burning widows (theoretically with their consent) on their husbands' funeral pyres. To contradict allegations that the practice was rare, Carey conducted a survey which showed that in 1803, 438 *satis* took place within a thirty-mile radius of Calcutta.[54] The Serampore missionaries' publicity on *sati* was widely used by Wilberforce in the charter renewal debates of 1812–13. However, the majority view of Company officials and directors remained that to prohibit *sati* would constitute an unwarranted and politically dangerous interference with the religious practices of the Hindu population. This view could not be countermanded until there was an overwhelming sentiment in public opinion and in Parliament that *sati* was in effect ritual murder on a vast scale which no government could tolerate. The creation of just such a sentiment was very largely the achievement of the speeches and writings of two Baptist missionaries – William Ward from Serampore, and James Peggs, a General Baptist missionary from Orissa. Without their publicity, Lord William Bentinck's prohibition of *sati* in Bengal in December 1829 would not have been possible. The governments of the Madras and Bombay presidencies followed suit in abolishing the practice in 1830.[55]

Missionaries agitated against *sati* on grounds of simple humanity. But *sati* was to the Christian mind merely one expression of an idolatrous religious system which seemed to foster a multitude of cruelties. Perhaps most notorious of all was the annual festival at the Hindu temple of Jagannath at Puri in the Cuttack district, where devotees occasionally threw themselves to their deaths under the wheels of idols' carriages.[56] The festival was shocking enough in itself; what touched evangelical nerves to the quick was the fact that the Company's government levied a tax on pilgrims to Jagannath and similar temples in the north of India, in order to support the temples in accordance with the practice of the previous Maratha rulers of the region. Evangelical opinion tended to identify India as the chief stronghold of idolatry, unique in the extent of its apostasy from the worship of the true God. It was, therefore, peculiarly shameful that the British government in India should be involved in the support of Hindu idolatry through the pilgrim tax and other subsidies to Hindu temples. Missionary agitation against the pilgrim tax went hand in hand with the campaign against *sati*, and was pursued with single-minded enthusiasm once *sati* had been abolished. James Peggs wrote to Bentinck in April 1830 that he rejoiced greatly in the abolition of *sati*, 'but the discontinuance of British connection with idolatry would save more lives and confer a greater boon upon India than even your Lordship's late popular measure'.[57] On this issue evangelical pressure faced not merely the Company's ingrained aversion to interference with Indian religion but also the more carnal obstacle of the profit motive. In the seventeen years up to 1831 the Company had made a net profit of £99,205 from the Jagannath festivals; the yield from the pilgrim tax at other temples was higher still.[58] Although the Board of Control, under the presidency of the Evangelical Charles Grant the younger (later Lord Glenelg), ordered the Governor General in 1833 to discontinue the pilgrim tax and all involvement of Company officials in the management of Hindu festivals and temples, the Indian government was permitted a fatal degree of discretion to implement the order at a gentlemanly pace. As a result, nothing was done to abolish the pilgrim tax until 1838–41, when renewed pressure from Christian opinion compelled the Whig government to prod the different presidency governments into action.[59] By 1841 the tax had been discontinued, but annual government grants to the Jagannath temple and numerous other temples throughout India continued through the 1840s and 1850s. According to a memorial to the Court of Directors from the Bombay missionary conference in February 1858, no less than 26,589 temples and shrines in the Bombay presidency alone were in receipt of financial support from the Company.[60]

The widespread Christian belief that East India Company rule had been lukewarm in its support for missions and continued to be compromised by its support for 'idolatry', forms the backcloth to an understanding of Christian responses to the Indian mutiny of 1857–58. Missionaries and their domestic supporters interpreted the mutiny as a divine judgment upon

Britain – not primarily for military aggression or territorial ambition, but for religious disobedience. Nonconformists were more likely than Anglicans to reflect on the 'inordinate, secular, selfish ambition' which had marked the course of British rule in India, but even those prepared to be this critical were almost unanimous in their acceptance of the providential legitimacy of British rule as a fundamental principle.[61] Despite the fact that the sepoy rebellion had been sparked off by fears of forcible conversion to Christianity, the missionary lobby stoutly maintained that the mutiny was the consequence of Britain having given India not too much Christianity, but too little. The reports of atrocities inflicted on British women and children shocked all sections of British opinion, but Christians could comment that such atrocities were not to be wondered at, since they were committed by a people long accustomed to the religious atrocities of *sati*, self-torture and the Jagannath festivals.[62] The events of the mutiny were thus portrayed as a natural overflow of the idolatry which Britain had so foolishly encouraged. Some discovered clinching evidence of the intimate connection between sin and judgment in the divine economy by reference to the case of a sepoy dismissed from the Bengal army in 1819 merely, it was alleged, because he had sought Christian baptism. 'Where did this incident take place?', asked the *Wesleyan Methodist Magazine* triumphantly, 'It was at Meerut; the very place where the flames of mutiny broke out with a red and fierce glare that lighted the world with consternation. They who cannot read the lesson of Divine retribution here, are dull indeed.'[63]

The ugliest aspect of British reactions to the mutiny was the reinforcement of crudely racist evaluations of the Indian character. The committee of the Peace Society observed with alarm the growth amongst the European community in India of a 'settled feeling of hatred and scorn' towards the native population, and made representations to the missionary societies to remind their Indian missionaries of the Christian duty to promote moderation and mercy. 'It is not impossible', the Society warned the LMS, 'that their own minds may to some extent have been tainted by that violent and vindictive spirit which is breathed everywhere around them.'[64] Such fears were probably justified, for missionary organs were quick to argue that optimistic secular evaluations of the Indian character had been refuted by the incontrovertible evidence of the sepoys' 'deeds of perfidy and blood'.[65] As with the Wesleyan missionaries' reaction to the South African Frontier War of 1834–35, the Christian doctrine of total depravity was exclusively applied to the 'heathen' party in a situation of armed racial conflict, with reprehensible results. The temptation to identify British troops with the armies of God was all the stronger when so many of the officers responsible for the military successes of the campaign were known evangelicals and missionary supporters – the Baptist Henry Havelock was the best-known example. The military victories of Christian men were seen as God's confirmation of the justice of the British cause in India – God had honoured those who had honoured him through their open profession of Christian faith in public office, and had thus given the stamp of his approval to Britain's role in India, provided that its true missionary objectives were adhered to.[66]

The logical deduction from the evangelical interpretation of the mutiny was that the road back to imperial prosperity in India followed the path of Christian duty. 'All recent events in India', affirmed the *Church Missionary Intelligencer* in 1860, 'have urged upon us this lesson ... that if we would rule in peace over the heathen entrusted to our charge, we must give to them the Gospel.'[67] Even Nonconformists, who were opposed on principle to any idea of promoting Christianity by government agency, urged that British rule in India must henceforth be discernibly Christian in character by its fearless pursuit of justice, even if this meant cutting across the prejudices of caste and religious sensibility. Between 1858 and 1860 the missionary societies applied considerable pressure on the British government (now in direct control in India) to forswear a policy of religious 'neutrality' and in particular to allow Bible teaching in government schools. They had little success, for the effect of the mutiny on government policy in India was to put the brake firmly on endeavours to regenerate India in a western image. At the level of public opinion, however, there was a substantial convergence between the evangelical imperative to make India secure by giving her the gospel and the economic imperative to make her secure by the promotion of public works and commercial development. British capital poured in its millions into Indian railway-building after 1858, while missionary periodicals commented enthusiastically that railways were an ideal instrument in the hands of providence for breaking down the isolationism which was the most serious obstacle to the gospel in India's caste-ridden society. Robert Arthington invested money in one of the railway companies in the hope that railways would both facilitate the growth of cotton production and promote evangelism and literature distribution. A navigation scheme in central India undertaken in response to commercial pressure from Lancashire cotton interests became the means of establishing a new CMS mission on the Godaveri River in 1861. India experienced its own version of 'commerce and Christianity'.[68]

Historians sometimes express surprise that the same missionary conscience which agitated so fervently against West Indian slavery failed to present any fundamental challenge to the central assumptions of British rule in India. Part of the answer lies in the very arbitrariness of the course of British annexations in India, which, as was stressed in chapter 3, seemed to confirm that the hand of God was at work. In India, as in South Africa, it was hard not to see 'a great law of Divine Providence' in operation, pushing the frontier of British rule ever onwards, despite the attempts of cost-conscious statesmen to call a halt to the process.[69] Evangelical missionaries were primarily concerned with the advance of the gospel and the moral responsibility of the nation before God. They directed their moral passion not against British imperial rule, but against those practices which palpably impeded missionary progress and threatened Britain's moral standing before God. West Indian slavery and government support for idolatry in India equally stood condemned on both counts, and missionary meetings spoke of the two in the same breath as comparable obstacles to the spread of the gospel.[70] It must also be emphasized that a quiescent political stance on the principle of British rule was the only option if missions were to gain a secure foothold in British India. Without it, there would have been no Christian presence in India to agitate for social and moral reform.

Concern for evangelistic progress was undoubtedly the primary generator of missionary involvement in social reform in nineteenth-century India.[71] However, simple Christian compassion for the needs of humanity is the only adequate explanation for missionary agitation against *sati* up to 1829, and was a powerful element in the later nineteenth-century missionary campaigns against the exploitation of the Indian peasantry by European indigo planters or *zamindari* landlords.[72] In seeking to undermine the caste system – an objective shared by all missionaries, though with disagreements over method – missionaries were confronting in the name of Christ a structural system which appeared to inculcate social divisiveness and racial hatred. One historian has aptly observed that 'one of the most striking features of the British missionary movement in India throughout the century is that so many men, influenced by an evangelical theology and a concept of mission which did not emphasize the importance of the struggle for social justice, should have become so caught up in "temporal" affairs and social protest'.[73] However much their theologies of mission and empire stand open to criticism, the fact remains that nineteenth-century missionaries in India left an imprint on the political ideals of the sub-continent whose influence can be seen in the commitment of the Indian constitution of 1949 to the principle of the fundamental rights and equality of all Indian citizens.[74]

4. Missions in China during the opium wars

In the eighteenth century, imperial China could claim with justice to be the greatest empire on earth. The Manchu or Ch'ing dynasty had constructed an Asian empire which easily outstripped its British, French or Dutch counterparts in terms of geographical extent or administrative sophistication. By the mid-nineteenth century the administration of the Chinese empire by the 'scholar-gentry' class was showing signs of stagnation, and British naval power posed a greater external threat to Chinese security. Nonetheless, the 'Celestial Empire' remained a supremely self-confident society, viewing with studied disdain the endeavours of Western barbarians to force an entry into its territory. The events of 1839 to 1860 were to administer an irreversible blow to that self-confidence, as the conservative, bureaucratized, formal imperialism of the Chinese empire came under challenge from the aggressive, informal, economic imperialism of the Western powers. The conflict between the two opened China to Christian missions.

British commercial interest in China advanced in step with the rise of the China tea trade from the late eighteenth century onwards. The East India Company paid for its increasing imports of China tea by exporting first cotton from Gujarat and then opium from Bengal to China. By the early 1830s the opium trade had become essential to the financing of the tea trade and scarcely less important as a source of revenue within India itself. Until 1834 the East India Company enjoyed monopolistic control of the China trade. However, cumulative pressure from free trading interests secured the breaking of the monopoly in 1834. The result was an immediate increase in the volume of the opium trade and a rush of new firms into the port of Canton. The Emperor required all foreign trade to be channelled through Canton, and in particular through the hands of a cartel of Chinese merchants known as the Cohong. The conflicts of the opium wars stemmed from the incompatibility between the attempts of the Chinese to continue to impose rigid regulation on all foreign trade and the irrepressible ambitions of Western free traders convinced that China was the *El Dorado* of the Orient.[75]

Protestant missions maintained only a toe-hold on the Chinese mainland by making use of the residential rights for foreigners available at Canton and the Portuguese enclave of Macao. Robert Morrison of the LMS worked in Canton or Macao from 1807 to 1834, engaged mainly in Bible translation, and was supported by his post as Chinese secretary and translator to the East India Company. The precariousness of the Western position in China compelled the earliest missionary pioneers such as Morrison to accept secular roles which in other missionary contexts would have been deemed unacceptable. Even more compromising than Morrison's was the position of the independent Prussian missionary Karl Gützlaff. From 1831 to 1833 Gützlaff sailed the China coast, first on a Chinese junk whose crew were opium users, then on a ship chartered by the East India Company to discover new northern outlets for the opium traffic, and finally on a merchantman actually engaged in the contraband opium trade. Gützlaff quite literally combined distribution of Chinese tracts and scriptures with interpreting duties for Jardine, Matheson and Company, destined to become the leading British entrepreneur in opium and other branches of the China trade.[76] Probably more significant in the long term was Gützlaff's work in bringing the needs of China before the attention of the Christian public in Britain and various other European countries. The published account of his three voyages along the Chinese coast, and a number of pamphlets published between 1835 and 1838, placed China firmly on the map of the British missionary conscience for the first time.[77]

By the late 1830s contraband opium imports into China had reached a scale sufficient to cause a serious drain of silver from the country and precipitate widespread economic dislocation in China's southern provinces. Economic more than moral concern lay behind the imperial government's decision in March 1839 to order the surrender of all imported opium. Events now moved rapidly to crisis point. In June all British merchants were expelled from Canton. By August the first British frigate had arrived off the port and opened hostilities. The first 'opium war' had begun.

The British government and British commercial interests stoutly maintained that the issue at stake in the war was not the opium traffic in itself but freedom and security for Western trade as a whole. The contention has more than a measure of truth, but it in no way diminishes the fact that Britain was fighting a war of aggressive economic imperialism. While the war was in progress, Christian opinion as to its validity was relatively quiet, although certainly not uncritical. Once news reached Britain of the signing of the Treaty of Nanking on 29 August 1842, however, Christian comment became vociferous and excited. On the one hand, there was relief at the termination of a war so embarrassing to Christian morality. 'We have triumphed', Lord Shaftesbury confided to his diary on 22 November 1842, 'in one of the most lawless, unnecessary, and unfair struggles in the records of History; it was a war on which good men could not invoke the favour of Heaven.'[78] On the other hand, there was uncontrolled excitement that the treaty guaranteed rights of foreign residence in five 'treaty ports'. The door was now open for missionary work in these five cities of Canton, Amoy, Foochow, Ningpo and Shanghai. There is evidence that the missionary societies faced substantial pressure from their constituencies from November 1842 to January 1843 to disregard financial constraints and commence operations in China. The LMS, exclaiming 'the voice of God to his Church is as distinctly uttered by his Providence as though we heard it from the Holy Oracle, "Behold I have set before thee an open door, and no man can shut it. Go forward!"', wasted no time in opening a special China fund; by the end of March 1843 the fund stood at £7,743.[79] The CMS was hampered by financial crisis, and, to the manifest displeasure of many of its supporters, declined to commence a China mission. However, a single donation of £6,000 soon enabled the Society to reverse its decision, and the first two CMS missionaries embarked for China in June 1844. The prospects of an opening China dazzled the Christian imagination no less than the commercial imagination of Manchester free traders. China remained in the forefront of the British missionary conscience until at least 1845. Even without taking special funds for China into account, missionary giving to the main English societies attained an exceptionally high level in real terms between 1843 and 1846.[80]

106

The British missionary movement (and also the American)[81] thus welcomed the favourable outcome for missions of a war fought in the cause of free trade – a war whose morality it had consistently criticized. To condemn this response as an unprincipled act of rationalization is to miss the significance for this episode of the evangelical theology of providence outlined in the previous chapter. According to this theology, there must have been some purpose behind the war of 1839–42, and, moreover, some purpose which was consistent with the known character of God's government. Samuel Wilberforce put the question to an SPG meeting in 1846:

> Will any reasonable man tell me that the providence of God led on a Christian people into that war in which so many of that unhappy people perished unavoidably, in order that the English people might buy that luxury [tea] some penny a pound cheaper than they could have bought it otherwise? I declare that it seems to me tantamount to denying the government of God to harbour such a thought.[82]

Providence, Melvill Horne had written in his *Letters on Missions* in 1794, is 'a mysterious book, not easily legible, and best understood when read backward'.[83] In retrospect the first opium war appeared to evangelicals to be an incontrovertible example of God's characteristic device of using the 'wrath of man to praise him' – God was bending 'the instrumentality of evils which have arisen through the sin of man and the devices of Satan' to his own saving purposes, and thus leading such evils to work out their own eventual destruction.[84] Even a leading peace advocate such as the Congregationalist John Angell James adhered to this view while continuing to denounce the injustice of the war.[85]

Despite the generous response to their special China appeals, the missionary societies found candidates for China hard to come by, and Christian interest in China tailed off in the later 1840s, as the exaggerated nature of the missionary expectations of 1842–43 became evident. Enthusiasm for China revived markedly in 1853, when reports began to reach Britain of the large-scale Taiping rebellion against the Ch'ing dynasty which had begun in Kwangsi province in 1850. The leaders of the Taipings proclaimed an ideology which contained elements of Christian teaching, and Christian opinion in Britain seized on the movement's more obviously anti-idolatrous and 'Protestant' features to speculate that a potentially Christian government might soon be established on the dragon throne. More sober and cautious evaluations of the rebellion were given by most missionaries on the spot and by the major missionary societies, and their caution was subsequently vindicated.[86] Nonetheless, the rebellion served to keep China near to the centre of missionary aspirations and stimulated hopes that, by one means or another, God would soon complete his work of opening China to missionary endeavour. Evangelical frustration at lack of missionary progress in China was expressed in renewed protests at the opium trade, which was now identified as an obstacle to the gospel as well as a national crime before God. The contrast between British immorality and the noble resistance of the Chinese emperor to the trade, complained the *Wesleyan Methodist Magazine* in 1856, was being 'held up to the confusion of our Missionaries when they attempt to glory in the cross of Christ'. 'Every chest of opium that is smuggled into China', agreed John Angell James, 'is a stone of stumbling thrown in the missionary's path.'[87] Moreover, providentialist logic suggested that what was so clearly contrary to national duty must also be contrary to national interest. The missionary lobby consistently ignored the indispensability of the opium shipments to the financing of the tea trade, and made opium the scapegoat for the failure of British manufacturers to penetrate the Chinese market on anything like the scale anticipated in 1842–43. The Bishop of Victoria (one of the two CMS pioneers sent to China in.1844) assured a CMS meeting in Manchester in 1857 that English manufactures were being 'beaten out of the field by the stronger force of sensual temptation'.[88]

As in Africa, Christian opposition to 'illegitimate' commerce was leading significant elements of the British missionary movement to endorse the expansionist designs of 'legitimate' free traders. The continuing British determination to secure a free hand for Western trade with China – whether legitimate or illegitimate – was the true cause of the second opium war, the Second Anglo-Chinese War of 1856–60. The immediate pretext for the war was the seizure by the Chinese authorities of the *Arrow*, a vessel which had been peddling opium under the British flag. The British Governor of Hong Kong, Sir John Bowring, responded to this 'insult' to the Union Jack by ordering the British navy to bombard Canton. Anglicans and Nonconformists, both on the field in China and at home, were equally divided in their reactions to this British behaviour. The Evangelical Anglican newspaper, the *Record*, and the *Wesleyan Methodist Magazine*, for example, defended the bombardment of Canton and the policy of the Palmerston government.[89] Open critics of the war included the editor of the *Church Missionary Intelligencer*, Joseph Ridgeway; John Angell James in his pamphlet *God's Voice from China*, published in 1858; and Edward Steane, secretary of the Baptist Union, in his successful proposal for a BMS mission to China in 1859.[90] As in 1842–43, however, there was universal Christian agreement that the outcome of the war constituted a singular over-ruling of divine providence. It was, after all, a nice irony that the war had been precipitated by the action of Sir John Bowring, a former secretary of the Peace Society and a known disciple of Richard Cobden's anti-imperialism.[91] Such irony became full of providential meaning in the light of the Treaty of Tientsin (1858) and Convention of Peking (1860), which gave European travellers virtually unlimited access to the Chinese interior and guaranteed security for Christian converts. In James's words, 'God's voice from China to the British churches' was now unmistakable. The result of the war enabled existing societies working in China, such as the LMS and CMS, to expand their operations, encouraged the BMS to enter China for the first time, and made possible James Hudson Taylor's vision of a mission to inland China, which came to fruition in 1865. Opium had indeed opened the way for the gospel.

China's experience between 1839 and 1860 (and indeed, thereafter) illustrates how potent a force imperialism can be even when territorial rule by the imperial power is not at issue. It is also a salutary reminder that imperialism has not been a European prerogative – the Taiping movement was both a reflection of the economic dislocation which the opium trade had caused in China's southern provinces and an indication that many Chinese still regarded the Ch'ing dynasty as an alien imperialism. More relevant to our purposes are the issues raised by the undeniably close association between the coming of Protestant Christianity to China and its forcible opening up by the power of Western commercial imperialism. It would be a mistake to concentrate too much fire on the morally ambiguous role of the eccentric Gützlaff, taking gospel pragmatism to its very limit in his combination of evangelistic, commercial and diplomatic functions. The real issues raised, as so often throughout this chapter, are theological ones. The missionary movement was unequivocal in its condemnation of the opium trade, and many Christians (though not all) were prepared to criticize the two wars of 1839–42 and 1858–60 as having no foundation in justice or morality. Yet, almost without exception, evangelicals accepted the outcome of those wars, believing that God had turned the evil of human design to the good of his saving purposes. Convinced that the gospel was the greatest and only lasting good that Britain could impart to Chinese humanity, Christians confidently deduced divine purpose from the consequences of the wars, and happily dispatched missionaries to work under the imperial umbrella of the 'unequal treaties'. Again it must be emphasized that the weight of responsibility for the eternal destiny of three hundred million Chinese souls was the ultimate moral consideration moving the evangelical conscience. Indeed, it was widely believed that the conversion of China would be the signal for the collapse of Satan's defences throughout the globe, and the dawning of millennial glory.[92] The question posed by the Christian history of nineteenth-century China is not so much whether or not missionaries compromised the gospel by collaboration with imperialist oppression, but whether they were justified in discerning the hand and purpose of God in specific historical events. If they were right, collaboration with imperialism was in a meaningful sense a duty imposed by the command of Christ and the claims of humanity.

5. Conclusion

These case-studies in the early period of British missionary history have illuminated two dominant motifs in the pattern of missionary attitudes: evangelical missionaries and their domestic supporters were concerned at almost any cost to see the progress of the gospel maintained; and most missionaries cast themselves in the role of defenders of native interests against the exploitative designs of European commercial or political forces. These overriding concerns resulted in widely differing political stances according to the precise configuration of the various imperial forces in any particular mission field, and the denominational background of the missionary. Nevertheless, it should be noted that in all four fields missionaries either saw or hoped to see these concerns satisfied by the exercise of some form of British intervention or control. In the West Indies, missionary pressure successfully brought the legislative power of the Westminster Parliament to bear against the economic colonialism of the plantation owners. In South Africa's more complex racial situation, missionary policy was caught between imperialism and settler colonialism; Philip's advocacy of direct British rule in native interests fell on deaf ears in his day, but foreshadowed things to come. Missionaries in India had an uneasy relationship with the East India Company, but welcomed the substitution of direct imperial control for Company rule after the mutiny, in the hope that responsibility before God rather than commercial profit would now be the governing influence on British policy. Lastly, in China, Christian opinion welcomed the outcome of British military intervention on behalf of British trade, because missionary opportunity seemed ultimately more important than the prolongation of humanitarian protest against a *fait accompli*.

The period from 1860 to 1895 was to see these two characteristic missionary concerns maintained just as strongly. However, just as British imperialism in the later nineteenth century more frequently assumed formal territorial expression, so the unchanging objectives of British missionaries now tended towards a more uniform set of solutions to particular missionary problems. Protection of the native was increasingly to imply annexation.

CHAPTER FIVE

From protection to annexation, 1860 to 1895

In missionary history, as in imperial history as a whole, the continuities between the earlier and later nineteenth century were more important than the discontinuities. The great majority of missionaries continued unshaken in their conviction that the offer of the gospel remained the only hope of salvation for all people – although by the 1890s the dissentient voices were more vocal and numerous. Similarly, most missionaries were still prepared to enter the political arena when missionary or native interests were directly threatened – although the new evangelicals of the Keswick school tended to be much more wary of political involvement. However, certain features of the missionary landscape were noticeably different in the later years of the century. Missionaries had only rarely been the sole European representatives in any field, but from the 1860s onwards the problems posed by secular white interests became more and more acute: settlers became more numerous and politically powerful, whilst trading interests more often took the form of chartered companies using military muscle to stake out claims for mineral rewards. Secondly, missionaries now found themselves having to respond, not to British imperial power in isolation, but to situations in Africa and the South Pacific where rival European powers were in competition for 'spheres of interest'. Thirdly, the spectrum of evangelistic situations was considerably more varied than in the early years of the missionary movement: some fields where success had been minimal suddenly began to present instances of mass conversion (India is the prime example); others, such as the LMS work among the Ndebele people of modern Zimbabwe, remained singularly unfruitful; others again, such as Buganda, offered success with a haste that brought its own problems. Evangelistic success placed a premium on the protection of new converts from harmful indigenous or alien forces. Evangelistic failure built up the pressure of missionary frustration, and increased the temptation to 'blow open' obdurate pagan societies by forceful means.

Two other developments must be borne in mind which relate more to domestic secular or ecclesiastical politics than to the mission field. Firstly, the extension of the parliamentary franchise in 1867 and 1884 and the great expansion of the press in Victorian England together rendered the missionary societies' supporting constituency both more aware and more influential politically than it had been previously. Opinion in the churches was not united in support of imperial expansion – in Nonconformity this was far from being the case – but it was capable of exerting substantial leverage on government policy in a humanitarian and pro-missionary direction, with consequences that were ultimately conducive to the growth of the empire. Secondly, Christian conceptions of the role of the state were themselves changing. The transformation was most marked among Nonconformists, whose history and principles had disposed them to favour a minimal role for the state in the ordering of society. While remaining opposed to all state regulation of religion, Victorian Nonconformists increasingly looked to the state to promote legislation that would extirpate public wrongs and provide a framework for a just and righteous society.[1] Nonconformists, as much as Anglicans, came to put their faith in the rule of law (and of British law in particular) as the means of enforcing Christian standards of justice and morality in society. The consequence, as far as foreign affairs were concerned, was growing Nonconformist support for measures which may appear to us as imperialistic, but were defended by many Victorian Christians as the simple dictates of justice and social order.

This chapter will examine four examples in which agitation by missionaries and domestic Christian opinion was wholly or partially responsible for the annexation of a territory by the British government. In each case a different denomination was involved. Fiji was the preserve of the Wesleyan Methodists. Bechuanaland was an LMS field and hence the particular concern of Congregationalists. Nyasaland was divided between the Church of Scotland and the Free Church of Scotland, and provides an instructive example of contradictory missionary responses to imperialism. Finally, Uganda was the scene of intense rivalry between the Evangelical Anglicans of the CMS and a French Roman Catholic mission.

1. Fiji, 1858–1874

In an age of singularly slow missionary progress, Fiji stood out as a spectacular example of evangelistic success. The first Wesleyan missionaries arrived in 1835 to find a society of palpable 'heathen darkness' in which infanticide, human sacrifice and cannibalism were endemic. Yet within twenty years Fijians were being converted in large numbers. By 1858 WMMS missionaries were waxing lyrical about the unrivalled place of Fiji in recent missionary history, and pleading for more workers to teach the flood of converts. Ten years later, out of a population in the islands of about 120,000, almost 106,000 were reported to be in regular attendance at public worship, and over 20,000 were enrolled church members or communicants meeting in class.[2] Political authority in the islands was disputed between

Cakobau, the Christian ruler of Bau and self-styled 'King' of Fiji, and M'afu, who held sway in the eastern part of the group with the backing of the King of Tonga. Before September 1858 there is little evidence of any pressure from the Wesleyan missionaries for Britain to assume sovereignty of Fiji. Although some missionaries were clearly imbued with ideals of a vaguely imperial nature, the question of annexation seems not to have been raised.[3] The burden of the message communicated from Fiji to the British public up to 1858 was rather the crying need for more missionary labourers.[4] As long as Fiji offered freedom for evangelistic action and some degree of political stability, the Wesleyan missionary presence was largely indifferent to imperial possibilities. The erosion of this indifference came about when these conditions were first threatened in 1858–59 and then progressively destroyed in the course of the 1860s.

Anxious letters written by the Wesleyan missionaries in September and October 1858 reported a two-fold threat to the political and religious freedom of Fiji. In September a French frigate had compelled Cakobau to sign a treaty granting French Roman Catholic missionaries equal rights and facilities in Fiji to those already possessed by the Wesleyans. The WMMS missionary, James Royce, reported that the frigate had had two Roman priests on board, and expressed the conviction of the missionary community 'that the Papists were at the bottom of this matter, and we may now look for something to follow in the wake'.[5] Evangelical anti-Catholicism, which assumed a particularly virulent form in Wesleyanism as a result of Wesleyan missionary experience in Ireland, now came into play to fuel fears that Catholic France might assume control of a Protestant mission field, as she had done in Tahiti in 1838–43 and New Caledonia in 1854. Within a few weeks of the visit of the French frigate, an American warship was in Fiji imposing terms of a different kind on Cakobau. The Americans were demanding speedy payment of a sum of 45,000 dollars in compensation for the ransacking of the house of the American consul in Fiji during a fire in 1849. The demand was accompanied, according to Royce, by threats of 'something very terrible from America'.[6] The British consul, W. T. Pritchard (himself the son of a former LMS missionary in Tahiti) promptly induced the fearful Cakobau to sign a treaty yielding the sovereignty of Fiji to Britain in return for Britain's assumption of responsibility for the American debt. Pritchard, who was supposed to be no more than a representative for British commercial interests, then set out for London to seek ratification of the deed of cession.

The proposed cession of Fiji to the British Crown was welcomed by the Wesleyan missionaries as a means of thwarting French Catholic machinations and of relieving Cakobau of the pressure of what they held to be manifestly unjust American claims. They also advocated British annexation as an instrument of political order which would safeguard 'the religious part of the people' from the 'oppression and murderous attacks' of non-Christian chiefs who refused to acknowledge Cakobau's supposed kingly authority.[7] These arguments were reproduced in a pamphlet published in 1859 by William Arthur, one of the general secretaries of the WMMS. Arthur claimed that if Britain did not annex Fiji, either France or America would, to the manifest disadvantage of British commercial and strategic interests. Arthur's most enthusiastic argument, however, focused on the desirability of supplementing the gift of Christianity with the benefits of Christian civilization: 'Fiji has received from England the greatest blessing of all, the gospel. It asks that which ranks next, peace and good government.'[8] Concern to make existing gospel victories secure against both external and internal threats had aligned the Wesleyan missionaries and their London masters with the cause of British imperialism in Fiji. The cause was, however, a hopeless one. In reality, the British government stood to gain very little from the acquisition of Fiji, and Pritchard returned to Fiji empty-handed at the beginning of November 1859. 'Everyone', commented one Wesleyan missionary, 'is sorely disappointed that Fiji is not accepted by our Government.'[9]

Pritchard, intent on building a personal empire in Fiji, did not give up. He succeeded in obtaining a renewed offer of cession from all the chiefs, which was more representative of the whole island group than Cakobau's previous offer could claim to be. This time Palmerston's government nibbled the bait and sent out Colonel W. J. Smythe to investigate the offer and report to London. However, Smythe's report strongly advised the government not to accept the cession, and any immediate prospect of annexation was accordingly ruled out.[10] It has been suggested that Smythe's recommendation reflected the views of the Wesleyan missionaries whom he met repeatedly during his stay in Fiji from July 1860 to May 1861.[11] In fact the missionaries appear to have retained a preference for British rule in principle while insisting that, if annexation meant the appointment of Pritchard as Governor, it was not worth having.[12] The threat from France or America had receded, and British intervention was no longer an immediate imperative. After 1861 the prospect of cession to Britain was laid quietly to rest, and missionary hopes focused on the creation of a strong and united native government.[13]

The reappearance at the end of the 1860s of missionary pressure for British rule was almost entirely due to the effects of economic change. The American Civil War of 1861–65 created a world shortage of cotton, and hence stimulated experiments in cotton cultivation in tropical areas recently penetrated by European influence. The impact of cotton on Fiji was immediate and profound. The number of white settlers in the islands rose from a mere 30 or 40 in 1860 to 2,000 in 1870.[14] A substantial white planter community brought two major problems in its wake, problems which were not to be resolved without the imposition of British rule.

Within Fiji itself the absence of any effective governmental authority or rule of law for the expanding settler population brought about numerous disputes over land, and a deterioration of relationships between Fijians and Europeans. In July 1867 a Wesleyan missionary, the Rev. Thomas Baker, and seven native agents were killed and eaten in the interior of Viti Levu, the largest of the Fijian islands. By 1869 missionaries were reporting a state of political turmoil in Fiji, with half of the eighty islands in the group under the control of M'afu and refusing allegiance to Cakobau.[15] Some way had to be found of imposing the rule of law if the missionary achievement of Fiji were not to founder amidst the bitterness of racial and territorial conflict:

> The Fiji of today, is not the Fiji of the past. The influx of a white population is testing the reality of our work, and the sincerity of our native converts. *Fire water* is a difficulty and a danger, and land disputes breed distrust and excite evil feelings. There is too much probability of New Zealand being acted over again down here, unless wise counsels prevail, and a good Government extend its sheltering wing over the group, keeping Judah from vexing Ephraim, and Ephraim from envying Judah.[16]

The WMMS recognized that the chances of the British government being prepared to extend its sheltering wing over Fiji were, in 1869, still slim. The Society's general committee accordingly adopted the more realistic tactic in March 1869 of urging the Foreign Secretary to 'devise some method by which British subjects in the islands may be made amenable to British law'; specifically the Society proposed that the British consul in Fiji should be granted magisterial powers.[17] The Gladstone government did in fact pursue this possibility in 1869 and again in 1871, but to no avail.[18] It took the second problem raised by the rapid economic development of Fiji to generate irresistible pressure for annexation.

The multiplication of cotton and other plantations in Fiji created an acute demand for cheap labour. To satisfy the demand, a labour traffic grew up among the south Pacific islands which was sufficiently unsavoury to be dubbed 'the Pacific slave trade'.[19] The branding of the labour traffic as a new form of the slave trade became the rhetorical platform on which a renewed and successful campaign for British annexation was built between 1872 and 1874. The parliamentary leader of the campaign was the Wesleyan MP, William McArthur. McArthur's arguments for annexation mixed strategic, commercial and humanitarian considerations, but for the missionaries on the field the dominant issue in these years was whether the British government was to put an end to 'disorder, anarchy, and *bloodshed*'.[20] What tipped the balance of forces in McArthur's favour was the progressive collapse of the attempts to maintain order by the white government formed in 1871 under Cakobau's titular headship. By 1874 the new Disraeli administration found itself confronted by a movement for British annexation of almost unstoppable momentum. In October 1874 the agreement was concluded whereby Fiji was to become a Crown colony on 2 January 1875. The jubilant missionaries sent McArthur a letter congratulating him for his efforts 'in the deep interests of humanity', and rejoicing in his success in securing for the law-abiding settler 'protection to property and life', and 'for the black man, deliverance from the bonds which, fastened on him by other hands than those of his chiefs, were eating into his soul'.[21]

Fiji provides a classic example of the way in which concerns characteristic of evangelical missionaries throughout the nineteenth century issued, in the changed conditions of the last third of the century, in more frequent and more explicit missionary support for the imposition of some form of British protection or rule. Fiji's Wesleyan missionaries and their domestic spokesmen were more prone than other Nonconformists to succumb to grandiose visions of imperial idealism, but this ideological inclination towards imperialism was not in itself sufficient to make the Wesleyan missionaries into consistent advocates of British intervention in Fiji. They pressed for British protection or rule only when Fijian stability and security were threatened – either by external aggression, as in 1858–59 – or by the breakdown of internal political order precipitated by the settler influx of the 1860s. The dominant motifs in the pro-imperial agitation of the WMMS missionaries were the need for protection against oppression, and the necessity of the rule of law. If these objectives could have been secured by something less than British formal control – either by granting the British consul jurisdictional authority or by the declaration of a protectorate – missionary opinion would have been satisfied.[22] However, as Fiji degenerated towards a position in which nobody appeared to possess or exercise effective jurisdiction, full British sovereignty became an increasingly compelling option. A society without law or sovereignty presented an appalling prospect of anarchy; as that grim spectre became more real, Wesleyan enthusiasm for the imagined benefits of British legality grew apace. Moreover, the half-way house of a protectorate seemed to British governments an unsatisfactory solution to the distinctive problems of Fiji, since it would have imposed unlimited responsibilities with only very limited power to discharge them.[23] In Fiji the dynamic of protection led to the final solution of formal sovereignty with a completeness and rapidity of logic that British governments were able for a time to resist in the different circumstances of tropical Africa.

2. Bechuanaland, 1878–1895

Between February 1884 and September 1885 Britain imposed her control on the whole of the semi-arid territory of Bechuanaland. Northern

116

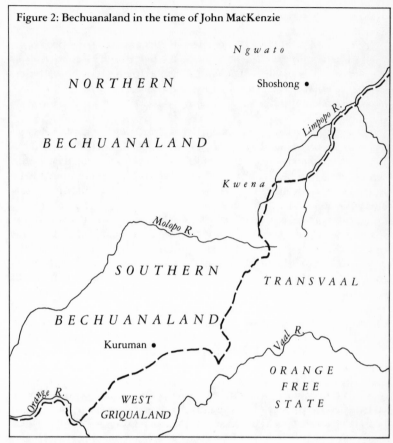

Figure 2: Bechuanaland in the time of John MacKenzie

Bechuanaland (modern Botswana) became a British protectorate; Southern Bechuanaland (now part of South Africa) became for a decade a British Crown colony. The story of the British annexation of Bechuanaland has become established as a classic instance of missionary imperialism. Heading the cast list in this imperial drama is an indomitable Scottish missionary of the LMS, John Mackenzie. Mackenzie commenced his work in 1858 among the southern sections of the Tswana people at Kuruman, the station pioneered by Robert Moffat, but in 1862 moved north to settle among the Ngwato clan of the Tswana at Shoshong. According to the most influential recent scholarly assessment, by Anthony J. Dachs, it was Mackenzie's mounting frustration at the resistance of the Ngwato and other Tswana groups to the gospel which made him into the principal advocate of British annexation.[24] The Tswana would not be converted until the power of their chiefs was broken, and that power could be broken only by the imposition of British rule. Mackenzie observed to the LMS in August 1876:

> On the whole, the old feudal power of the native chiefs is opposed
> to Christianity, and the people who are living under English law
> are in a far more advantageous position as to the reception of the
> Gospel than when they were living in their own heathen towns
> surrounded by all its thralls and sanctions.[25]

Mackenzie's tireless agitation for formal British involvement in Bechuanaland, conducted initially from Bechuanaland itself, and then from 1882 to
1884 in Britain on furlough, was thus the device of a frustrated evangelist,
compelled to resort to political means to vanquish Tswana resistance to the
gospel. Missionary imperialism, concludes Dachs, was, in this case at least,
a response to missionary failure.[26]

This interpretation of Mackenzie's motivation is not without plausibility.
Mackenzie *did* recognize that Tswana living under the rule of a pagan chief
were less likely to respond to Christian preaching than were those Africans
subject to formal British control, and *did* hope to undermine the communal
cohesion of the Tswana clans by promoting the 'healthy individualistic
competition' of economic enterprise based on individual land tenure.[27]
Furthermore, there can be little doubt that LMS missionaries in the 1890s
supported the designs of Cecil Rhodes's British South Africa Company
within Zambesia (modern Zimbabwe) precisely because there seemed no
other way of breaking down the despotism of the militaristic Ndebele state,
which had baulked all missionary progress. However, there was a
considerable difference in degree between Ndebele and Bechuana resistance
to missionary evangelism, as Robert Moffat's son J. S. Moffat pointed out in
1888.[28] LMS missionaries had achieved some very significant successes in
Bechuanaland before Mackenzie launched his final campaign for British
annexation in 1882. Sechele I, chief of the Kwena, had been baptized as
early as 1848; by 1882 three of the five main divisions of the Tswana had
Christian chiefs – among them Kwama, chief of the Ngwato, destined to
become perhaps the most celebrated Christian chief of late nineteenth-
century Africa.[29] There is little hard evidence for Dachs's argument that
Mackenzie resorted to advocating British rule out of evangelistic despera-
tion; on the contrary, one of the key-notes of the LMS-inspired public
campaign on behalf of Bechuanaland in 1882–83 was the need to preserve
and protect 'the precious and substantial results of the labours of two
generations of Christian missionaries in Bechuana Land'.[30] The imperialism
of John Mackenzie was too idealistic to be merely a pragmatic response to
missionary failure. His principled enthusiasm for British rule arose in large
measure out of the reality of the Bechuanaland mission-field, but it owed less
to evangelistic strategy than it did to humanitarian concern.

Mackenzie's first decade of missionary service in Bechuanaland had convinced him that the crucial question was not whether the Tswana were to be ruled by the white man, but rather which white men were to do the ruling. At the outset he had hoped he might be able so to 'elevate' one of the Tswana tribes that 'they could endure the shock of meeting the wave of European cultivation, *etc.*, and not be driven away by it' – with missionary help Tswana tribalism might perhaps be preserved intact. But experience convinced Mackenzie that his initial hopes were unrealistic: the advance of white power and the mingling of races appeared to be irresistible forces which he could only assume to be the will of God.[31] If Britain failed to assume control of these momentous processes of change, others with less benevolent intentions would do so instead.

These imperialist convictions reached maturity after Mackenzie was moved back to Kuruman by the LMS in 1876. Within two years he found himself in the centre of a rising by traditionalist elements of the southern Tswana against those of their leaders who had associated with missionaries, settlers and the British government of neighbouring West Griqualand. By September 1878 the administrator of West Griqualand had invited Mackenzie to assist him in the pacification and 'settlement' of the southern Tswana.[32] The Tswana were threatened by encroachments on their traditional grazing and hunting areas by land-hungry Boer farmers from the Transvaal. Mackenzie became convinced that the only hope of security for the Tswana lay in the introduction of a European system of individual title to land in 'guaranteed' territories supervised by Britain. For nearly a year he assisted the Griqualand authorities in the resettlement of the Tswana on these principles, before writing to the LMS requesting sanction for his existing activities and the Society's permission to accept a formal salaried post as 'commissioner' of Southern Bechuanaland.[33] Not surprisingly, the LMS Directors took a decided objection to Mackenzie's combination of the roles of missionary and government official, and withheld their permission.[34] A disgruntled Mackenzie warned the Directors in February 1880 that they had made a 'grave mistake' which would prove injurious to native interests.[35]

It was clear to Mackenzie by 1880 that the 'missionary road' to the north along the line of the Bechuanaland mission stations was threatened by two equally unacceptable forces. On the one hand, there were the Boer 'freebooters' of the Transvaal, whose incursions on Tswana territory were becoming more frequent and penetrating. On the other, there was the new menace of the economic imperialism of Cecil Rhodes, already carving out a political career for himself in the Cape Town parliament and extending his ambitions to the newly-discovered gold and diamonds of the southern African interior. Rhodes's imperialism, founded on a belief in the intrinsic superiority of the British race, was destined to clash repeatedly with the equally ambitious but fundamentally humanitarian imperialism of John Mackenzie.[36]

Missionary alarm at the plight of the Tswana became much more general after Britain and the leaders of the Transvaal signed the Convention of Pretoria in 1881. Although the status and boundaries of the Transvaal Republic were defined for the first time, the Convention stipulated the withdrawal of the small British force maintaining order in Southern Bechuanaland: the Boer freebooters had been given an open door, and they duly entered it. The LMS Bechuanaland District Committee responded in May 1882 by appealing to the British government to intervene as 'Protector of the Native Tribes', and in July Mackenzie set out for home on furlough, determined to rouse British Christian and humanitarian opinion on behalf of Bechuanaland.[37]

From September 1882 to early 1884 Mackenzie and the LMS mounted a skilful campaign to put pressure on the Gladstone government to declare a British protectorate over Southern Bechuanaland. The resolutions passed at public meetings of the LMS or Congregational Union urged the government to fulfil its treaty responsibilities to the Tswana as defined in the Pretoria Convention; they also emphasized, even more than the need to defend the substantial fruits of missionary labour in Bechuanaland, the claims of 'humanity and justice'. The resolutions did not even call specifically for the imposition of a protectorate, but merely for the government to take such action as would effectually protect the Tswana from Boer marauders.[38] The public voice of the campaign thus fell far short of Mackenzie's personal vision of 'Austral Africa' – of British rule, not just in Southern Bechuanaland, but over the whole of Africa south of the Zambezi – a vision which very few shared.[39] Yet by ultimate implication the agitation was calling for a protectorate to be declared, and even Gladstone's anti-imperialist government could not hold out indefinitely. In February 1884 Britain declared a provisional protectorate over Southern Bechuanaland, and Mackenzie was appointed to the post barred to him in 1879 – that of resident British Commissioner.[40]

The Bechuanaland story has acquired the reputation of a notoriously blatant case of missionary imperialism, and there can be no denying that Mackenzie was a fervent imperialist, animated by the dream of a grand imperial federation in southern Africa under the direct control of Britain. However, the starkness of Mackenzie's Christian imperialism ought not to be permitted to conceal three qualifying points of some substance. First, this was no case of the missionary 'working hand in hand with the imperial power'. Mackenzie's distinctive imperial recipe for southern Africa won no support from any British government and was directly contrary to Rhodes's plans for supremacy by the Cape Colony. Mackenzie soon proved an embarrassment as Commissioner, and in August 1884 was ditched in favour of Rhodes.[41] Although Southern Bechuanaland became a British colony in September 1885, Britain annexed the territory on the clear understanding that there should be no obstacle to its eventual transfer to the Cape Colony.

That transfer duly took place in 1895 - Rhodes had triumphed and Mackenzie had failed.[42] Thus the Bechuanaland case illustrates pointedly a second truth of more general application: there was not one imperialism but many competing and conflicting imperialisms. By the end of the 1880s humanitarian imperialism of the Mackenzie variety was becoming increasingly attractive to missionaries as the best alternative to unregulated exploitation by other white interests, whether these were settler farmers, such as the Boers, or chartered companies, such as Rhodes's British South Africa Company.

The third qualification may appear tendentious, yet must be faced. Historical hindsight forces upon us the question whether Mackenzie was not in fact correct in his belief that the Tswana would be better off under British protection than in a white supremacist South Africa ruled from either Cape Town or Johannesburg. Ironically it was Northern and not Southern Bechuanaland which escaped the clutches of both Boers and Rhodes to survive as a British protectorate, which eventually became the independent state of Botswana. That protectorate, imposed in January 1885, had nothing to do with Mackenzie's arguments, and was Britain's pre-emptive response to the beginnings of German involvement in South-West Africa (now Namibia).[43] Nonetheless, Mackenzie welcomed the protectorate as a fulfilment of his ideals. Without that act of British imperialism, Northern Bechuanaland would have become part of South Africa and experienced a degree of exploitation which it never knew under British rule.

3. Nyasaland (Malawi), 1874-1894

If the missionary role in imperial politics in Bechuanaland has acquired a certain notoriety among historians, the contribution of Christian missions to the making of modern Malawi has attracted an even greater volume of scholarly applause. The leading historian of Malawi - John McCracken - commends the political activities of the Scottish missions in Malawi as 'outstanding for their pugnacity and integrity'.[44] An African writer on missions and politics in Malawi considers the Scottish missionary record in Malawi to be 'perhaps the only case of unbroken pursuit of equity in a colonial cause by a group of people who were themselves by race and upbringing members of the imperial power'.[45] Yet missionaries played no less prominent a part in the absorption of Nyasaland into the British empire between 1889 and 1894 than they had played in Bechuanaland approximately a decade earlier. The more favourable verdict passed on Christian missions in Nyasaland/Malawi is coloured by the exceptionally forthright stance taken by Scottish missionaries in the mid-twentieth century in resisting imperial plans for a Central African Federation and promoting the cause of Malawian independence. In the late nineteenth-

Figure 3: Nyasaland (Malawi) 1874–1894

century period which is the subject of this chapter, the missionary response to imperialism in Nyasaland was complex, diverse, but in no way uncharacteristic.

Protestant missions in Malawi can trace their origin to David Livingstone's vision of the Zambezi river as a highway for 'commerce and Christianity' into the heart of Africa. Baulked in that intention by the impassable nature of the Cabora Bassa rapids to steamer traffic, Livingstone had turned instead to the Shire river and the adjacent highlands at the southern end of Lake Malawi. A missionary and trading presence in this region offered alluring prospects for destroying much of the East African slave trade at its source. During Livingstone's life-time these plans remained unfulfilled. The newly-founded Universities' Mission to Central Africa abandoned its Zambezi mission in 1863. James Stewart, a Scottish admirer of Livingstone's, went out to the Zambezi in 1861 to prepare for a Scottish industrial mission, but returned in 1863 a disillusioned man.[46] Two things were necessary before Livingstone's missionary vision for the Lake Malawi region could be brought to birth.

The first, paradoxically, was Livingstone's own death in Central Africa in 1873. It was after attending Livingstone's funeral at Westminster Abbey in April 1874 that James Stewart deemed the time ripe for reviving the idea of a Scottish mission to Central Africa, and persuaded the Free Church of Scotland to sponsor a 'Livingstonia' mission in memory of the man whose death had won him near-mythological status.[47] In the same month as the Free Church approved Stewart's proposals, the General Assembly of the Church of Scotland authorized the establishment of a mission 'among the natives of that part of Africa which has been hallowed by the last labours and death of Dr. Livingstone'.[48]

The second precondition for the opening of East Africa to missionary enterprise was more prosaic. The opening of the Suez Canal in 1869 brought East Africa within the reach of European economic aspirations. In 1872 the British India Steam Navigation Company established a monthly steamer service between Aden and Durban via Zanzibar. Its chairman, William Mackinnon, was one of a group of Scottish businessmen and industrialists whom Stewart recruited to provide the independent financial base of the Livingstonia Mission (which until 1914 was autonomous of Free Church funds). The connection between business ambition and the origins of the Mission must not be overplayed – Mackinnon was the only wealthy supporter to have direct economic concerns in East Africa, and his interest in the Nyasa region was not sustained after 1878.[49] Nonetheless, the missionary advance into East Africa in the 1870s and 1880s would not have been possible without the improved communications with the Indian Ocean which the economic and strategic concerns of France and Britain had created.

The Livingstonia Mission established its first station at Cape Maclear at the southern end of Lake Malawi in 1875. The Church of Scotland set up its mission a year later, further south at Blantyre in the Shire highlands. Both missions had the original aim of combating the slave trade in the region by means of 'Christian colonies', which would be centres of legitimate commerce, and settlements where Africans could acquire the skills of Western civilization and industry. The linkage between Christianity and commerce was symbolized in Livingstonia's case by the incorporation in 1878 of a trading company, known subsequently as the African Lakes Company, and owned by the same industrialists as financed the Mission itself.

Neither at Blantyre nor at Livingstonia was this initial missionary approach successful. At Blantyre the policy of running the Mission as a Christian colony in which missionaries assumed powers of civil jurisdiction over Africans proved disastrous, and compelled the General Assembly to intervene in 1881 to put the Mission's house in order.[50] Livingstonia suffered from the less than Christian behaviour of some of the employees of the African Lakes Company, and the Mission failed to make any impact on the Yao people of the Cape Maclear region. The Yao chiefs owed their power to the east coast trade in ivory, copper and slaves, and the missionaries' demands that they should repudiate the slave trade struck at the roots of their authority.[51] In 1881 the Mission recognized the inevitable and transferred its headquarters from Cape Maclear to Bandawe, halfway up the west coast of the lake. There the Tonga people proved far more receptive to the missionary presence, eagerly welcoming the political protection and educational opportunities which the Mission provided. But the Tonga were themselves under threat from the Ngoni, warlike immigrants from far to the south, and it is significant that there were no actual conversions among the Tonga till 1889.[52] In the mid-1880s, after a decade of missionary activity, the Scottish achievement in Nyasaland still appeared remarkably slender. Frustration at lack of evangelistic progress was to be one variable determining missionary responses to the coming of British imperial power in the course of the next decade, but it was not the only, nor even the most important variable.

Between 1884 and 1889 the political context of missionary activity throughout East Africa changed profoundly. A situation of relative security and freedom of operation gave way to one of danger and instability, which was in its turn resolved only by the imposition of formal partition by the European powers. It was argued by Professor Roland Oliver in a now classic work of missionary history, *The Missionary Factor in East Africa*, that the primary cause of this transformation can be traced to the sudden arrival in 1884–85 of Bismarck's Germany on the colonial stage.[53] At the end of 1884 a German colonial adventurer named Karl Peters negotiated for himself a series of treaties with African rulers on the coast of what is now Tanzania, promising German protection in return for trading privileges. By the end of February 1885 Bismarck had ratified the treaties and hence endorsed the status of the territories as German protectorates.[54] The German intrusion, argues Oliver, had a knock-on effect far inland, transforming the Arab chiefs of the East African interior from traders to empire-builders, and hardening their attitudes to all things European. Christian missions bore the brunt of this new Arab militancy, being on occasion openly attacked, and everywhere threatened by what looked like a campaign for Islamic rule orchestrated by the Sultan of Zanzibar. By 1888 the African Lakes Company found itself fighting a virtual war against Mlozi, the most powerful of the Arab chiefs; missionaries throughout East Africa began to draw the conclusion that 'the choice for Africa was not Europe or independence, but Europe or Zanzibar'.[55]

Germany's entrance into the East African arena had a further consequence which alarmed the Protestant missions in Malawi. Portugal, who for three centuries had occupied the coastal territory around the mouth of the Zambezi, now asserted a claim to the entire Zambezi hinterland as far north as the Shire highlands. The Scottish missions thus faced a dual threat – from the Arabs to the north of Lake Nyasa, and from the Portuguese to the south. Their parent churches in Scotland joined forces in 1888–89 to apply private and public pressure on Lord Salisbury's government to take steps 'to secure the safety of British subjects and interests in Nyasaland'.[56] Deputations, petitions and public meetings demanded that Britain should force the Portuguese to withdraw their troops from the Shire region and declare Nyasaland, not a protectorate, but a British 'sphere of influence' into which Portugal could not enter. This was a distinction without a difference. Salisbury's government remained sympathetic but reluctant to intervene.[57] In May, Cecil Rhodes offered the British government a way out of its impasse. Rhodes applied for a royal charter for a British South Africa Company to promote British interests both north and south of the Zambezi river at no expense to the British exchequer; he proposed to absorb the African Lakes Company into his own company, and offered up to £9,000 a year to finance the government of the territory north of the Zambezi. Compliance with Rhodes suited Salisbury's current South African policy, and offered a means of thwarting Portuguese and German ambitions at minimum cost.[58] Rhodes gained his charter, and in June the government dispatched Harry Johnston with authority to declare a protectorate over Blantyre and the Shire highlands on behalf of the British South Africa Company.[59]

The Scottish missions had gained their immediate political objective of excluding Catholic Portugal, with its known lack of commitment to the anti-slavery cause, from the Nyasa field. Missionary response to the advent of company rule was, however, far from uniform. Opinion in the Blantyre Mission was hostile from the outset, complaining that 'the relegation of all interests ... to the sole judgement of a large monopolizing Commercial concern is not and never has been considered help at all, certainly not protection'.[60] The Blantyre missionaries, under the brilliant but dictatorial leadership of David Scott, distrusted Johnston, both personally and as an examplar of aspects of Western civilization which they had no desire to see introduced to Africa. The Mission retained much of its original character as a Christian colony under the theocratic rule of the missionaries. The coming of Johnston's government to the immediate vicinity of the Mission challenged its temporal status and imperilled its working relationships with the surrounding chiefs. Blantyre maintained a consistent opposition to chartered Company rule and Johnston's policy of destroying African political authorities, and advocated instead a full British protectorate founded on respect for indigenous authority.[61]

In contrast, the Free Church's Livingstonia Mission displayed an essentially positive attitude to chartered Company rule. From as early as

125

1885, the Mission had supported the African Lakes Company in its attempts to obtain a charter bestowing governmental authority, and accordingly welcomed Rhodes's initiative in 1889. Robert Laws, the dominant missionary personality at Livingstonia, supported most of Johnston's policies and in turn received Johnston's accolade as 'the greatest man who has yet appeared in Nyasaland'.[62] The nexus between commerce and Christianity had always been tighter at Livingstonia than at Blantyre, with the result that the Free Church missionaries appear not to have shared their Blantyre colleagues' convictions about the moral unfitness of a commercial company to rule. Livingstonia had, moreover, broken more radically with the theocratic model of a missionary community when it moved from Cape Maclear to Bandawe; missionaries who had themselves disclaimed responsibility for secular jurisdiction were more likely to welcome an alternative Western source of law and order. Furthermore, Livingstonia viewed the imagined benefits of Company rule from a safe distance. Johnston's writ did not yet run on the western shores of the lake, so that the harsher realities of the Company's regime were hidden from Livingstonia's view.[63]

In Nyasaland, as elsewhere in Africa, the device of proxy rule by chartered company proved inadequate as a long-term means of securing British interests. Johnston's government was starved of funds. In 1891 an initial compromise was reached whereby the Foreign Office assumed responsibility for administration of the protectorate, with the aid of a subsidy from the British South Africa Company. In 1894 the process of absorption into the empire was completed when the British government accepted full financial responsibility for the Nyasaland protectorate.

Two groups of missionaries from similar theological and social backgrounds thus responded to the crucial early years of the colonial impact on Malawi in markedly contrasting ways.[64] It would be unhelpful to label one group as more 'imperialistic' than the other. The Livingstonia missionaries were less able than their Blantyre counterparts to perceive the liabilities of identification with commercial interests, yet it must be remembered that any profits made by the African Lakes Company in excess of a 5% dividend were to be paid into mission funds; in fact the Company paid no dividend at all for its first eight years.[65] The Blantyre missionaries were more 'enlightened' in their respect for aspects of African political systems and culture, yet their concern to 'protect' the African degenerated more easily into an authoritarian paternalism.[66] In the long term both missions achieved distinction as humanitarian champions of African interests in the era of white settler power and nascent African nationalism. The distinctiveness of Malawi in missionary history is that some of the leading pioneers of the 1880s and 1890s were still on the field in the 1920s or even 1930s – Laws of Livingstonia and Hetherwick of Blantyre, for example, did not retire till 1928.[67] The missionary imperialists of the late Victorian age were, in Malawi, the very same people who brought nationalist politics to birth in the twentieth century.

4. Uganda, 1877–1894

In Bechuanaland missionaries had promoted the concept of a British protectorate in order to thwart the forces of economic imperialism represented by Cecil Rhodes. In Nyasaland one mission was fundamentally opposed to chartered company rule while the other was broadly sympathetic. In Uganda the Protestant missionary interest in the form of the Church Missionary Society was strongly supportive of the economic imperialism of the Imperial British East Africa Company. The variety of missionary responses is to be explained, not primarily by reference to differing denominational propensities to imperialism, but in terms of the distinctive political circumstances which affected the three fields. Uganda is unique in Victorian missionary history, not merely for the nature of the relationship between missionaries and the agents of British commercial imperialism, but for the range of political and religious forces which helped to make its CMS missionaries into such ardent advocates of British imperial expansion in the region.

The first CMS missionaries arrived at the court of Kabaka Mutesa I of Buganda (the dominant kingdom at the heart of what is now Uganda) in 1877. Two years later they were joined by the first Roman Catholic missionaries of the French White Fathers mission. Initially the Catholics made greater headway. The CMS pioneer A. M. Mackay reported in June 1881 that 'converts we have not yet found but half-believers many'.[68] However, after the baptism of the first five Protestant converts in March 1882, the CMS mission received a steady flow of conversions, most notably from the influential entourage of the Kabaka. By the time Mutesa's son, Mwanga, acceded to the throne in 1884, the royal court had divided into three religious parties: the Protestants, the Catholics and, most numerous of all, the Muslims, evidence of the extent of the penetration of Arab power even into inaccessible Buganda. Mwanga himself adhered to none of the new faiths and felt threatened by them all. In 1885 he had James Hannington, first Anglican bishop of Eastern Equatorial Africa, murdered; in the following year at least forty-six Protestant and Catholic converts were slaughtered. When, in 1888, Mwanga began to plot still bloodier massacres of Christians and Muslims alike, the Muslims took the initiative in deposing him and installing his brother as Kabaka in his stead. Within a month the Muslims had expelled both Christian parties from the court and embarked upon a comprehensive programme intended to transform Buganda into an Islamic state.[69] In Buganda no less than in Nyasaland it seemed by late 1888 that Christian missions stood on the brink of extinction at the hands of a militant and resurgent Islam – all Protestant and Catholic missionaries had been forced to leave the country. 'These events', reflected Mackay, 'render the question paramount: Is Arab or European power henceforth to prevail in Central Africa?'[70]

It was into this volatile context that representatives of both British and German imperialism stepped in 1889–90. Britain and Germany had signed an agreement in 1886 delimiting their respective spheres of influence in East Africa, but Buganda and all territory west of Lake Victoria lay beyond its scope. Anxious to forestall anticipated German designs on Buganda, the British government pinned its hopes on Sir William Mackinnon's Imperial British East Africa Company (IBEAC), which had received its royal charter in 1888. The Company had little economic incentive to become involved as far inland as Buganda, but Mackinnon was animated by grander visions than immediate profitability: his company was to fulfil David Livingstone's vision of opening up East Africa for commerce and Christianity, and its initial dividends would be paid in philanthropy rather than pounds.[71] Mackinnon thus did not require too much governmental persuasion to fulfil his pre-emptive role and dispatch an exploratory expedition, under F. J. Jackson, which arrived in Buganda in April 1890. Even before Jackson reached Buganda, both Protestant and Catholic leaders had appealed for his aid in the civil war against the Muslims. However, Jackson arrived in Buganda to find that the German adventurer Karl Peters had got there first. Peters had presented the Catholics with a realistic alternative to British political patronage and thereby hardened the Protestants in their support for the IBEAC cause. Both Peters and Jackson attempted to impose treaties favourable to their respective countries, but the scales were not tipped in Britain's favour until the arrival of a more permanent IBEAC force under Captain F. D. Lugard in December 1890. Lugard succeeded in detaching the more moderate Catholic chiefs from their pro-German alignment, and imposed on the reluctant Mwanga (now back on the throne with Christian support) a treaty declaring that Buganda was now under the 'protection' of the IBEAC acting on behalf of the British Crown.[72]

The new Anglican bishop, Alfred Tucker, arrived in Buganda only a fortnight after Lugard to find the country 'like a volcano on the verge of an eruption'.[73] Tucker's overwhelming impression was that the Protestants had so identified themselves with the Company's cause that they were compromised in the eyes of all other Baganda, and faced certain massacre if the Company were to withdraw its forces.[74] This personal conviction of Tucker's was to be of crucial importance in determining the destiny of Uganda. The civil wars were still far from over – Christians fought Muslims until May 1891, and Protestants fought Catholics early in 1892. The Protestants, fighting under the IBEAC flag and with the help of Lugard's Maxim guns, were predictably victorious. The victory, however, seemed destined to be a hollow one, for the Company, despairing of ever making a profit out of war-torn Uganda, had informed the Foreign Office in July

1891 of its decision to withdraw its forces. Bishop Tucker was back in England when the news of the Company's decision broke; his predictions of disaster in Uganda now became unconditional.

There is some uncertainty about the precise configuration of the events which ensued in Britain. Some part was played by a meeting in August 1891 between General George Hutchinson of the CMS and General Sir Arnold Kemball, now the dominant figure on the IBEAC Board. It is possible that Kemball had conceived a deliberate strategy of depicting the Company's imminent withdrawal from Uganda as a betrayal of Protestant interests, in order to use Christian public opinion as a lever to force the Salisbury government to intervene. He certainly warned Hutchinson that the IBEAC needed more than the sympathy of the CMS if disaster were to be averted.[75] It may be doubted, however, whether Kemball's strategy was more than a perception of how Anglican feeling was already moving under Tucker's direction. The following month Sir William Mackinnon met Tucker and two members of the CMS Committee fortuitously while touring the Scottish highlands. Mackinnon offered £10,000 of his own money if the CMS would donate £15,000 to enable the Company to remain in Uganda for one more year after which, he hoped, the government would intervene. When the CMS representatives indicated that the Society's funds could not legitimately be put to such a purpose, Mackinnon asked whether the friends of CMS would be prepared to raise the sum independently. Tucker and the others replied that 'this might be possible'.[76] On 18 September the CMS wrote to Mackinnon promising a strong letter to Lord Salisbury and undertaking to try to raise £10,000–15,000 if the Company would commit itself to remain in Uganda at least till the end of 1892.[77]

The initial response from CMS supporters to this unorthodox appeal was slow, but on 30 October Tucker addressed the anniversary meeting of the CMS Gleaners' Union (a recently-formed league of committed CMS supporters), and invited promises for the Uganda appeal to be sent up to the platform. 'The greatest enthusiasm prevailed', and within half an hour, £8,000 had been promised. Within ten days the sum had reached £16,000. The Company was able to reverse its decision, and announced its intention to remain in Uganda until the end of December 1892. Uganda had been 'saved', though only for a year. 'It may be truly said today', asserted Eugene Stock with untroubled pride in 1899, 'as Bishop Tucker has often said, that England owes the great empire she now rules over in Central Africa to that memorable meeting of the Gleaners' Union in Exeter Hall on October 30th, 1891.'[78]

Tucker had won no more than a temporary reprieve for the Company's Ugandan operation. Its survival depended on the availability of government funding for the construction of a railway linking Uganda to the coast. Salisbury's Conservative government obtained parliamentary approval for a mere £20,000 for a survey of the route, but was then defeated in the general election of July 1892. The new Liberal administration was hopelessly divided on the Uganda question. Gladstone led most of his party in opposing an imperial solution; Lord Rosebery, the Foreign Secretary, strongly supported one. The CMS sent a deputation to Rosebery on 23 September, warning of fearful bloodshed in Buganda if the Company withdrew. Similar predictions came from the British Consul-General in Zanzibar. Impressed but still divided, the Cabinet agreed on 30 September to pay the Company to remain in Uganda for three more months, but with ultimate evacuation still in view.[79]

There followed in the autumn of 1892 a remarkable campaign of public pressure and agitation for the retention of Uganda. Resolutions from public meetings poured into the Foreign Office. Their burden was that to abandon Uganda would be a breach of national faith and a disastrous set-back for the cause of Christianity and civilization in Africa. The most prominent motif of all was fear of a revival of the slave trade consequent upon British withdrawal. It was known that the peace imposed by Lugard in Buganda was fragile in the extreme – the Muslims in fact made one more armed attempt to gain ascendancy in 1893 – and there seemed every likelihood that a British withdrawal would throw the country into a worse anarchy than any experienced during the civil wars. There is little evidence that the CMS orchestrated the campaign, although the Society fully supported its objectives. It was a largely spontaneous outburst of Protestant, anti-slavery and pro-imperial sentiment.[80]

On 7 November the Cabinet agreed to send a Commissioner to Uganda to report on the desirability of evacuation or retention. The Cabinet's decision was made before most of the resolutions urging retention had been received, but the results of public pressure were clearly seen in Rosebery's private instructions to the Commissioner, which regarded the matter as virtually settled.[81] Furthermore, when the Commissioner, Sir Gerald Portal, reached Uganda, his chief adviser, according to one source, was none other than Bishop Tucker, still singing the same song of 'the tragic consequences which must ensue if the British government did not assume control on the Company's withdrawal'.[82] Tucker's guiding hand on events can be discerned right up to April 1894, when the final decision was made that Uganda should be retained, no longer through the intermediary of the IBEAC, but as a full protectorate of the British Crown.

The imperial outcome in Uganda was shaped by the force of missionary and domestic Christian opinion to an even greater degree than was the case in Fiji, Bechuanaland or Nyasaland. Nevertheless, it can be plausibly argued that the real reasons for the Liberal government's *volte-face* had more to do with a hard-headed perception of French threats to the upper Nile region than with a genuine concern for Uganda itself.[83] Be that as it may, some assessment of Anglican attitudes in this rather unsavoury episode of missionary history is clearly called for.

130

Nonconformist support for the Anglican campaign for Uganda was at best lukewarm, although Tucker and Eugene Stock tried to paint a different picture.[84] Tucker himself took pains to rebut the criticism that the CMS, by appealing to the Government to take steps to protect its missionaries, had depended on the 'arm of flesh'. He pointed out that the Society never dreamt of requesting government intervention after the martyrdom of Hannington and other CMS pioneers, and insisted that the issue was whether Britain would 'keep faith' with the terms of Lugard's December 1890 treaty, which 'solemnly pledged' the protection of the IBEAC, as the authorized representative of the British government, to the Kabaka and his chiefs, and to the Protestant chiefs in particular.[85] This was a distinctly rose-tinted view of a treaty which was accepted with resentment by the Kabaka and most of his chiefs. Indeed, Tucker's last line of defence of Lugard's treaty abandoned humanitarian principle for nationalistic sentiment: had it not been signed, he reflected, Uganda would probably have become 'a dependency of the French Republic or an appanage of the Imperial crown of Germany. At any rate, the head waters of the Nile would have passed into other hands than those of Great Britain.'[86]

The CMS missionaries who found themselves caught up in the infinite complexities of Bugandan politics in the period of the 'scramble' were simple evangelicals of well-to-do backgrounds but no political sophistication. George Pilkington (killed in the last Muslim rebellion against Christian ascendancy in 1897) spoke for all of his missionary colleagues in 1894 when he exclaimed 'Politics, how I hate them.'[87] Pilkington had offended Lugard in 1892 by telling him to his face that he did not regard him as a converted man, and Protestant missionary relationships with Lugard grew steadily worse as he leaned over backwards to win the support of Catholic chiefs for his settlement.[88] These evangelical Christians had set out with a genuine resolve to 'keep out of all political questions', but found it was, in practice, impossible to resist the pressure from the Baganda to act as their advisers on matters of external political relations.[89] 'As a general rule', asserted Alfred Tucker, missionaries should stay aloof from interference in indigenous politics; yet there are times when it is the duty of the missionary 'to cast in the whole weight of his influence on the side of humanity, justice and Christian duty'.[90] That principle would command almost universal Christian acceptance today, but with markedly different political consequences.

Tucker's repeated insistence that the Protestant party had been compromised into a position of dependence on British protection was true enough, and the spectre of anarchy and Islamic resurgence following a British withdrawal was real enough. Whether the desirability of averting these anticipated disasters justifies the means employed remains the crucial moral issue, and it is a very similar issue to that faced by many twentieth-century Christians who believe themselves to be *combating* colonialism in the name of justice and humanity. The appropriate criticism of the Ugandan missionaries and their domestic supporters is not that they cared nothing for justice and righteousness, but that in their self-consciously moral stand for justice and righteousness they too readily accepted the distortions which the prevailing imperial ideology imposed on these concepts. Professedly non-political missionaries swallowed too easily calculated arguments for national advantage when they were cloaked in the moral vocabulary of evangelical humanitarianism. Moreover, the political and religious naivety of the CMS missionaries rendered them reluctant to sanction a settlement which treated Catholics with the same justice as they demanded for Protestants; it was ironically the more even-handed imperialism of Lugard which subsequently won the applause of Protestant Baganda who had come to enjoy the considerable fruits of the *pax Britannica*, and even the more objective applause of some modern historians.[91]

5. Conclusion

The examples of Fiji, Bechuanaland, Nyasaland and Uganda reveal with increasing clarity the ambiguities which the age of competitive European imperialism posed for the evangelical Christian conscience. Evangelical Christians remained as staunchly committed to the causes of liberty for the gospel, freedom for the slave, and protection for the native as they had been in the age of Wilberforce or Knibb. But those same concerns were now drawing them more frequently and more enthusiastically into the advocacy of explicitly imperial solutions. As the stability of indigenous societies became more fragile, and the competition for their economic or strategic rewards more intense, Christian commitment to the liberating rule of justice could become almost indistinguishable from commitment to the imposition of British law. Few missionaries then perceived that such an outcome ran the risk of becoming ultimately more injurious to liberty and justice than the perils it was supposed to avert.

In the twentieth century, as the hollowness of many of these imperial solutions became apparent, Christian missions were to find themselves unable to deflect the attacks of nationalist politicians who took up Western ideals of justice and liberty and used them to assail the whole system of Western imperial control. The fact that many of the nationalists owed their education and political apprenticeship to the missions did nothing to soften the force of the onslaught when it came.

CHAPTER SIX

Missions and the nationalist revolutions, 1895–1960

1. Missions in a twentieth-century landscape

In the twentieth century, European imperialism reached the zenith of its power. The European colonial empires grew in size, sophistication and ideological self-confidence, and the British empire was the grandest of them all. But their strength was illusory. Formal territorial control had often been a reluctant response to competition from rival powers, and its expense or instability now amply justified the initial reluctance. Furthermore, formal imperial rule proved to be consistently effective in transmitting at least one Western political assumption into the tropical atmosphere. One of the driving forces behind Western imperialism was European nationalism. The struggle for national identity and independence in nineteenth-century Europe had given birth to new nation states such as Italy and Germany, and imparted the edge of popular fervour to the scramble for tropical influence. Yet the underlying premiss of nationalism was the belief that any group which felt itself to be a people had the unquestioned right to govern itself as a nation. At the end of the nineteenth century such self-consciousness of national identity was largely absent from Africa, and present in Asia only in embryonic form (as in India), or in a form which was conservative and isolationist (as in imperial China). The creation throughout Africa and Asia of nationalist sentiment and activity on the Western progressive model was the paradoxical achievement of European colonial rule. Christian missions in the twentieth century frequently had to operate in a context shaped by emergent nationalism as much as by Western imperialism. Initially indigenous nationalism seemed to be the fulfilment of the aspirations of colonial rulers and missionaries alike; eventually it was to lead to nationalist revolutions which would bring colonial rule to an end and challenge the assumptions and even the existence of Western missions.

Missions made their own direct contribution to the growth of nationalism, primarily through the medium of education. From the late nineteenth century onwards most missionary societies devoted more and more of their resources to education, particularly at the secondary and tertiary levels. Strategically, this emphasis was a function of their belief in the priority of establishing a truly self-governing church: educated indigenous leadership was a prerequisite of progress towards autonomy. Theologically, it often reflected a waning of confidence in traditional evangelism, or at least a shift of focus towards a programme of 'Christianization' of the fabric of national life. Many of the products of mission secondary schools or Christian institutions of higher education did indeed achieve prominence in church or political leadership; but they frequently became the articulators of nationalist protest in a way that some of their missionary mentors had failed to anticipate. The missionary endeavour to Christianize national life through educational enterprise believed itself to be more enlightened than the more confrontational approach of earlier and more conservative missionaries, but it tended to idealize the values of Anglo-Saxon Protestant civilization as the imagined solution to non-Western 'backwardness' – an assumption which the course of twentieth-century European history would reduce to tatters.

Missionary education produced many of the leaders of the nationalist revolutions. Missionary ecumenism helped to weld those leaders together into cohesive elites. The twentieth century witnessed the transformation of the informal interdenominationalism of the nineteenth-century missionary movement into actual unions or federations of churches on the mission field. National church leaders of different denominations were brought into closer contact and discovered common grievances and aspirations. United churches or councils of churches could speak with greater weight and forcefulness to missions or colonial authorities. Yet theological developments in the sending churches distorted this picture of growing ecumenical co-operation on the field. Between 1895 and 1930 the essential unity of nineteenth-century evangelical Protestantism fragmented as conservative and liberal evangelicals went their separate ways. The 'faith' missions distanced themselves from their more liberal denominational partners, and tended to hang back from ecumenical involvement and the devolution of authority towards the national churches; they were also comparatively uninvolved in advanced educational work. As a result, their missionaries were less sensitive to the mounting groundswell of opinion against imperialism and their converts less prominent in the growth of nationalist politics.

Another consideration which fundamentally affected missions (and especially British missions) in the first half of the twentieth century was the impact of the two World Wars. The First World War had surprisingly little effect on the income of the major British societies: most recorded a steady increase in income during the war years, which was sustained into the 1920s.[1] It is also clear that the war did not in itself spell the end of the optimism characteristic of Victorian Britain, for it was succeeded by a resurgence of hope that war could be eliminated from the international scene by the exercise of human goodwill and co-operation between states.

Not until after 1928, with the advent of catastrophic economic depression and the subsequent growth of fascism in Europe, did the mood change and the missionary societies experience a serious falling off in both income and recruits.[2] Nevertheless, on the field the immediate impact of the war was serious: the supply of funds to the field was interrupted, missionaries were withdrawn, and some areas (such as East Africa) themselves became theatres of conflict. National churches were thrown onto their own resources, creating opportunities for accelerated progress towards autonomy which the societies did not always buy up after 1918.[3]

The war had two further consequences which were more fundamental still. In the first place, the ideals of Anglo-Saxon Protestant civilization which many national Christians before 1914 had imbibed enthusiastically from their missionary mentors, now became less compelling, thus making the search for Asian or African Christianities which were authentic to indigenous culture attractive and urgent. Secondly, the war marked the watershed between the era of British dominance in the missionary movement and the age of American missionary supremacy, which has continued to the present day. The shift in the balance of Protestant forces had its own independent causes, but the war hastened the process by its impoverishment of the European economies and relocation of the hub of Western economic power in New York.[4]

The Second World War and its aftermath completed the transition from British to American global pre-eminence. The war precipitated the British exodus from India, although only in retrospect can it be said to have heralded the end of the British empire itself: the decision of the Attlee government to pull out of India was in fact accompanied by a determination to strengthen British imperial commitments in Africa and the Middle East.[5] In spiritual terms the war appears to have reinforced rather than undermined the appeal of orthodox Christianity in Britain: the 1950s were perhaps the most Christian decade Britain had experienced since the early years of the century.[6] Yet the war inevitably proved extremely disruptive for the British missionary movement, which was now thoroughly overshadowed numerically by its American counterpart.

The twentieth-century missionary landscape exhibited one further feature which had not been generally present in the previous century. Christianity was no longer the sole alien ideology on offer to non-Western peoples. Islam now presented a serious challenge as an alternative pathway to political modernization. Muslim competition had been familiar enough to Victorian missionaries in East or West Africa, but in the nineteenth century the Islamic faith had been irredeemably associated with the slave trade, and hence more feared than welcomed by animistic peoples. British colonial rule effectively banished the slave trader, but in so doing opened the way for the Muslim trader or teacher to ply his wares unhampered by the old associations. Furthermore, British colonial policy in some areas, such as northern Nigeria, seemed actively to favour Islam by the device of employing Muslim emirs as lynch-pins of the system of 'indirect rule'. Missionaries complained with some justification that the *pax Britannica* was doing more to advance the cause of Islam than the gospel of Christ.[7]

In Asia a still more serious rival arose in the early 1920s. The success of the Bolshevik revolution in Russia in 1917 soon had repercussions beyond the borders of the new Soviet Union. In 1919 the Communist International (Comintern) was established to co-ordinate the international revolutionary cause. With remarkable rapidity Communist ideology became the most effective vehicle for the expression of anti-colonial and nationalist protest, initially in the Far East, and then farther afield. From now on ideas which owed their origin, to a greater or lesser extent, to the Marxian tradition were to provide the motive power behind opposition to both Western imperialism in general and Christian missions in particular.

The remainder of this chapter selects two case studies which exemplify some of these general themes with peculiar clarity. The first goes outside the boundaries of the formal British empire, but is of central importance to the whole subject of missions and imperialism. In China the years between 1895 and 1927 were of formative importance for the evolution of nationalist responses to the informal imperialism of the Western powers, and hence also for missionary thinking and strategy. Events in China during these years foreshadowed the culmination of the anti-Christian movement after the Communists had assumed power in 1949. The second case study, though of less far-reaching significance, will illuminate the relationship between missions, the colonial state, and emergent nationalism in British Africa: Kenya between 1918 and 1931 provides a telling example of the complex pressures encountered by missions which found themselves 'under the flag' of British colonial rule in its maturity.

2. China, 1895–1927

Between 1895 and 1927 China threw off the ancient imperial yoke of the Ch'ing (Manchu) dynasty, and took her first steps towards becoming a modern nation state capable of reversing the accumulated humiliations inflicted by the new imperialism of the Western powers. These were thus crucial years for the missionary enterprise in China. The missionary movement had accepted the forcible opening of China by the European powers between 1842 and 1860 as evidence that God had over-ruled the evil of man for his own salvific purposes (see chapter 4, section 4, pp. 104–109). Whether this interpretation was theologically legitimate or not, the consequences of the retrospective missionary acceptance of imperial aggression haunted Christian missions in China for nearly a century to come. The 'unequal treaties' which now governed China's relations with the Western powers were also the guarantors of religious freedom for the missionaries and their Chinese converts, and most missionaries before the 1920s felt no qualms about appealing to their treaty rights.

One such treaty, concluded in 1843, had secured to Britain a position of unique privilege by specifying that any concession which China might grant to any other power must thereby also apply to Britain. British missionaries had used this 'most-favoured-nation' clause to claim the right to own property outside the treaty ports, on the grounds that the same right had been conceded to the French in 1860. The Chinese, however, contested the validity of the concession, and missionaries found themselves embroiled in periodic disputes with the Chinese authorities over property matters. They also found themselves compelled on occasion to invoke treaty rights to protect their converts from official persecution, thus giving the impression that they were willing to employ treaty privileges to remove national Christians from Chinese legal jurisdiction. Protestants, at least initially, appear to have been less involved in disputes of this kind than Catholics, but Chinese resentment made no theological distinctions. By the 1890s the British position of informal commercial pre-eminence in China, concentrated on the Yangtze river, was threatened both by the instability which missionary problems were creating and by growing competition from the other European powers.[8]

In 1895 China suffered her gravest national humiliation yet, when she was defeated in the Sino-Japanese War. She was now regarded by the European powers as ripe for the picking; France, Germany and Russia led the race for territorial and economic concessions. For a time it seemed as if China might go the way of tropical Africa and be formally partitioned by the Western powers. British missionaries did not welcome this prospect, yet many believed that, once the process had begun, Britain ought not to opt out. Thus the veteran LMS missionary, Griffith John, wrote in April 1898 that if the Yangtze valley were to fall into British hands, it would be 'a cause of great rejoicing'. In January the President of the CMS, Sir John Kennaway, had asked Lord Salisbury, the Prime Minister and Foreign Secretary, if it were not possible, 'now that conditions were altered' in the country, to persuade China to grant missionaries property rights outside the treaty ports. The Foreign Office in this case declined to exploit Chinese vulnerability to confirm disputed missionary privileges, but was more prepared to exploit missionary grievances when national advantage was at stake. Thus the British government used the murder in November 1898 of the CIM missionary, W. S. Fleming, as a pretext to enforce its interpretation of the disputed northern boundary of the Kowloon peninsula in Hong Kong. The original concession of the peninsula to Britain had nothing to do with missionary questions, but the Fleming incident had the effect of associating the missionary movement with the unholy scramble for territorial concessions currently being waged by the Western powers. Few missionaries then perceived how damaging the association would prove to be. Few of the Chinese political and military leaders, who since the early 1880s had been advocating China's 'self-strengthening', had included Christianity in their recipes for national recovery; rather Christianity appeared to be a contributor to China's humiliation.[9]

One British missionary who had a highly distinctive prescription for China's ills was the former BMS missionary, Timothy Richard. Richard had served in Shantung and Shansi provinces since 1870. His first-hand experience of the catastrophic famine which hit northern China in 1876-77 had convinced him that China could find national salvation only through a massive programme of Westernization and economic modernization. China needed the gospel of forgiveness, but she also needed the gospel of material progress and scientific advance. Whereas in the West it was the problems of urban life which gave rise to the social gospel movement, in China the social gospel, as pioneered by Richard and a few other missionaries of advanced views (such as the American Presbyterians Calvin Mateer and Gilbert Reid), was a response to the predicament of the rural peasantry. With time this distinctive vision for the regeneration of China became highly influential.[10]

From 1879 Richard's missionary programme gave unique emphasis to preaching the virtues of Western science and technology to the 'scholar-official' class – the powerful bureaucrats who had surmounted the formidable hurdles of the imperial examination system and controlled the state apparatus. The response of high-ranking officials to Richard's overtures in the 1880s was generally disappointing. By 1890 he had concluded that he must cast his net more widely to reach the younger generation of Chinese intellectuals through the medium of the Chinese-language press. At the same time Richard was in trouble with his BMS colleagues, who regarded his theology as unsound and his missionary methods as misguided. A solution was found in 1891 when the BMS agreed to second Richard to be secretary of the Society for the Diffusion of Christian and General Knowledge among the Chinese (subsequently the Christian Literature Society for China). In his new capacity Richard wrote, edited or translated a stream of titles which propagated the values of Western civilization. The most influential was his translation in 1895 of Robert Mackenzie's *The Nineteenth Century: A History* (1880), which was a rhapsodic eulogy of that century as the great age of progress, and of Britain as the exemplar of the blessings that would flow to nations which espoused Christianity, scientific enlightenment and liberal political values.[11] Richard's message to the intelligentsia was clear: the road to 'self-strengthening' followed the path of Westernization. His message to the missionary community was equally forthright: the kingdom of God in China would never be built through the traditional means of seeking the conversion of individuals; 'conversion by the million', as Richard entitled a two-volume collection of his writings published in 1907, would be the consequence of a broadly-based educational strategy aimed at the intelligentsia.[12]

For a time the ideas of national reconstruction advocated by Richard and his associate, Gilbert Reid, enjoyed the support of a growing party of reformers at the imperial court. One of the reforming leaders, K'ang Yu-wei, succeeded in giving the new Western ideas of evolutionary progress legitimacy by claiming to find them in the true (rather than the received) text of the Confucian classics.[13] In 1898 K'ang was appointed tutor to the Emperor Kuang-hsu, and, for a heady period of one hundred days, modernizing reform swept all before it in China. But the climate changed dramatically on 21 September, when the Empress Dowager, a champion of traditionalism, seized control in Beijing and executed several reforming leaders; K'ang fled to Japan. A new wave of anti-foreign feeling swept through China, and attacks on missionaries multiplied.

The anti-foreign feeling unleashed in September 1898 culminated in the 'Boxer' rising of 1899–1900. The 'Boxer' movement was composed of devotees of heterodox sects who practised occult rites (which included boxing-like gestures). Originally they were opposed to the ruling Ch'ing dynasty, but the imperial administration succeeded in restricting their hatred to the foreign community, and in particular to missionaries, whom the Boxers vilified as secret agents of the Western powers. Both Catholic and Protestant churches in the North suffered severely at the hands of the Boxers. The Catholics lost nearly fifty missionaries and perhaps 30,000 national Christians; the Protestants lost fewer converts – approximately 2,000 – but recorded an even higher toll of missionary martyrs – 135 adult Protestant missionaries and fifty-three missionary children lost their lives.[14] Inevitably the Western powers intervened to protect their nationals. On 14 August 1900 a Western force captured Beijing, and the imperial court fled. The foreign troops executed reprisals on the Chinese scarcely less brutal than the Boxer massacres themselves. The powers imposed a settlement on China, which provided for the punishment of the chief perpetrators of anti-foreign outrages and the payment of extensive indemnities as compensation to all foreigners for lives lost and property damaged.

Once again China had been humiliated at the hands of the West. The forces of reaction were now thoroughly discredited and the momentum of pro-Western reform unstoppable. In 1905 the old system of civil service examinations was abolished, and a new Ministry of Education established to promote Western as well as Oriental learning. New schools and universities on the Western model were founded, and a new student class emerged eager to appropriate what Western knowledge had to offer. The tide of change in China was now running so strongly that the survival of the Ch'ing dynasty began to look precarious. Its weakness was compounded by the almost simultaneous deaths in November 1908 of the Empress Dowager and the Emperor, leaving an infant, P'u-yi, on the imperial throne. In 1911–12 the dynasty finally collapsed, and China became a republic.

The suppression of the Boxer rising appeared to mark the beginning of happier days for Christian missions in China. The next two decades were indeed to see spectacular church growth and an enormous expansion of missionary influence. Beneath the surface, however, the seeds of future troubles were germinating. The readiness of most of the missionary societies to make substantial claims on the indemnity money inevitably perpetuated the impression among hostile observers that the missions were prepared to live off the fat of Western military conquest. Only the CIM (which had suffered greater losses than any other mission) adopted the policy, under Hudson Taylor's leadership, of refusing to make any corporate claim for compensation, in order to emphasize the Mission's distinctiveness from the temporal power, and to exemplify to the Chinese 'the meekness and gentleness of Christ'.[15] All missionaries and their converts continued to enjoy the special protection afforded them by the 'unequal treaties'. The Shanghai missionary conference of 1907, representing all Protestant work in China, resolved that 'the time has not come when all the protection to Christian converts provided in the treaties can safely be withdrawn', though it insisted that any appeal to treaty rights must be regarded as a last resort, and hoped that such appeals would soon be unnecessary.[16]

James Bashford, the American Methodist Bishop of Beijing, told the World Missionary Conference at Edinburgh in 1910 that in the Far East 'more than one-fourth of the human race stands at the parting of the ways. Not since the days of the Reformation, not indeed since Pentecost, has so great an opportunity confronted the Christian Church.'[17] The church in China (which Bashford had chiefly in mind) was indeed growing rapidly, despite the ravages inflicted by persecution. Between 1889 and 1905 the communicant membership of the Protestant churches had increased fivefold; by 1915 the aggregate membership stood at 268,652 and the total Protestant community numbered over half a million. Missionaries flocked to China to seize these unprecedented opportunities: the number of Protestant missionaries in China rose from 1,296 in 1889 to 8,158 in 1925. Americans accounted for a large proportion of the increase: in 1905 45% of Protestant missionaries in China were British, and 35% from the USA; by 1922 only 18% were British, but 51% were now American.[18]

Increasingly this expanding Protestant missionary force was engaged, not in directly evangelistic work, but in education. The CIM – easily the largest missionary body – was the sole but important exception. Christian high schools, colleges and universities multiplied to satisfy the new hunger for Western learning. Amongst the student population, and the younger professional class generally, membership of the YMCA (introduced to China in 1895) became popular, especially after the 1911–12 Revolution. The new missionary programme, spearheaded by the YMCA, was in many ways a fulfilment of the ideals of Timothy Richard. Fletcher Brockman, YMCA national secretary in China, consulted closely with Richard in 1901 on the problem of how to reach the traditional student class (the scholar-officials of the future) with the Christian message. Richard's advice was to the effect that lectures on Western science must be the first priority. When John Mott, secretary of the World Student Christian Federation and the dominant figure in the American YMCA, revisited China at the end of 1901, he agreed to Brockman's request that he should search for a scientist who was a Christian to become a YMCA science lecturer in China. He did, however, resist Richard's suggestion that the YMCA should devote all its energies to science lectures. Mott found his man in C. H. Robertson, a keen YMCA member and professor of mechanical engineering at Purdue University. From 1903 onwards Robertson's lectures on Western science were received by educated Chinese with immense enthusiasm. His lectures formed an important adjunct to highly successful evangelistic campaigns conducted by Mott and George Sherwood Eddy after the Revolution.[19] At its peak between 1913 and 1915, YMCA evangelism unashamedly presented Christianity as the religion of modernization, the great ideological engine which, in partnership with Western science and education, would drive China into the modern world of freedom and prosperity.

This missionary recipe for China's modernization also had its attraction for the political leaders of the new China. President Yuan Shih-k'ai lent his public patronage to the YMCA evangelistic campaigns, and in 1913 even issued an appeal to Chinese Protestants to make Sunday 27 April a day of concerted prayer for him and his government – an appeal which aroused great interest and rejoicing throughout Protestant America.[20] Yuan Shih-k'ai's flirtation with Christianity proved short-lived, but more enduring was the impact of Christian ideas on the most influential of China's early republican leaders – Sun Yat-sen.

Sun Yat-sen spent most of his early life outside imperial China. Educated in Christian schools and colleges in Honolulu and Hong Kong, he had by 1894 adopted a nationalist stance dedicated to the overthrow of the Ch'ing dynasty, the restoration of China to the Chinese, and the setting up of a republican government. Compelled to seek asylum in the West, he was in the USA when news of the 1911 Revolution broke. Sun hurried back to Shanghai, and was actually installed as President in January 1912. In the event he yielded the presidency to Yuan Shih-k'ai, who remained in power till his death in 1916. During the decade of civil war and chronic instability which ensued, when power in China fell increasingly into the hands of provincial 'warlords', Sun established himself as the acknowledged leader in the south of China, and his Kuomintang (Revolutionary Party – KMT) as the primary vehicle of the Chinese nationalist revolution. Sun died of cancer in Beijing in 1925.

The day before he died, Sun Yat-sen proclaimed: 'I am a Christian; God

141

sent me to fight evil for my people. Jesus was a revolutionist; so am I.'[21] In reality Sun's creed was a mish-mash of ideas culled from progressive social Christianity and a variety of Western secular thinkers such as Darwin, Marx and Henry George. Indeed, relatively little separated Sun's eclectic ideology from the advanced modernism of the YMCA in China, whose theology by the 1920s struck one CMS missionary, A. F. Lutley, as 'more Confucian than Christian' and unbalanced in its portrayal of Jesus as a political revolutionary.[22] By late 1923 Sun, in response to overtures from the Comintern, was turning away from the West towards Soviet Russia as the most likely champion of Chinese nationalist aspirations; it may not be wholly coincidental that, at the same time, some Protestant modernists in the USA were also proclaiming the spiritual affinity of Christianity and Communism.[23]

The missionary programme of the YMCA and the philosophy of Sun Yat-sen both reflect the triumph of ideas which, when first expounded by Timothy Richard in the 1880s, were the preserve of a heterodox minority. Once the suppression of the Boxer rising had ensured the victory of reform over reaction in Beijing, Richard's prescription of targeting the educational elite with the message that Christianity was the pathway to modernization became both palatable and effective. Hence the decade after the 1911–12 Revolution saw growing numbers of Chinese, students especially, accepting the modernist premiss that Christianity alone could build a new, prosperous and progressive China out of the chaos left by Western imperial incursions and the collapse of the Ch'ing regime. Protestant Christianity became a significant influence on the 'New Culture' movement, in which China's new educated elite sought to integrate the ideas of Western liberalism within China's young nationalism. Only as the 1920s unfolded did it become apparent just how vulnerable this apologia for the Christian faith was. The ideals of social evolution and human progress so enthusiastically disseminated by Richard could easily be turned against Christianity. The blind faith in Western science inculcated by the YMCA left the door wide open for the claims of scientism and positivism that Christianity was intellectually indefensible. Above all, the presentation of Christianity as the guarantor of national regeneration was a standing invitation to any rival ideology which could present itself as able to deliver the same goods, and at the same time promise an end to the humiliations inflicted on China by Western imperialism.[24]

Between 1922 and 1927 these possibilities were realized as China experienced the last major upsurge of militantly anti-Christian feeling before the Communist take-over in 1949. The prime movers in this anti-Christian movement were the very same recipients of Western-style higher education to whom the Protestant missions had looked as the pioneers of national reconstruction. By 1922 many of the student class had become disillusioned with the slow pace of reform, the protracted disruption inflicted by the warlords who controlled much of the country, and the continued refusal of the Western powers (displayed at the Washington Conference in 1921–22) to abandon their extraterritorial rights in China. In response, some turned to the ideas of leading Western opponents of Christianity, such as Bertrand Russell, who conducted a lecture tour in China in 1920. Others were attracted by the writings of Lenin on capitalism and imperialism, recently translated into Chinese, and joined the Chinese Communist Party (CCP), founded as a result of a Comintern mission sent to China in the spring of 1920. The title and tone of a Protestant publication in 1922 celebrating the missionary achievement in China – *The Christian Occupation of China* – merely stoked the flames of anti-Christian resentment. The final trigger for the formation of the anti-Christian movement was the decision of the World Student Christian Federation to hold its annual meeting at Tsing Hua University in April 1922. As a direct riposte, the Anti-Christian Student Federation was established in Shanghai in March, closely followed by the formation in Beijing of the Great Anti-Religion Federation, which set up branches in universities throughout China. Both bodies were strongly influenced by Communist ideology, and large rallies were held to attack Christianity as incompatible with modern science, and denounce Christian missions as the handmaiden of imperialism and capitalism.[25]

This first wave of the anti-Christian movement was confined largely to the universities, and tended to lose momentum after the end of the 1922 summer term. Its second and more significant wave came in the wake of the reorientation in late 1923 of Sun Yat-sen's KMT towards a pro-Russian alignment and a coalition with the CCP. Opposition to imperialism now became the central motif of the Chinese Nationalist movement, and the two parties singled out for special attack the 'cultural imperialism' of the numerous Christian schools and colleges, which allegedly 'denationalized' Chinese youth and made them the 'running dogs' of the imperialist powers; membership of the YMCA slumped by 34% between 1924 and 1928.[26] Under the slogan of 'Restore Educational Rights', a campaign of educational boycotts and disruption was organized. It reached its greatest intensity after the May 30 incident in the Shanghai International Settlement in 1925, when British police fired on a crowd of Chinese demonstrators, killing twelve and wounding seventeen. Within a few days nineteen Chinese staff and over 500 students had withdrawn from the Episcopalian St John's University in Shanghai, in protest at the president's refusal to fly the Chinese flag at half-mast in commemoration of the dead. The Nationalist tide was now running with unprecedented strength; what had begun as a purely educational movement now assumed a broader significance.

In July 1926 the Nationalist armies, under the leadership of Chiang K'ai-shek, embarked on a major expedition northwards from Canton with the aim of unifying China under Nationalist control. As they advanced, often with left-wing KMT party activists in their train, anti-Christian incidents multiplied: churches and mission properties were looted. The most serious incident occurred on 24 March 1927, when six Europeans were killed in anti-foreign riots in Nanking after Nationalist troops had taken over the city. The crisis precipitated an exodus of over half the Protestant missionary force from China; by July 1927 about 5,000 Protestant missionaries had left the country or at least retreated to the comparative safety of the treaty ports. In the large parts of China now under Nationalist control, mission schools had to accept government registration and agree to teach the 'Three People's Principles' of Sun Yat-sen – the People's Nationalism, the People's Sovereignty and the People's Livelihood.

In mid-1927 it seemed as if the missionary era in China's history was about to be abruptly terminated. In fact, the anti-Christian movement evaporated rapidly after 1927. Threats of armed intervention by the Western powers compelled the new Nationalist government, formed in 1928, to pursue a more conciliatory line. Chiang K'ai-shek himself became more favourable to Christianity, and in October 1930 was baptized into the Methodist Church. Most important of all, the Nationalists, fearing a Communist take-over of the Chinese revolution, repudiated their coalition with the CCP, and purged left-wing elements from the KMT. A more favourable stance towards Christianity was the inevitable corollary. Throughout the 1930s China's Nationalist government maintained a broadly conciliatory attitude towards the churches. The tradition of anti-Christian invective was kept up by the CCP, although even the Communists temporarily relaxed their opposition to Christianity during the years from 1937 to 1945, when the Japanese occupation of Eastern China relegated all other issues to a secondary place. Only after 1949 was the torrent of anti-Christian feeling, which had been dammed up since 1927, unleashed in its full force.

What took place in China between 1922 and 1927 set the agenda for the anti-religious programme adopted by the Communist regime after 1949. It was also decisive in alerting missionary opinion to the seriousness of the issues which Western imperialism had posed for the church in China. The clamour against the unequal treaties which followed the May 30 incident in 1925 precipitated some drastic rethinking by the missions: within a few months almost all the major British societies had endorsed resolutions prepared by the Conference of British Missionary Societies, expressing a desire that missionary activity in China should no longer be buttressed by the religious provisions of the existing treaties, and that extraterritoriality should be abolished; most of the American mission boards took the same view.[27]

The crisis also prompted the missions to accelerate their existing programme of devolution of responsibility towards the Chinese churches. Both British and American Protestant missions had for some time been committed in theory to the 'Three-Self' principles of building a self-supporting, self-governing and self-extending indigenous church. The 'Three-Self' formula can be traced back to the writings of Henry Venn in Britain and Rufus Anderson in the USA in the mid-nineteenth century; its use in China was pioneered in the early 1880s by the Presbyterian missionaries, John Campbell Gibson and John L. Nevius.[28] Only in the critical climate of the 1920s, however, did missions take swift and decisive steps towards the creation of an autonomous church. The existing structures of ecumenical missionary co-operation made possible the establishment in 1922 of a National Christian Council, and the formation by 1927 of the Church of Christ in China, uniting churches of sixteen denominations. The partial missionary exodus of 1927, followed in 1928 by the crisis in missionary funding caused by the world depression, necessitated further devolution of authority to indigenous leadership. The Chinese churches were rapidly severing their damaging associations with Western imperialism, but new political associations were being forged in their stead which carried dangers of their own. The National Christian Council became the organ of pro-Nationalist Christian sentiment, and its modernist theological orientation soon led to the withdrawal of the CIM, many of whose missionaries belonged to the conservative evangelical Bible Union of China, formed in 1920.[29] The Council survived to welcome the Communist revolution of 1949, although by 1954 its role had virtually been supplanted by the Committee of the China Christian Three-Self Patriotic Movement, whose chairman was Y. T. Wu, a former YMCA staff member and firm supporter of the Communist regime.[30]

By 1927 Protestant missions had at last awoken to the gravity of the charges being levelled against them. But hasty attempts to devolve responsibility to the Chinese church were a superficial response to the crisis. Most of the missions had perceived belatedly that reliance on the protection afforded by the unequal treaties was ultimately counter-productive, but few missionaries seem to have grasped that the real problem lay at a deeper and more ideological level. Anti-foreignism was a long-standing and powerful element in China's cultural make-up. Missionary Christianity, and especially its increasingly dominant liberal variant, had self-consciously and deliberately presented itself as the central ingredient of an integrated package of Westernization. It had thus played straight into the hands of Chinese anti-foreignism. Once Soviet influence had succeeded in detaching Chinese nationalism from its initial pro-Western stance after the 1911–12 Revolution, there could be no doubt that a version of Christianity so unashamedly wrapped in Western cultural and political values would ultimately be dismissed as incompatible with the aims and identity of the new China. That outcome was delayed until after 1949, but it was between 1922 and 1927 that the writing appeared on the wall. The events of the anti-Christian movement of those years ought to have been a warning, not just to China missionaries, but to the missionary movement as a whole. The new nationalisms of the non-European world would to a large extent follow the trail which China had blazed. All Western missions, whether British or not, now faced the challenge of a world which repudiated more and more of the premisses undergirding even the most beneficent aspects of Western imperialism. Missionaries working within the boundaries of the formal British empire faced that challenge in a rather different way, but fundamentally the issues were the same.

3. Kenya, 1918-1931

China was never integrated into the formal empire of Britain or any other power. For this very reason, British Christians were probably less conscious of any national moral responsibility towards China than they were in relation to the territories of Britain's tropical African empire. It was there that the moral vocabulary of imperial trusteeship was most frequently appealed to and employed by both missionaries and others with human-itarian interests. The grand test-case of British trusteeship was Kenya.

The completion of the Uganda railway in 1901 opened the interior of Kenya (then the British East Africa Protectorate) to penetration both by Christian missions and by secular European interests. The Protestant missionary presence, originally confined to the coastal strip around Mombasa, now acquired a new concentration in Kikuyuland, the fertile area north of Nairobi. Operating within a fairly confined geographical area, the various Protestant missions were speedily attracted by the prospect of some form of union, or at least federation. In 1913 the four principal Protestant missions – the CMS, the Church of Scotland Mission (CSM), the United Methodist Free Church Mission, and the interdenominational Africa Inland Mission (AIM) – participated in a conference at the CSM station at Kikuyu, and agreed proposals for a federation of their respective churches. The Kikuyu scheme was torpedoed by the public opposition of Frank Weston, the Anglo-Catholic Bishop of Zanzibar, but a much looser form of interdenominational co-operation was salvaged from the ensuing controversy, in the shape of an Alliance of the four missions, concluded in 1918.[31] The formation of the Alliance meant that the missionary response to the problems which surfaced in the 1920s could not be an entirely uncoordinated one.

By the 1920s Kenya possessed a white settler community more powerful than any in the continent outside South Africa or Southern Rhodesia. Proportionately to the African population their numbers were not large – only about 12,500 amongst an indigenous population of some three million in 1925.[32] Their political influence, however, was out of all proportion to their numbers, once Britain had rewarded the settlers for their defence of

British interests during the First World War with the award of full colonial status to Kenya in 1920.[33] The priorities of the settler community were to achieve the maximum possible degree of self-government and to tune the plantation economy to meet the rising demands of production for the world market. The inescapable contradiction between these priorities and the ideals of imperial trusteeship soon became apparent. Missionaries and humanitarians professed to believe, in the words of W. E. Owen, head of the CMS Nyanza mission, that 'the only Christian justification for Empire over backward peoples is that it may serve them – not exploit them'.[34] The depth and sincerity of this conviction were put to the test by a variety of challenges which made Kenya a microcosm of the dilemmas encountered by missions living 'under the flag' of twentieth-century colonial rule. Missionaries had to respond almost simultaneously to a growing settler appetite for African land and labour, the emergence of African nationalist politics, and the outbreak of a major crisis in the relationship of Christian moral standards to indigenous cultural practices. As in China, policy choices made in the 1920s by missionaries, national Christians and nationalist politicians carried implications which were fully revealed only in the 1950s and 1960s.

On 7 February 1918 Norman Leys, medical officer for Nyasaland and a convinced Christian Socialist, despatched a massive letter to the Colonial Secretary expressing serious concern at the situation in Britain's Crown Colonies in East Africa.[35] Leys had considerable experience in British East Africa as well as Nyasaland, and conditions in Kenya were in fact the chief preoccupation of his letter. Leys's anxiety focused on the twin problems of land and labour. Under the Crown Lands Ordinance of 1902, Africans had been deprived of any permanent legal title to land throughout British East Africa, apart from a ten-mile wide strip along the coast. Only in the 'native reserves' demarcated by the Protectorate government could the African population be sure of a reasonable degree of protection from the depredations of the settlers, and even there some of the best land had been appropriated by the missions.[36] More serious still, in Leys's view, was the existence in Kenya of a system of virtual forced labour: 'There is no slavery under our flag, but labour is performed under conditions which produce and even exaggerate some of the evils of slavery.'[37] The demand for cheap plantation labour was so high that the settlers had induced the government to instruct its district officers to 'encourage' labour migration; in practice they could do so only by ordering the chiefs to provide the requisite supplies of labour.

Norman Leys's letter never received the courtesy of a reply from the Colonial Office. Nevertheless, he had correctly identified the issues which were to lie at the root of the politics of Kenya, and above all of Kikuyuland, until the 1950s. Indeed, in 1919 the settler lobby extracted a further sanction from the colonial government: in October the Chief Native Commissioner issued a circular, urging government officials in the native reserves to 'exercise every possible lawful influence to induce able-bodied male natives to go into the labour field'; Africans were now to be virtually compelled to work for two months each year either for the government or for a settler.[38] The missionary response came in the form of a memorandum issued by Bishop Willis of Uganda, Bishop Heywood of Mombasa and J. W. Arthur, head of the CSM. The memorandum expressed serious concern at the abuses which were likely to arise from a system of compulsory labour implemented by the chiefs, and warned that for a native

> to leave his house unthatched, his crops unreaped, his wife unguarded perhaps for months at a time, in return for cash he does not want to see on the 'advice' of his chief – which he dare not disregard – is not a prospect calculated to inspire loyalty to the Government from which the advice emanates.[39]

The memorandum confined its criticisms to the proposed procedures for labour recruitment – in particular to the position in which it placed the chiefs – and held back from condemning the government's policy in principle. Indeed, Arthur wrote privately to the governor, assuring him that the missions were not against the principle of compulsory labour. Arthur later defended his view by asserting that 'work was a necessary part of Christianity. To Christianize natives, to educate them and to make them work were complementary principles.'[40] For Arthur, the pagan African was a naturally idle fellow who needed the gospel of work alongside the gospel of redemption. Kenya, like China, had its share of missionaries who were still unshaken in their conviction that European civilization – at least in its economic values – was a divinely-appointed remedy for non-Western 'backwardness'.

Some strands of Christian opinion were more uncompromising in their opposition to the forced labour policy. Bishop Frank Weston condemned his two fellow bishops as 'traitors', and published a pamphlet asserting that 'some of us who are missionaries will not agree to any such policy. We regard forced labour ... as itself immoral.'[41] An even more influential dissentient from the bishops' memorandum was J. H. Oldham, a former YMCA missionary in India, and now editor of the *International Review of Missions*. Oldham drew much of his information on Kenya from Handley Hooper, CMS missionary at Kahuhia; Hooper believed strongly that the growing forces of industrial and commercial civilization had to be resisted if Kenya were not to fall victim to economic selfishness.[42] By 1920 Oldham was, in the words of Adrian Hastings, 'the spider at the heart of almost every non-Roman missionary web',[43] and it was he who orchestrated a major propaganda campaign in 1920 on the Kenyan labour question. At the heart of Oldham's campaign was a memorandum, approved by the Conference of British Missionary Societies, and then signed by a galaxy of figures towards the left of British public life, entitled 'Labour in Africa and the Principles of Trusteeship'. It was an appeal to the British government to be true to its own profession of the ideals of imperial trusteeship by ensuring that native interests in Kenya were not sacrificed on the altar of settler demands.[44]

Oldham's sustained pressure made its mark. In September 1921, the 1919 circular on native labour was withdrawn. Whatever the ambiguities of the initial missionary response to the circular, there can be no doubt that it was Christian opinion and organization which were primarily responsible for bringing the issue to the forefront of public debate. Oldham's influential hand was again much in evidence two years later, when the settler lobby rallied its forces against government concessions of enhanced political rights to the Indian community in Kenya. Oldham's influence, mediated through Archbishop Davidson of Canterbury, was decisive in securing from the Colonial Office the famous 'Devonshire Declaration', which stated:

> Primarily Kenya is an African territory, and His Majesty's Government think it necessary definitely to record their considered opinion that the interests of the African natives must be paramount, and that if, and when, those interests and the interests of the immigrant races should conflict, the former should prevail.[45]

Oldham's fearless championship of the idea of trusteeship ensured that the public Christian response to the intensifying threats to African interests in Kenya was clear-cut and politically effective. Although it was many years before the British government was prepared to give full cash value to its assertion of African paramountcy, the 1923 Declaration did at least preserve Kenya from going the way of Southern Rhodesia as a self-governing white colony. Oldham was not in principle opposed to either imperial rule or white settlement, but believed, with W. E. Owen, that empire could be justified only on the basis of a harmonious partnership between the interests of all racial groups.[46] Few missionaries disagreed, but the benevolent paternalism of some was threatened by Oldham's political stridency, and even more by the emergence in the course of the 1920s of indigenous champions of African interests. For part of the legacy which the First World War bestowed on Kenya was the birth of nationalist politics.

The conditions of post-war Kenya were ripe for the development of African political consciousness. Among the Kikuyu especially, the intensified European pressure on African land and labour coincided with a heightened responsiveness to the Christian message, and a new hunger for the educational opportunities which the missions presented. As a result, Christian ideals provided the inspiration, and Christian education the tools, for the first steps in nationalist political initiative. The first 'modern' political association in Kenya, the Kikuyu Association, originated in 1919 in protests against the alienation of Kikuyuland made by Christian chiefs and headmen in the region of the CMS station at Kabete. Missionary patronage was accepted from the outset, and the Association remained moderate in tone and fundamentally Christian in orientation throughout the 1920s. Far more threatening was the entry into the political arena of a younger generation of Kenyans who had received a missionary education, but were not prepared to remain under permanent missionary tutelage.

The pioneer of this more militant brand of nationalist politics was a mission-educated telephone-operator in Nairobi, Harry Thuku. Thuku founded two associations in 1921 which blazed the trail for subsequent nationalist politics – the Young Kikuyu Association (YKA), and the more broadly based East African Association. Thuku focused on much the same issues of land, labour, wages and taxation as the Kikuyu Association, but underlying his agitation was a fundamental hostility to European rule. He drew his supporters primarily from mission adherents, initially in Nairobi, and then most notably from the CMS stations at Kahuhia and Weithaga in northern Kikuyuland. Handley Hooper reported to Oldham on 4 March 1922 that a large element in the Christian community at Kahuhia had cast Thuku in the role of a prophetic deliverer, and warned that the future of the mission was 'trembling in the balance'.[47] Hooper regarded rebellion as a distinct possibility, but had sufficient sympathy with Thuku's political objectives to maintain close contact with him and attempt to direct his protest into constitutional channels. At Weithaga the senior missionary, A. W. McGregor, was an older evangelical, less sophisticated and less liberal in his sympathies than Hooper. McGregor, fearing 'an insurrection against the government with possibly an enormous loss of life', saw it to be his duty to collect incriminating evidence on the activities of the YKA and pass it to the government.[48] On 14 March 1922 Thuku was indeed arrested, an event which provoked a riot in Nairobi, in which twenty-five Africans were shot dead. Thuku was deported to the coast, and for a time the voice of Kenyan nationalism was silenced.

When nationalist politics re-emerged in 1924–25 in the shape of the Kikuyu Central Association (KCA), the same variety of missionary response was evident.[49] The KCA had its roots in the Kahuhia mission, where Hooper and his successor, Francis Green (after Hooper left to become Africa Secretary of CMS in 1926), maintained good relations with the KCA leadership. Although radical by comparison with the Kikuyu Association, the KCA was at heart neither anti-missionary nor anti-colonial: its objectives were to secure for Africans a fair share of the benefits of the colonial regime, not to overthrow it. Jomo Kenyatta, general secretary of the KCA from 1928, had been educated by the CSM, and was too concerned for Kikuyu unity to adopt an intrinsically anti-Christian stance. Nonetheless, the majority of missionaries regarded KCA membership as inconsistent with full Christian obedience, and interpreted the increasing politicization of the African church as a symptom of incipient worldliness. Broadly speaking, the most theologically conservative missionaries were least likely to manifest sympathy with the new nationalist politics, whereas those who proclaimed their disdain for 'fundamentalism', such as W. E. Owen in Nyanza, tended to give active encouragement to moderate, constitutional nationalism, and earn the wrath of the settlers in the process – they nick-named him 'Archdemon Owen'.[50] Paradoxically, the success of more liberal missionaries in keeping African criticism of the colonial regime within legitimate, constitutional channels did more to preserve the stability of British rule than the overtly pro-colonial stance of more conservative missionaries, such as McGregor, which tended to drive African politicians into dangerous isolation from Christian influence. The watershed in Kenyan politics was reached when the initiative began to pass from moderate hands to a new form of militancy based on cultural, as much as political, protest. That point was reached between 1929 and 1931, and it was in Kikuyuland that the crisis broke.

Conversion to Christianity demanded of any Kikuyu a radical shift in cultural values. As elsewhere in Africa, the tension between Christian standards and traditional culture was most evident in the sphere of marriage and sexual relations. In Kikuyuland the tension was particularly acute because the Kikuyu practised not only male but also female circumcision (or clitoridectomy).[51] For a girl, circumcision marked the transition to womanhood; to remain uncircumcised was to renounce tribal identity and accepted moral constraints. Most missionaries, however, regarded the practice as barbaric, degrading to women and medically dangerous. In 1918 the Alliance of Protestant Missions had indeed resolved to seek government legislation abolishing female circumcision. Such drastic government intervention was never a real possibility, and as a result the missions could not evade the challenge of formulating their own policies of church discipline on the issue.

From the early 1920s the CSM, closely followed by the AIM, endeavoured to outlaw the practice of female circumcision among its church members. However, it was not until 1928 that the question became a major test of Christian allegiance within the mission. In April 1928 the Kirk Session at Tumutumu mission demanded that all church members make a declaration repudiating circumcision on pain of suspension. About 200 people, 7% of the membership of the local churches, refused to do so and were accordingly suspended. From this point the crisis escalated rapidly to serious proportions. A court case involving a girl circumcised, allegedly against her will, led J. W. Arthur to take a public stand in the press against circumcision. The KCA, no friends of Arthur's, were quick to politicize the question in response. In the autumn of 1929 the CSM decided to force the issue by requiring, first its church leaders, and then ordinary church members, to forswear the practice of circumcision. The Kikuyu showed their protest by withdrawing their children *en masse* from the mission's outschools in the villages. The AIM took a similarly hard line, and met with the same response. Large numbers of AIM outschools were closed, and many adherents left the mission. Attacks on missionaries became common, culminating in the murder of Hulda Stumpf of the AIM on 2 January 1930.

Neither missionaries nor Kikuyu Christians were united on the circumcision issue. Some church leaders were amongst its most vehement opponents. Others drew a parallel with Jewish circumcision in the New Testament, arguing on the basis of Galatians 5:6 that circumcision was a 'thing indifferent', which should be left to the conscience of the individual Christian. Within the CMS there was a wide variety of opinion. At one extreme was John Comely, missionary at Kigari, who in January 1931 felt led by prayer and the backing of his church elders to take an absolute stand against female circumcision. The result was a fall in school attendance from 1,734 in 1930 to 346 in 1931, and a decline in adult baptisms from 107 in 1930 to 54 in 1931, and only 14 in 1932. At Kabare, on the other hand, the church elders, with the approval of their missionary, W. J. Rampley, surmounted the problem by instituting a private and Christianized version of the circumcision rites for both boys and girls. The Kabare solution was so successful that the official CMS policy, as laid down by Bishop Heywood, threatening church discipline against those who permitted their daughters to be circumcised, became unenforceable. Overall, the position of the CMS on the issue remained less than clear-cut, to a degree which outraged Arthur and strained the unity of the Alliance.

The significance of the circumcision controversy of 1929–31 is that it provoked the first signs in Kenya of an anti-Christian, or at least an anti-mission, movement. Wherever the missions took a hard line against circumcision, dissident Kikuyu Christians took the lead in establishing independent schools, and, in some cases, in forming Kenya's first independent churches. The CMS missionary T. F. C. Bewes claimed that these independent schools were the nurseries of the Mau Mau resistance movement of the 1950s, 'teaching deliberate anti-Government and indeed anti-Christian propaganda', and his claim is supported from a different perspective by the African nationalist historian Arnold Temu.[52] Mau Mau was essentially and passionately anti-Christian, a movement which revived and re-cast the symbols of the pre-Christian past – notably the secret oath of blood-brothers – to mobilize Kikuyu resistance to the British. The connection between the circumcision controversy and the Mau Mau movement is undeniable.

By setting Christianity and traditional Kikuyu values in such open confrontation, the circumcision crisis dictated that emergent African nationalism in Kenya would in future contain a dominant streak of indigenous cultural assertion. That streak was implicitly antagonistic to Christianity, and became overtly and violently so during the anti-colonial war of the 1950s. The circumcision controversy had also undermined the relationship of trust between the more moderate strands of Kikuyu nationalism and the liberal mission leadership. The political generation which came to maturity in the aftermath of the controversy owed an enormous debt to the missionary tradition symbolized by W. E. Owen – a tradition of liberal evangelicalism and fearless opposition to white racialism. Through Carey Francis, headmaster of the Alliance High School established at Kikuyu in 1926, that tradition was mediated to some of the key personalities in the Kenya African Union, which took over the mantle of Kenyan constitutional nationalism in 1944, and led the country to independence in 1963. But the legacy of the circumcision controversy made certain that the movement which Jomo Kenyatta now led would not toe the line of missionary counsel.

The relationship between missions and the colonial state in Kenya was far from being one of unambiguous harmony. Missionaries suspected the colonial administration of being half-hearted in its commitment to distinctively Christian objectives, and too inclined to yield to settler pressure – and their suspicions were well-founded. Colonial officials distrusted missionaries as purveyors of dangerously egalitarian doctrines which threatened the basis of white supremacy: 'Are your pupils taught that all men are equal?' was one of the anxious questions put to the Anglican bishops by Kenya's first Director of Education in 1912.[53] Such fears may have contributed to the apparent British policy of giving Muslims preferential employment in the police, the King's African Rifles, and personal service to government officials. Norman Leys was shrewd enough to warn the Colonial Office that Islam was likely to develop into a militantly nationalistic creed more threatening to the West than African Christianity could ever be; nevertheless, he believed that Christianity, if true to itself, was inescapably at odds with the theoretical basis of colonialism, precisely because it taught that 'there is no difference, Jew nor Gentile, slave nor free'.[54] That conviction would command widespread Christian agreement today, but in 1918 Leys was almost a lone voice. Even Oldham, perhaps Leys's closest associate on East African questions, saw no fundamental contradiction between Christianity and colonialism, provided that Christian public opinion ensured that colonial government was conducted with scrupulous regard to the good of the subject people, and not merely with a view to the interests of the ruling race.[55] The missionary calling was to keep the flag in check, not to haul it down.

The missionary challenge to the colonial state in Kenya came from those at the liberal end of the now broad spectrum of evangelicalism. In this respect, Kenya might appear to present almost the exact mirror image of China at the same period, where, as we have seen, the apolitical conservative evangelicalism of the CIM avoided the unbridled Westernizing enthusiasm of the missionary majority. The contrast is more apparent than real. Transplanted to a Kenyan context in the 1920s, Timothy Richard would no doubt have been just as sharp a thorn in the settler flesh as Owen was. Conversely, it is not hard to imagine an Oldham or an Owen in China sedulously propagating the rational benefits of Western education, science and liberal political philosophy. Owen's overall verdict on Britain's African empire was positive, precisely because it could be shown to have delivered goods of this nature:

> With all our mistakes there is a very high and noble record of achievement on behalf of Africans. Gone is the slave trade, and gone inter-tribal wars. A new era of civilization has dawned for Africa, and out of the sleep of ages Africa awakes to find laid at her feet the rich treasures of knowledge and achievement which it has taken us hundreds of years to acquire.[56]

If these same arguments were deployed to justify the missionary enterprise itself (and this was increasingly so as soteriological arguments became less popular), Christian defences could begin to appear vulnerable. To defend missions on the basis of their ability to transmit to the 'younger' races the treasures of civilization and technology which had been a Western prerogative since the Enlightenment was perilous in two respects. It invited African nationalists to call the white man's bluff in the same way as the Communists did in China: they could blaze alternative pathways to economic and educational progress which did not involve so high a cultural price as conversion to mission Christianity. Even more seriously, such an intimate linkage between Christianity and the supposedly self-evident advantages of Western civilization exposed the Christian faith to attack, as Western culture progressively lost its self-confidence, and African cultures re-asserted their integrity with new vigour and militancy. Hence in Kenya the political and cultural protest which was Mau Mau, directed its especial hatred against Christians, and Kikuyu Christians more than missionaries, for the former stood accused as traitors to tribal loyalty. The most courageous African opposition to Mau Mau came from Christians identified with the Revival movement which originated in Rwanda in the early 1930s.[57] The Revival brethren were uncompromising in their repudiation of everything in African culture which carried pagan associations, yet were truly autonomous of missionary control.[58] They were also true to the Keswick missionary tradition from which they sprang, in being largely indifferent to political concerns – they were hardly represented in the ranks of the Kenya African Union. The Revival Christians have understandably been criticized for their failure to preach a holistic message relevant to social and political concerns, but perhaps it needed a movement of such intense spirituality to withstand the immense pressures applied by anti-Christian cultural nationalism.[59] In China similarly, the churches which refused to align themselves with the Three-Self Patriotic Movement tended to be those founded by the CIM or other theologically conservative and apolitical missions.

Missions in the twentieth century thus had to relate, both to the mature forces of Western imperialism which enveloped them, and to the emergent forces of indigenous nationalism which they helped to bring to birth. Whether operating 'under the flag' of formal colonial rule or not, missionaries had hard choices to make on questions which were essentially political, such as the use of treaty privileges in China, or the labour question in Kenya. But in Kenya certainly, and arguably in China also, the issues which did most to fuel the growth of anti-Christian sentiment were at bottom less political than cultural. In the final analysis the missions and imperialism debate is not about armies and governments, but about cultural assumptions and attitudes. For that reason, the next chapter is devoted to the subject of Christianity and culture.

CHAPTER SEVEN

Christianity and culture

The relationship of British missions to political or economic imperialism continues to provoke a good deal of scholarly debate and disagreement. But over the contribution of the missionary movement as a whole to cultural imperialism the academic consensus is overwhelming. Historians, anthropologists and theologians unite in their judgment that missionaries have been guilty of foisting their own cultural values on their converts. They have upset the stability of indigenous social systems, and saddled the younger churches of the Third World with a thoroughly 'foreign' Christianity. Few Christian commentators would disagree that one of the highest priorities for the Third World churches today is to unwrap the gospel from its alien cultural packaging and develop expressions of the Christian faith which are genuinely indigenous to their particular cultural contexts. The charge of cultural imperialism is levelled against missionaries irrespective of their country of origin or their field of service. British missionaries operating within British colonial territories were perhaps more likely to disseminate 'Britishness' than their compatriots working in more hostile environments, but fundamentally this issue is broader and deeper than formal colonial alignments: it concerns the assumptions and values which underlie human behaviour. The aim of this chapter is to look afresh at the historical evidence relating to the cultural attitudes of British Protestant missionaries of the last two centuries, and draw some theoretical conclusions which may help to inform current discussion of the relationship between Christianity and culture.

The gospel of civilization

There can be little dispute that, for most of the nineteenth century, British Christians believed that the missionary was called to propagate the imagined benefits of Western civilization alongside the Christian message. It was assumed that the poor, benighted 'heathen' were in a condition of massive cultural deprivation, which the gospel alone could remedy. At present they were shockingly different from civilized Europeans; in years to come, when gospel power had done its work, those differences would be largely eliminated. However, this fundamental theological conviction that Christianity would exert a standardizing influence on other peoples was in practice modified, to a greater or lesser extent, by the impact of actual experience of other societies. The attitudes of early Nonconformist missionaries in the South Seas and in India provide two differing but complementary examples.

The Congregationalist and Wesleyan missionaries who were present in some numbers in Melanesia and Polynesia from the 1820s onwards, found apparently conclusive evidence of the moral degradation of 'heathen' society. In many of the islands cannibalism, infanticide, human sacrifice, and homosexual practice were endemic. The prevalent evangelical belief that God had given up non-Christian, idolatrous peoples to the consequences of their own depravity seemed amply confirmed.[1] Satanic dominion had brought the islanders to the nadir of moral and cultural decline; the missionary task was to reverse the process. Moral elevation implied, not merely the elimination of blatantly inhumane practices, but also the inculcation of the virtues which these lower-middle class missionaries regarded as akin to godliness – industry, sobriety and decency. The missionaries created opportunities for the men of the islands to engage in honest manual labour, in the hope that this would cure their lamentable 'indolence'.[2] They also attempted to persuade the islanders to abandon their traditional dwellings in favour of limestone block houses, built and furnished on the model of the typical English artisan's cottage. On occasion they even tried to enforce such a policy with disciplinary sanctions. Thus in 1823 John Orsmond, LMS missionary in the Society Islands, wrote in his journal:

> Today agreeably to a law the church established last church meeting I have with a book and pencil been to every house ... and have noted down under the name of each member what has been done. The condition of the house and its furniture and it is resolved [sic] that if they do not from this time forth begin to hurl paganism in all its abominable shapes from our City such person shall not be a member of the church. The house must [be] plastered in and out, have doors and windows, bedrooms with doors and shutters, and a garden encircling the house.[3]

With time, however, the realization dawned that in a tropical climate traditional dwellings had their advantages, at least for the native inhabitants. In practice most missionaries were prepared to modify their definition of civilized standards to accommodate the realities of life in the South Seas. On the question of clothing, for example, the conventional image of the prudish missionaries covering up the uninhibited islanders in 'Mother

Hubbard's' or other unsuitable and unhealthy clothes is not wholly accurate. Missionaries did regard Western clothing as a mark of civilization, and wrote home in shocked tones recounting the more striking instances of native immodesty in dress. But the strongest pressure to adopt full European dress came, not from the missionaries, but from the religious public in Britain and, significantly, from the islanders themselves. Western dress inevitably became a symbol of prestige and social advancement, and it is more common to find missionaries deploring the inhabitants' insatiable appetite for European clothes than to find them deploring the immodesty of native dress.[4]

If the early Baptist missionaries in India spoke less frequently than their South Sea contemporaries of the need for civilization, it was because India presented them with a sophisticated religious system which constituted a challenge of a different kind from the 'primitive barbarism' of the South Pacific. Yet India possessed its own barbarism, to which the Baptists reacted with equal indignation, as their campaign against *sati* witnesses.[5] At the root of India's ills was the caste system, which Carey termed 'one of the most cursed engines that ever the devil invented to enslave the souls of men'.[6] Carey and his colleagues longed and prayed for the destruction of the caste system, and its replacement by a society with no artificial barriers to stand in the way of conversion to Christ. Their initial evaluation of the Indian national character was negative: 'Avarice and servility are so joined in, I think, every individual, that cheating, juggling, and lying, are esteemed as no sins with them.'[7] Like countless Western missionaries of a later generation, the BMS pioneers interpreted as innate deceitfulness the Oriental propensity to give in conversation the answer which is known to be desired, rather than that which corresponds to the objective 'facts', as a Westerner would perceive them.[8]

The Baptists' evaluation of Hindu sacred literature was scarcely more favourable. They had sufficient interest to translate the Ramayana epic into English, but they did so primarily in order to promote Christian understanding of the Hindu mind, with a view to more effective evangelism. The profits from the sale of the poem were devoted to the support of the Serampore Bible translations, thus giving Joshua Marshman the opportunity to reflect gleefully that Satan cannot have intended that his 'vile and destructive fables' should contribute to the circulation of 'the oracles of Truth'.[9]

Yet the moral aversion of the early Baptist missionaries to so many aspects of Hindu culture and society did not imply a principled hostility to all things Indian. At an early date they adopted the position that converts should be allowed to retain their Indian names, many of them names of Hindu deities. They observed that Gentile converts in the New Testament bore names derived from the Greek gods, and provided further justification of their decision by enunciating a general principle:

159

> We think the great object which divine Providence has in view in causing the gospel to be promulgated in the world, is not the changing of the names, the dress, the food, and the innocent usages of mankind, but to produce a moral and divine change in the hearts and conduct of men.[10]

No present-day missionary anthropologist would dissent from such a statement. The readiness of the Serampore Baptists to distinguish between those aspects of Indian society which were intrinsically antagonistic to Christianity and the 'innocent usages of mankind' helped them to perceive that Indians would be the only effective evangelists of their fellow-countrymen. William Ward confessed in 1802 that he was

> ready to doubt whether Europeans will ever be extensively useful in converting souls by preaching in this country. God can do all things. Paul could become a Jew to win Jews, and as a Gentile to win Gentiles; but, however needful, we cannot become Hindoos to win them, nor Mussulmans to win Mussulmans.[11]

Ward had penetrated close to the heart of the problem of cross-cultural communication. The BMS pioneers in India were ahead of their time in the extent of their cultural awareness, but they do not represent fundamental exceptions to the normal pattern of early nineteenth-century missionary attitudes. Missionaries in this period anticipated a complete transformation of pagan society through the civilizing agency of the gospel, yet most permitted their personal experience of other cultures to re-define their norms of civilization to the limited extent that their moral and theological convictions allowed.

Theoretical statements by missionary society secretaries or writers on mission tended to affirm the orthodox position that Christian missions could be relied upon to transform heathen barbarism into Christian civilization – but to omit the qualifications that serving missionaries found to be necessary in practice. The three society secretaries who testified to the parliamentary select committee on aborigines in 1836–37 were unanimous and unqualified in their confidence in 'the tendency and efficacy of Christianity to civilize mankind'. A ringing statement by William Ellis of the LMS summed up the missionary consensus of the early and mid-nineteenth century: 'No man can become a Christian, in the true sense of the term, however savage he may have been before, without becoming a civilized man.'[12]

Four assumptions

The close association in missionary thinking between Christianity and civilization depended on at least four prior assumptions. The first of these was the belief that the cultures which missionaries were penetrating were in no sense religiously neutral – rather they were under the control of the Evil One. 'Heathen' societies were the domain of Satan in all their aspects – not merely religion, but also economics, politics, public morals, the arts, and all that is embraced by the term 'culture'. The South Pacific and Bengal both provided vivid illustration of the fact that unchecked 'idolatry' resulted in inhumanity and moral degradation on an awful scale. Modern responses to this first assumption tend to be clouded by the current unacceptability of idolatry as a category for understanding other faiths. But the legitimacy or illegitimacy of idolatry as a concept is strictly irrelevant to the underlying issue, which is the claim that no culture can be religiously neutral. It will be argued below that this claim is irrefutable.

The second underlying assumption was the supposition that nineteenth-century Britain constituted a model of Christian culture and society. Missionary magazines sometimes contained descriptions, graphically illustrated, of what early Britain was thought to have been like before the coming of Christianity – primitive, barbarous and idolatrous. It was Christianity, and above all that national recognition of God and of the Word of God in the Protestant Reformation, which had made Britain what she was. The Bible had made Britain great. She was the archetype of the Christian nation, and God's design was to create more Christian nations on the same pattern. To a twentieth-century observer, such assertions appear sanctimonious and wilfully blind to the social evils of the first industrial nation. But they possessed this much truth: the culture of Victorian Britain *was* shaped by the Bible and by evangelical Protestantism to a degree which finds no parallel in any other period of British history (with the possible exception of the Cromwellian era), and very few parallels in world history. 'Victorian England was religious', as Professor Chadwick reminds us.[13] As a result, the equation between Victorian culture and Christian values was by no means an implausible one to contemporaries.

The confidence of British Christians in the essential benevolence of their own culture rested, thirdly, on the implicit faith in human progress which was one of the legacies of the Enlightenment to Christian thought.[14] Evangelicals professed to believe that all people shared equally in the depravity of original sin, but they found it hard to resist the conclusion that centuries of Christian influence within a society had held in check the human sinfulness that was given a free rein in 'heathen' countries. Long before Darwin's theory of evolution, the thinkers of the Scottish Enlightenment had popularized a theory of social development which posited a progression from a primitive or hunting form of subsistence, via two subsequent stages of pastoral and agrarian forms of economy, to the highest or commercial stage of civilization.[15] When integrated within a Christian theological framework, this approach implied that 'heathen' societies remained frozen in an ice age of primitivism, which the warmth of gospel light had long since thawed in Protestant Europe. The modern understanding of the positive function played by rites and customs in giving a society identity and cohesion was almost entirely absent. By the third quarter of the century, social anthropology was beginning to emerge as an academic discipline, but its researches did nothing to assist Christians to adopt a more sympathetic stance towards alien cultures. On the contrary, much of late nineteenth-century anthropology was devoted to expounding the principles of so-called 'scientific' racism, which threatened the Christian insistence on the essential unity of all mankind, and whose exponents (such as the African explorer Richard Burton) regarded the attempts of missionaries to uplift the 'savage' as wholly futile.[16]

The fourth assumption underpinning Christian faith in efforts to civilize the 'heathen' was quite simply the pragmatic one that such efforts could be shown to have worked. The most plausible evidence to this effect was provided by the rapid growth of the church in Sierra Leone.[17] The colony's population comprised at first black settlers from Nova Scotia and Jamaica, and subsequently former slaves from all over West Africa, liberated by the British naval squadrons. It is not surprising that a hotch-potch population of uprooted individuals, separated from their own people and lacking any collective cultural identity, responded enthusiastically to Christianity and the cultural values of its missionary representatives. In consequence, an African mirror-image of respectable, middle-class, English Christianity developed in the colony. There were inevitable distortions to the image, but it was sufficiently recognizable to provide visible proof that 'heathen savages' could be transformed into model Christian gentlemen. When Samuel Crowther, the Sierra Leonean ex-slave who became the first black Anglican bishop in Africa, stood in black frock coat before the British Christian public for the first time in 1851, the whole missionary enterprise, as Professor Walls points out, seemed justified.[18] The peculiar historical circumstances which had produced the exotic character of the Krio church in Sierra Leone were not at first understood, and there seemed no reason why the story should not be repeated elsewhere.

Missionaries and race

How did each of these four assumptions fare in the course of the nineteenth century? The first assumption – that non-Christian cultures were not religiously neutral but permeated by satanic influence – survived intact mainly in theologically conservative circles. The essence of the claim that other cultures were under the direct control of evil spiritual powers remained most plausible in Africa, where late Victorian missionaries were still engaged in first-hand encounters with peoples they had no hesitation in describing as 'savages'. Societies marked by such features as domestic slavery, cannibalism, trial for witchcraft by ordeal, and the forcible burial of wives or servants in the graves of deceased chiefs, inevitably struck missionaries as depraved and cruel. George Grenfell, the pioneering BMS missionary, later observed that the recording of practices such as these on the Congo river in the 1880s made his old diaries 'blood-curdling and horrible' to read. Significantly it was this state of 'lawlessness and misery' that disposed Grenfell to become such an earnest advocate of the Congo Free State established by King Leopold II of Belgium.[19]

The impression made by the 'darkness' of African society could be so overwhelming that some missionaries were tempted to adopt the racialist categories which many of their secular contemporaries had espoused, especially when they were confronted by conspicuous failures in the quality of African Christian leadership. The sad dissensions which split the CMS Niger mission after 1887 and undermined the authority of Samuel Crowther as bishop were fomented by young and zealous missionaries sceptical of the intrinsic capacity of the negro to rule.[20] James Lowry Maxwell, one of the first missionaries sent out by the Sudan United Mission in 1904, confessed to his diary on one occasion that the atmosphere of lying and duplicity which surrounded him invited the bitter conclusion that 'we can trust nothing with a black skin on it'. Maxwell at least tried to resist this conclusion, and consoled himself with the reflection that even the darkness of the African night was illuminated by the stars – the lives in which divine truth was at work.[21] Maxwell's colleague, Karl Kumm, habitually described the Sudan in terms whose racial overtones are profoundly disturbing: 'The Land of Darkness ... dark are the bodies of the people who live there, darker are their minds, and darker still their souls.'[22]

Evangelical missionaries were not exempt from the racial prejudice which had become so deeply engrained in British society by the close of the nineteenth century. The majority, however, were clearly distinguished from the scientific racists by their refusal to accept any notion of genetic inferiority. They continued to believe that African darkness was the result of the reign of the prince of darkness; ultimately it would be dispelled by the work of the missionary 'lightbearer'.[23] When in 1901 George Grenfell drafted a paper on missionary strategy and the race question, he was quite prepared to concede that the intellectual attainments of the black man were markedly inferior to those of the white race, but attributed the differential to the contrasting impact of centuries of oppression as compared with centuries of civilization; he saw no insuperable obstacle to the black man reaching the same standard attained by the white, and asserted that evangelical Christianity was the only force that had proved itself capable of the comprehensive regeneration that was required.[24] Grenfell's position was essentially the same as that expounded by the missionary society secretaries to the aborigines' committee in 1836–37.

Christianity and world religions

In Africa early nineteenth-century categories of religious understanding survived well into the twentieth century. Missionaries working in the more sophisticated civilizations of Asia were quicker to abandon the old terminology of idolatry and heathenism, and to develop in its place a wholly new approach to other religions. The first steps towards such a new theological understanding had been taken as early as 1845 by F. D. Maurice in his Boyle Lectures on *The Religions of the World in their Relations to Christianity*. Maurice had maintained that all religions contained elements of goodness and truth, posing questions which found their ultimate answer only in Christ. Maurice's more positive evaluation of other faiths was related to his reinterpretation of the doctrine of eternal punishment, and the doubts which now began to assail traditional teaching on hell grew alongside the mounting unease with the summary dismissal of other religions as possessing no salvific value.[25]

From the 1870s onwards, individual missionary voices in India began to conceive of the relationship between Christianity and Hinduism in terms of fulfilment rather than confrontation. The most complete statement of this view was made by the former LMS missionary, J. N. Farquhar, in his *The Crown of Hinduism* (1913), which presented Jesus as the embodiment of the highest ethical aspirations of Hinduism. Those who adopted this new theological approach tended also to view the caste system in a more favourable light than did the traditional missionary apologetic: it had preserved the vitality of Hindu civilization for centuries, and contained in embryo notions of human brotherhood that could now find their fulfilment in Christian ideas of the universal fatherhood of God and brotherhood of man. Admittedly, the demands of modern man for equality and justice could be satisfied only through the establishment of a Christian social order, but this would come in India by the transcending rather than the destruction of caste.[26]

Liberalization of the missionary attitude to other religions tended in India to produce a more positive evaluation of Hindu culture and society. But these advanced missionary thinkers still expected fundamental change in Indian society, and did so in a way which reflected their own cultural background. The liberal missionary creed of 'fulfilment' typified the evolutionary cast of mind so beloved of the late Victorian intelligentsia. Farquhar believed that educational progress in India would compel Hindus to acknowledge the religious and ethical superiority of Christianity. Hinduism was thus destined to wither away, to be replaced by the 'higher' religion of Christianity. The Christ whom Farquhar presented as the crown of Hinduism was the dogma-less Christ of social gospel liberalism, a teacher of ethical idealism and social justice who could command the devotion of all men.[27] As the case-study (in chapter 6) of Timothy Richard and the YMCA in China showed, modernist Christianity could fall prey to its own, more subtle brand of cultural imperialism. The fact that its values were more inclusive ones softens, but should not disguise, the reality that it too wished to fashion the non-European world in a particular Western image – the image of enlightened liberal optimism.

Apostles of a new cultural strategy

The second assumption undergirding the close linkage between Christianity and civilization – the belief that Britain represented a model of a Christian society – became increasingly vulnerable as the nineteenth century drew to a close. By the 1890s almost all branches of the Christian church had developed a keen social conscience which left Christians only too aware of the moral evils embedded in the fabric of national life. Some missionaries were now more hesitant about reproducing in their converts cultural patterns which might inhibit their evangelistic effectiveness. As early as 1888, W. Holman Bentley, the pioneering Baptist missionary in the Congo, warned against the danger of 'denationalizing' the first converts of the Congo church by dressing them up as 'black white men'.[28] Nonetheless, before the First World War, the fundamental self-confidence of British Christianity and national identity was such that few British missions questioned the basic theoretical premiss that God intended non-Christian nations to follow a path of development towards civilization broadly similar to that pioneered by the Protestant West. Missionary magazines in the immediate pre-war years could still be found assuring their readers that 'what God had done for English savages centuries ago, could He not do for these black men today?'[29]

However, the first signs of missionary scepticism towards the values of Western civilization had appeared long before, not surprisingly in a context where Western identity was a distinct evangelistic liability – in imperial China. James Hudson Taylor horrified the foreign community in Shanghai in 1855 when he shaved his head, apart from the obligatory pigtail, and adopted Chinese dress.[30] Taylor's decision was primarily a strategic one, but it may also have reflected the influence upon him of a theological tradition (that of the early Brethren movement) which had little room for notions of the advance of Christian civilization. Taylor's missionary approach significantly became most popular amongst missionaries influenced by the holiness movement, which emphasized personal consecration rather than social regeneration. After the foundation of the CIM, Taylor attempted to make the adoption of Chinese dress an 'absolute prerequisite' for work in the interior, but encountered considerable resistance from candidates from lower-class backgrounds. The requirement of Chinese dress was not enforceable until after the influx in the 1880s of wealthier and more genteel candidates eager to demonstrate the reality of their spiritual consecration by abandoning the distinctive badges of missionary status.[31]

The holiness ethic encouraged a similar policy of maximum cultural identification on other mission fields. CMS missionaries in the Niger mission at the end of the 1880s adopted the dress and title of the recognized Muslim teachers of the Hausa country – the *mallam* – and followed the Hausa diet and lifestyle. By living alongside the people on totally equal terms, they were confident that the power of the indwelling Christ would be transparently evident to the Hausa.[32] The tragic irony is that the advocates of such cultural flexibility were on the Niger the very same missionaries who showed an inflexible impatience with the deficiencies of African church leadership. Those who were losing faith in the virtues of European civilization were losing faith also in the capacity of indigenous leadership to fulfil the rigorous standards of holiness which the new evangelical spirituality set itself.[33] Christians who had become disillusioned with the Enlightenment creed of progress were also more pessimistic about the potential for progress in the spiritual lives of their converts.

The criteria of human progress

It should be evident by now that the third assumption mentioned above – that Christian nations had unlocked the secret of human progress – experienced mixed fortunes in the later years of the nineteenth century. At the one extreme were liberal missionaries, such as Timothy Richard, who took with them into the twentieth century a serene assurance of the blessings which Western science and political values would impart to the waiting world. They frequently regarded the civilizations of Asia with respect, even affection, yet at heart they were committed to the view that such civilizations were destined to give way to the Christian civilization of the West, which alone could guarantee technological and economic advance. The theological counterpart to their evolutionary optimism was the liberal hope that the great religions of the world would, under sympathetic missionary tutelage, locate the fulfilment of their highest ideals in the teachings of Jesus Christ. At the opposite extreme were those conservative evangelicals who had espoused a premillennial eschatology that removed the prospect of human progress beyond the parousia. They were prepared to divest themselves of their cultural identity for the sake of the gospel, but discovered that cultural identification was a more complex and painful business than the mere adaptation of dress and lifestyle. In between these two extremes lay a whole spectrum of theological positions that struck a variety of compromises between an underlying theoretical confidence in the fact of human progress and some degree of recognition that the reality of Western society fell short of Christian ideals.

George Grenfell's comments on the race question in 1901 may serve as one illustration of these intermediate standpoints. Having stated his conviction that the negro was in principle capable of material and intellectual achievements on a par with those of the West, Grenfell continued:

> But, after all, it is neither in the realm of things material nor of matters intellectual that true and vital progress is made manifest. It is not because we have steamships, telegraph, electric light, five editions of a newspaper in a single day or the thousand and one things of which the past century boasts itself, nor because we have a greater average ability for mental gymnastics as evidenced by the examination papers of our schools and colleges that we are really in advance of our forefathers.

True progress, Grenfell insisted, was a matter of moral and spiritual development, and it was in this area that he was most sanguine for the future of the black race.[34] Human material progress was not to be questioned, but neither was it to be accorded ultimate value. Christian missions might make the world more prosperous and technologically efficient, but these gains would be of minimal importance if Christianity failed to make men and women more noble in character.

Grenfell's view may be taken as broadly representative of the evangelical (but non-conservative) mainstream of the missionary movement at the turn of the century. The fundamental confidence in human moral progress which he expressed was dented but not destroyed by the First World War; it continued to buoy the spirit of British missions well into the inter-war period. Between the 1930s and the 1960s this residual Christian confidence in the moral advance of humanity through the dissemination of Western values progressively evaporated. Many in Britain in 1939–40, whether Christian or not, saw the struggle against Hitler as ultimately a crusade for the defence of Christian civilization.[35] But after the war, as the full enormity of the Nazi holocaust came to light, discussion of Christian civilization became less frequent and less confident, for it was hard to deny that Christian Europe stood in some sense responsible for the holocaust and for the horrors of the war itself. By the 1960s the defence of Christian civilization was a theme scarcely heard outside the white enclaves of South Africa and Rhodesia. Western culture had lost its self-confidence, and as a result missionary thinking entered the period of profound re-evaluation which has continued to the present day.

A halt to Westernization

On the mission field the gradual disintegration of Christian confidence in Western cultural values was first evidenced by a new willingness on the part of missionaries to perceive that the cultures in which they were working were in many respects closer to the world of the Bible than were their own cultures. This was particularly so in Africa, where aspects of tribal society began to appear less 'dark' and indeed preferable to the secular modernity of the West.

The fourth assumption underlying the linkage between Christianity and Western civilization – the pragmatic one that Westernization could be shown to produce a healthy indigenous church – had in fact failed to outlive the nineteenth century. The problems of the CMS Niger mission had discredited the Sierra Leone ideal of 'black Europeans'. A similar settlement for freed slaves, established by the CMS at Freretown on the Kenyan coast in 1875, produced the same enthusiasm for European ways on the part of the converts, but to the dismay rather than the delight of the missionaries. They sought to preserve the original tribal identities of the freed slaves, and on occasion even encouraged traditional tribal dances. In part they were motivated by fear of the advance of Islam down the East African coast: 'detribalized' Africans, they observed, were more susceptible to Muslim proselytism. But they were also well aware that the hankering after all things European had too often led to a nominal Christianity devoid of true spiritual life. Thus when in the 1890s some of the Freretown converts took to wearing trousers, hats, boots and carrying walking sticks, the CMS missionary H. K. Binns determined to put his foot down. On the grounds that 'many think our religion consists of wearing a pair of trousers', Binns urged that all mission employees be compelled to wear loin cloths. Even though it might 'shake the mission to its foundation', he insisted on making willingness to renounce European dress a test of 'who are truly on the Lord's side'.[36]

Missionary disapproval of converts imitating European ways was nothing new. What was new was the intense moral absolutism with which missionaries now battled to forestall the emergence of nominal, cultural Christianity. The Freretown story provides further evidence that greater missionary sensitivity to cultural differences could imply an increase in missionary authoritarianism rather than the reverse. Nevertheless, missionaries in the coming decades displayed an increasingly positive appreciation of many aspects of African culture. 'We live in Old Testament times out here in many ways', confided one CMS missionary to her diary in 1925.[37] Rural Africa enabled evangelical missionaries to recapture the world of the biblical narratives in a way they could never do at home in the increasingly industrial West. Canon T. F. C. Bewes reflected on his years in Kenya:

We often used to say to each other, 'This is Gospel country.' There is no need to look further afield for analogy and parable; it is all here – the rich man gathering into barns, the sower in the fields, the stall for the fatted calf, girls getting ready for a wedding, children playing in the market place. Sheep are always getting lost; thieves may still beset a traveller on a lonely road; the father waits for news from Nairobi of his foolish prodigal boy; there are wild and gorgeous lilies in the field. ... These might be His own fields and valleys, and the winding paths of Galilee where Jesus walked.[38]

At a more profound level, however, the parallels between African culture and the cultural values of the Old Testament in particular raised some of the most perplexing issues of twentieth-century mission policy. Africans taught by evangelical missionaries to regard the Scriptures as their final authority turned to the Old Testament when it became available in their own language, discovered that the patriarchs were polygamists without apparently being condemned for being so, and were not always convinced by their missionary mentors' attempts to prove that the biblical norm remains monogamy. W. E. Owen actually urged a delay in the translation of the Old Testament into Luo in 1925 for fear that it would provide a justification for 'backsliding' into the 'polygamy of the surrounding pagan society' of the Nyanza district.[39] The Luo tribe has in fact proved fertile soil for the growth of African independent churches. It may not be entirely coincidental that the completion of the Luo Old Testament in 1953 was followed in 1957–58 by a major secession from the Anglican Church – the Church of Christ in Africa – which permits polygamists to be baptized and to receive communion, though not to hold church office.[40]

The independent churches of modern Africa have raised with peculiar sharpness the theological and hermeneutical questions that lie at the root of the problem of Christianity and culture. Much of their appeal has clearly derived from their ability to combine fervent Christian commitment with the preservation of traditional African values. On such matters as marriage, sickness and healing, the importance of the spirit world, and the place of ritual and symbolism in religion, the independent churches have offered a form of Christianity that is not merely radically different from Protestant missionary religion but even claims to be more authentically biblical. In Africa, as in every continent, Western missionaries are at last being compelled to submit their own cultural tradition – as well as that of others – to the scrutiny of the biblical revelation. The concluding section of this chapter will attempt a theological assessment of the historical record we have examined, and endeavour to suggest some positive conclusions for today's church.

What is culture?

All discussion of the relationship between Christianity and culture needs to recognize that the culture of any people embraces far more than those relatively superficial matters of lifestyle which the alien observer first notices. Definitions of culture are legion, but that adopted by the Willowbank Report on 'Gospel and Culture' in 1978 is as good as any:

> Culture is an integrated system of beliefs, of values, of customs, and of institutions which express these beliefs, values and customs, which binds a society together and gives it a sense of identity, dignity, security and continuity.[41]

The customs and social structures of any cultural unit are the visible expression of underlying beliefs and values, which together comprise the 'world-view' of that group of people. It follows that religion and culture are inextricably linked. In the words of Stephen Neill, 'There has never yet been a great religion which did not find its expression in a great culture. There has never yet been a great culture which did not have deep roots in a religion.'[42] Conversion from one set of religious beliefs to another must have profound cultural implications, both for an individual and for a group of people. If it is accepted that the task of the Christian missionary is (in the baldest possible terms) to induce people to renounce their existing religious (or irreligious) allegiance in favour of Christianity, then there can be no question that the missionary is in principle committed to the promotion of cultural change. This conclusion can be resisted with logical consistency only by repudiating the exclusive truth-claims of New Testament Christianity. To attempt to distil out a 'pure' Christian message, unadulterated by any cultural accretions, would, as Lesslie Newbigin points out, be not merely a hopeless quest, but an actual abandonment of the gospel of the word made flesh within a particular historical and cultural context.[43]

Any evaluation of the historical record of Christian missions on this subject thus needs to beware of the illusion that it was desirable or even possible for missionaries to propagate a culture-free gospel which could be absorbed painlessly by the non-Christian cultures that received them. Other illusions of equivalent falsity must also be pointed out. Perhaps the most pervasive is the supposition that indigenous cultures prior to the missionary impact were in a condition of static perfection. This mythical view is itself a peculiarly arrogant form of cultural imperialism, founded on the notion that non-Western societies knew nothing of change or innovation until brought into contact with the modernizing West. On the contrary, almost all cultures exist in a state of perpetual flux, and represent an amalgam of diverse and often contradictory influences. The choice confronting indigenous cultures has not been between change and no change, but between a number of possible directions of change, some evidently more beneficial than others. This point carries general validity, but it clearly has particular relevance to the period of Western imperial expansion, when missionaries were very rarely the sole agents of alien cultural change to impinge on 'primitive' societies; in almost every case they formed part of a broader Western impact, often seeing themselves as brokers easing the transition of relatively isolated peoples to participation in an expanded community.[44] The appropriate basis for evaluating the missionary impact thus cannot be whether missionaries promoted cultural change or not, but whether the direction of that change was generally beneficial or not. By this standard, certain aspects of the cultural transformation produced by missionaries can scarcely be denied a positive evaluation. The missionary contribution to health care, primary and secondary education, and more recently, agricultural development has been substantial, and such material benefits have inevitably and rightly altered existing values and patterns of behaviour. To insist that missionaries should not have promoted cultural change is, at the very least, to insist that these improvements in the quality of human life in the societies which received them should have been withheld.

It should also be apparent from this chapter that the responses of British missionaries to cultural problems have not been monolithic: they frequently disagreed amongst themselves, and even those who were most deeply committed to the prospect of transforming 'heathen' societies were prepared in practice to delineate a greater or lesser area of the 'innocent usages of mankind', which they saw no need to change.

These provisos are important, and should be given due weight before any negative judgment is passed on the missionary record on cultural questions. They do not, however, obscure the dominant impression made by a study of the cultural attitudes of the British missionary movement of the last century: with very few exceptions, British Christians accepted that non-Christian societies stood in need of a comprehensive regeneration – they needed to be transformed by the process of 'civilization'. This transformation was not so much an independent process which ought to parallel the proclamation of the gospel as its necessary and inevitable consequence: the gospel in itself was held to be the civilizing agent. The missionary model of civilization followed the pattern set by the post-Enlightenment, industrialized West, and specifically, in the case of British missionaries, by Victorian society as perceived by the religious middle classes.

Two pleas for the defence

The self-deception and myopia inherent in this approach are immediately apparent to people in the late twentieth century, not least because they are profoundly sceptical of the claim that Western civilization has brought unparalleled benefits to the world.[45] However, two mitigating pleas ought to be heard in defence of this missionary tradition before final sentence is passed. The first is the fact that these missionaries had grasped that the gospel of Christ has reference to all areas of human life, and that there can be no exclusions from his claims to sovereignty. Despite Lesslie Newbigin's insistence in *The Other Side of 1984* and *Foolishness to the Greeks* that the post-Enlightenment Protestant tradition has relegated Christianity to the role of a private set of other-worldly beliefs for the individual, the mainstream of British Protestant missions before 1914 was in fact marked by intense enthusiasm to see the gospel leaven working its results in the fields of commerce, manufactures, government and family life.[46] Whatever its defects, this theology of mission certainly did not sever all connection between the kingship of Christ and the contemporary world.

The second point to be made in defence of this missionary tradition is related to the first. Part of the package of civilization which Christianity was thought to bring in its train was freedom and justice. Missionaries in this tradition were generally, as previous chapters have shown, fervent human-itarians, and often became imperialists for that very reason. They were also fundamentally opposed to the growing secular assumption that the dark races of the earth were destined to perpetual inferiority to the white man: for such an assumption contravened their most cherished convictions about the universal regenerative power of the gospel. Paternalistic they often were, but their faith in the potential of the reclaimed 'savage' was exalted enough to be the object of general derision by secular critics.

It should be noted that the alternative missionary tradition, arising out of the holiness movement and identifiable by the 1920s as 'conservative evangelical', can, broadly speaking, be shown to be deficient at precisely these two points where the mainstream of the missionary movement was strong. It too easily reduced the Christian message to a matter of the relationship of the individual soul to eternity; and hence it left its adherents vulnerable to the prevailing winds of secular thinking in other areas. Those conservative evangelical missionaries who did lapse into racialist categories of thinking had been ill-prepared by their theological tradition for the challenges that confronted them on the mission field. Conversely, the more conservative strand of the British missionary move-ment often emerges with considerable credit at the very points where the more liberal mainstream was found lacking. Its adherents frequently displayed a healthy scepticism for the much-vaunted achievements of Western civilization; they helped the missionary movement as a whole to recognize the handicap which an overtly Western Christianity imposed on the development of the indigenous churches; and in situations of fierce nationalist antagonism, such as in China or Kenya in the 1950s, their converts displayed remarkable fortitude and strength of conviction.

Evangelical Christendom?

What, then, was the essential error of the 'Christianity and civilization' school? Was it, as one writer has claimed, to confuse Christianity and Christendom, to fail to distinguish a belief system from a cultural tradition?[47] The problem about such a distinction is its suggestion that strictly religious beliefs can be conveniently separated from the broader cultural values that give expression to those beliefs. It is, therefore, not easy to resist Newbigin's implication that to refuse the privatization of Christianity must mean to accept the validity of the search for some form of Christendom, even if, with Newbigin, we concede that no return to the absolutism of medieval Christendom is possible or desirable.[48] However, theology cannot accept the idea of Christendom (with its ultimate implication that humanity in its natural state is in principle redeemed) without betraying convictions about the necessity of the new birth which evangelical Protestants, at least, would regard as central to their faith. The challenge confronting Christians today is to discover a 'third way' between the pursuit of Christendom (which must eventually lead back to medievalism) and a retreat into a purely private Christianity. That third way for Christian mission will involve the construction within each society of a Christian counter-culture to exemplify the absolute values of the kingdom of God within that particular cultural context. The error of nineteenth-century missionaries, as of so many other architects of a Christian social order, was to mistake the contingent values of one particular philosophical tradition – the Enlightenment – for the eternal values which the Christian counter-culture must seek to express. It was not that they abandoned the public sphere to current secular judgments, but rather that, in their anxiety to claim the public sphere for Christ, they intermingled distinctively evangelical insights with assumptions which Enlightenment thought had woven into the fabric of Victorian discourse about human social development. The most baneful of these confusions was the assumption that the regenerative power of the gospel would propel a society along essentially the same path of economic, technological and political 'progress' as Britain had herself followed. Missionaries proved unable to resist the temptation to push their converts and churches along that path which they believed the dynamic of the gospel had already selected for them.

Christianity and culture today

The heart of the problem confronting the missionary endeavour of the

173

Western churches has been that Western cultures contain a complex amalgam of Christian and secular influences. There are emphases central to the Western cultural tradition – such as the infinite worth of the individual, or the insistence that leadership in church or state is ultimately accountable to both God and man – whose origins are more Christian than secular. Yet these emphases have been overlaid and re-interpreted in the West by assumptions derived from non-Christian sources, so that a stress on the value of the individual becomes individualism, or the demand for accountable leadership becomes a rigid application of Western-style democracy in societies accustomed to finding other paths to consensus. There are other features of Western culture – such as the insistence that all reality is explicable by scientific, rational analysis – which are in principle antagonistic to the biblical world-view. Missionary experience has now compelled Western Christians to re-examine their rationalistic presuppositions, and to recognize that non-Western attitudes to such phenomena as spirit possession may be much closer to biblical conceptions than previous missionary generations have been prepared to admit.[49] The temptation currently confronting some sections of Protestant Christianity may in fact be to run so fast in the flight from Western rationalism that they fall into the arms of non-Western world views which contradict biblical norms at other points. Thus to reject the Western assumption that all sickness or accident has a natural, material explanation should not entail an adoption of the contrary predilection of animist cultures for treating all misfortune as the result of malign spiritual influence, with the consequence that human moral responsibility is undermined.

To investigate these questions adequately would require another book. What the record of history should do is to emphasize how complex is the amalgam that we label 'Western culture', which, for all its loss of self-confidence, continues with remarkable resilience to fashion human societies throughout the globe in many aspects of its image. The story of the last two centuries of missionary history should also inculcate a sense of extreme caution as this Christian generation makes its own endeavour to draw the outlines of Christian counter-cultures for today, for we are in principle no less likely to fall prey to cultural imperialism than our forebears.

CHAPTER EIGHT

Empires and missions under human and divine judgment

This book is itself a characteristic product of its time: it addresses those questions about the Western missionary movement which, though they may not ultimately prove to be the only important questions to ask, are high on the agenda of contemporary debate. Its primary aim has been to encourage the formation of a better informed and more discerning historical understanding of the relationship between Protestant missions and British imperialism. Judgment that is passed without some measure of accurate understanding is by definition no more than prejudice. Careful analysis of the historical evidence is important, not least because current judgments of the relationship of Christian missions to imperialism are inevitably distorted by the preoccupations and limitations of contemporary ideologies. The preceding chapters have, therefore, concentrated on the explanation of Christian attitudes and convictions which may appear strange or downright unacceptable to late twentieth-century minds. To a certain extent, these chapters have suspended moral judgment on the issues raised by those beliefs. There is a sense in which all Christian writing of history ought properly to suspend judgment on the moral record of men and women in the past, for Christianity asserts that judgment is ultimately a divine prerogative. Yet it is also true that to abdicate all responsibility for reaching a verdict would itself be immoral. The historian is called to form provisional judgments on the basis of the limited knowledge at his disposal, and, indeed, the nature of historical writing dictates that he can hardly avoid doing so. The Christian historian writing about Christian history is even more strongly obliged to arrive at some theological evaluation of the substance of his narrative. This brief concluding chapter will, therefore, survey some of the broader questions posed by the argument of this book, and offer some provisional answers from a specifically Christian perspective. The first of these four questions relates to imperialism itself, and the remaining three arise more directly from the relationship of British Protestant missions to imperialism.

1. Is all imperialism necessarily illegitimate?

Most contemporary writing, whether Christian or not, assumes that all imperialism is devoid of moral and political legitimacy and therefore deserving of censure. To the extent that imperialism has been founded on human pride, aggression and greed, such a negative verdict is both understandable and appropriate. The problem, however, is that pride, aggression and greed are, in some measure at least, characteristic of all human political rule, not merely of those forms of political authority which we choose to label as 'imperial'. The issue thus arises of how to define the boundary between legitimate and illegitimate political rule. Conventional condemnations of imperialism assume that the boundary is essentially territorial or ethnic – *viz.* that political authority is legitimate when exercised over one's own people within their natural geographical borders, but illegitimate when exercised over others outside those borders. This distinction is valid and tenable when the globe is made up, as it now is, of sovereign nation states which are generally recognized as the legitimate authorities for ruling their subjects, since the latter are conventionally viewed as one people, defined by their national identity.

However, this modern approach to the problem of political legitimacy is itself the product of a historical process culminating in the nineteenth-century movements of nationalism and liberal democracy.[1] It tends to disguise the fact that few modern nation states represent one (and no more than one) historical 'people'. Most are the product of complex processes of evolution which brought together a number of different peoples within a single political unit. In many cases these modern nation states are segments of former empires, in which the original inhabitants of a territory have been reduced to subjection by colonial invaders (the USA, Australia and New Zealand are obvious examples, but the same can be said of the various parts of Britain itself if we go back far enough in history). In certain cases, some of the constituent peoples of such states retain very distinct ethnic identities, and continue to regard the rule of the nation state as, in some measure at least, a colonial imposition (for example, the Sikh population of the Punjab in India, the Estonian, Lithuanian and Latvian peoples of the USSR, or the Catholic population of Northern Ireland). Such examples render the conventional basis of differentiation between legitimate and illegitimate rule unworkable as a standard of historical judgment. In reality it is the passing of time that has bestowed legitimacy on political units which originated in imperial expansion of one kind or another. Some other standard of judgment is required. For Christians, the quest for such a standard must be founded on God's self-revelation in Scripture.

A nationalistic basis of differentiation between legitimate and illegitimate political authority was unknown in the pre-modern world, and is hence absent from the Bible. There are, admittedly, one or two references in

Scripture to God having 'set the boundaries of the peoples' (Deuteronomy 32:8 and possibly also Acts 17:26).[2] Although these verses imply that God is opposed to territorial aggression, they can offer little specific guidance to modern Christians on how to define the boundaries which God has set. A more dominant strand in biblical teaching is that political legitimacy is bestowed or withheld by God himself: he raises up kingdoms and empires, and in time brings them to nothing again. The Old Testament recognizes the exercise of political rule over alien peoples as a recurrent feature of a sinful world, and indeed on occasion presents such rule as specifically commissioned by God, whether that commissioning is acknowledged or not, and whether that rule is exercised in a moral fashion or not. Israel herself was commanded to conquer and possess Canaan, a land which was not hers by any modern standard of judgment. Cyrus of Persia is described in Isaiah 45 as anointed by God to subdue nations and hence forward his purpose of liberating his people from Babylonian exile. That Babylonian power, according to Habakkuk 1:5-11, was raised up by God as an instrument of his judgment on his chosen people, yet Babylon would itself be judged for the lawless and violent manner of its imperial rule.

According to the Old Testament, therefore, empires are judged on the basis of their degree of obedience to the divine purpose allotted to them, and according to the justice or injustice of their rule over their subjects – the prophecies against the nations in Amos 1 and 2 are an excellent example. To be sure, the injustices identified often include the evils of plunder, aggression and cruel treatment of subject peoples (Isaiah 10:13-14; Amos 1: 3, 6, 9, 11, 13), but the emphasis of judgment falls more on the manner and spirit of imperial rule than on its actual existence. The Assyrian empire is condemned in Isaiah 10, not so much for its aggressive acts against Israel and Judah, which are asserted to be authorized by God himself, as for its limitless ambition and arrogance in claiming that its conquests were won by its own might and wisdom rather than by divine permission. Nevertheless, the Old Testament seems to imply that empires, simply because of their greater political scale and absolute power, are more liable than smaller political units to fall prey to such arrogant and lawless attitudes: the depiction of empires in Daniel 7 as ferocious beasts suggests that empires, although frequently allotted roles of special importance in providential history, are also subject to judgment of peculiar severity.

In comparison, the New Testament has little to say on matters of international politics. However, it should be noted that the ministry of Jesus was located within an imperial context, and that Jesus' statement that the things that were Caesar's should be rendered to Caesar signified an explicit refusal on his part to deny all legitimacy to the Roman imperial regime in Palestine (Mark 12:13-17). Paul's assertion in Romans 13 that all governing authorities were established by God similarly refers to the representatives of the Roman imperial state. His letter was, of course, addressed to Christians in Rome, who by modern political standards can be reckoned 'legitimate' subjects of that state; but other New Testament letters addressed to Christians who were living in the Roman colonial territories, such as Asia Minor or Crete, show precisely the same attitude to the state authorities (1 Peter 2:13-14; 1 Timothy 2:1-2; Titus 3:1). In the New Testament, as in the Old, empires have no less (and no more) intrinsic political legitimacy than any other political unit: all are expressions of God's sovereign rule of the world, yet are themselves subordinate to that sovereign rule and its exacting standards of justice. All authorities, whether spiritual or temporal, have been created by God and are subject to his rule in Christ (Colossians 1:16). However, the book of Revelation, in repeating the warning of Daniel that judgment within history is a reality for kingdoms and empires, contains the same implication that the largest political units are liable to be the most arrogant, and that their fall will be correspondingly more severe (Revelation 17 and 18). Yet empires are measured by precisely the same standard as all human kingdoms – by their degree of adherence to the values of justice, righteousness and compassion which characterize the kingdom of God.

It may be suggested, therefore, that the appropriate standard of judgment for the British empire is not fundamentally different from that which should be applied to all human governments. In so far as imperial policy-making was dictated by considerations of national self-interest rather than concern for native welfare, British imperialism merits the same negative verdict as is earned by all governments which subordinate the needs of the less powerful to the interests of the more powerful. However, that negative verdict must be qualified by some recognition of the force of humanitarian imperatives in ensuring that questions of native welfare could never be totally ignored by colonial policy makers. There were situations – such as the Cape Colony in the 1830s, Bechuanaland in 1884–85, and possibly even Uganda in 1892–94 – in which British annexation may indeed have been the most advantageous for the native populations of the political options currently available. Equally there were other contexts, such as nineteenth-century India, where annexation cannot conceivably be justified on any grounds other than Britain's own commercial and strategic interests. Nevertheless, it would still be possible to argue that an imperial position built up by a series of morally unjustified annexations turned out in the long run to be for the ultimate relative good of the colonized people. It would be at least worthy of debate to claim that the benefits to India of British rule – in terms of the creation of national identity, the establishment of parliamentary democracy and the encouragement of economic development – ultimately outweighed the short-term cost in terms of exploitation and racial humiliation. Such an argument – whose essence was in fact put forward by nineteenth-century Christians in relation to India – would possess greater acceptability if founded on a Christian view of history which posits that God in his providence brings good out of human evil.

This discussion thus leads us to the second question of a theological nature raised by the subject of this book.

2. How biblical was the concept of providence held by nineteenth-century missionaries?

It will be evident from the preceding chapters that British evangelical missionaries had a highly developed concept of providence which saw the hand of God at work in current events, especially those which related to the extension of British imperial influence or control. They believed that Britain's imperial role had been thrust upon her by divine appointment in order to further the spread of the gospel, that Britain was called to be a faithful steward of her imperial trusteeship, and that unfaithfulness would be met by divine judgment on Britain as a nation. They only rarely questioned or opposed the fact of British imperial rule; but they consistently challenged and criticized the morality with which it operated, with particular regard to its treatment of subject peoples. 'The missionary calling was to keep the flag in check, not to haul it down' (see above, chapter 6, p. 153).

It is clear that this theology of history was modelled quite self-consciously on Old Testament patterns. Evangelical Christians in imperial Britain had no doubt that God continued to work in history in the same way as he did in Old Testament times, raising up empires to promote his purposes of mercy and judgment. This may have been a false assumption, but the New Testament offers no specific grounds for believing that it was: although the historical nation of Israel is no longer the focus of God's providential activity to the same degree that it was before the coming of the new age in Christ, the basic principle that political authorities are both instruments of God's purposes and subject to his judgment is re-affirmed by the New Testament.

To this extent the theology of providence that underpinned the missionary acceptance of Britain's imperial role can be defended as essentially consonant with biblical Christianity. Two fundamental questions must, however, be posed before it can be endorsed in the form adopted by the historic missionary movement.

The first is to ask whether Christians are granted the same clarity and certainty of prophetic vision as enabled the Old Testament prophets to discern and interpret the hand of God in current political events. Were British and American Protestants correct, for instance, to assert that the outcome of the two opium wars of 1839–42 and 1858–60 represented a clear case of God turning human evil to the good of his own purposes of grace for the inhabitants of China? On the one hand, it seems entirely reasonable for the Christian observer to deduce from the revelation of God's mode of operation given in Scripture that, 'when good surprisingly emerges from evil, God is evidently at work'.[3] If we allow present-day Christians (as surely we must) to reflect that in twentieth-century China God has used the anti-Christian movement of the Communist revolution to enable a truly indigenous Chinese church to develop and flourish as never before, then we can hardly deny to Victorian Christians the right to claim that in their own day God had similarly (though in diametrically opposing circumstances) turned the wrath of man to praise him by using Western aggression and commercial exploitation to bring the gospel to China. Yet a question-mark must remain against the supreme confidence with which Victorian Christians interpreted the purpose of God in particular episodes of imperial history. Although the gift of prophecy remains available to the church, Christians are not granted infallible insight into the spiritual significance of contemporary events. An element of provisionality must qualify their judgments in a way that was not true of the inspired prophets of ancient Israel. That degree of provisionality should induce a proper humility when attempting to read the 'mysterious book' of divine providence.[4] Rather more of that humility would have helped missionaries in China to distance themselves more clearly from those secular forces whose immorality they deplored but whose status as instruments of providence they wished to assert.

A second question that ought to be addressed to the theology of history espoused by the missionary movement is whether it took sufficient account of the fact that, although empires may be instruments of divine providence, they are no more than that. No nation apart from God's historic people of Israel may be accorded any uniquely privileged or necessary part in his purposes. Christians in the fourth and fifth centuries tended to view the Roman empire, not just as an instrument used by God to propagate Christianity, but as an institution of abiding importance within God's saving purposes, with the Christian emperors being invested with almost messianic significance. The fall of Rome to Alaric's Goths in AD 410 thus struck many Christians as a disaster with fearful implications for the future of the kingdom of God. One of the chief aims of Augustine of Hippo's great work, *The City of God*, was to rebut this 'sacral' understanding of the Roman empire: the empire had indeed been raised up by God for his own purposes, but the kingdom of God did not come crashing down when the Roman empire fell.[5] Neither, we may add, did it do so when the missionaries were expelled from China between 1949 and 1952, or when the British empire was hastily dismantled in the 1960s. The destiny of the city of God, argued Augustine, is not tied to the fortunes of any human empire or power structure.

The temptation confronting British Christians convinced that their nation had a role to play in serving the purposes of God in their generation was similarly to invest that role with a permanence and a grandeur that it did not warrant. The responses of British Christians to the Indian mutiny of 1857 revealed that many had come to equate Britain's role in India with that of Israel in the idolatrous land of Canaan. Many of the sermons preached on the day of national humiliation held on 7 October 1857 used Old Testament texts to call on God to defend the honour of his name by coming to the defence of the British forces in India.[6] But no nation, however central to the purposes of God at a particular time, can claim the privileged, sacred status which now belongs to the new international people of God, the church. To be used by God, whether for judgment or salvation, ought to inculcate nothing but humility in those so used. Instead, the record of history suggests that 'servant' nations tend to become arrogant nations, either because they are unaware that their role is not of their own making – as with Assyria in Isaiah 10 – or because they take undue pleasure in the consciousness that they are being distinctively used by God – as was the case in Victorian Britain. In the second half of the twentieth century, evangelicals in the USA have faced a similar temptation: conscious of the immense global influence exerted by their nation in both the political and the religious spheres, some have cast their country in the role of God's chosen vessel for the defence of liberty and the propagation of biblical Christianity. It is not inconceivable that they are right, but the danger lies in the hubris which such a belief so easily encourages.

The understanding of divine providence, which was so marked a feature of missionary attitudes to imperialism, was, therefore, biblical in its essential outlines, but distorted by the mechanistic imprint of Enlightenment thought and by the national pride encouraged by Britain's pre-eminent world power. It would be unfair, however, for late twentieth-century Christians to fasten on the weaknesses in the theology of providence held by our Victorian forebears as our chief line of attack against their Christian imperialism. For our predecessors at least held unshakeably to the biblical conviction that God is at work in human history on a grand scale, whereas we have virtually abandoned any attempt to construct a meaningful theology of providence for today.

3. Were missionaries of earlier generations motivated more by secular motivations than by the gospel?

Chapter 2 emphasized that imperialism is a much more complex and elusive phenomenon than is implied by the conventional condemnations of the missionary movement for collaboration with imperialism. Later chapters have reinforced the point that there was not one imperialism, but many: frequently the dilemma confronting missionaries and their supporters was not whether or not to sanction an imperial presence in a particular mission field, but rather to know which political option among the several competing for imperial influence, offered the best prospects for peace, justice and the interests of the gospel. The fact that they generally opted in such circumstances for some form of British protection or rule could be attributed merely to undiscriminating nationalism. Undoubtedly such partisan motives were present in varying measure: they were clearly demonstrated, for example, in the Anglican campaign on behalf of Uganda in the early 1890s. Yet concern for national prestige was rarely uppermost in Christian minds when considering imperial issues. Even in the Ugandan case, the most powerful motivations were those which stemmed from the heart of the historic evangelical conscience – in this case, concern for the interests of the Protestant faith, and a determination to thwart any revival of the slave trade. Where missionaries supported imperial annexations, they did so because they firmly believed that imperial rule, far from being an instrument of oppression, was in fact God's provision for human liberation. Such a fervently moral imperialism, far from leading British missions into a hand-in-hand collaboration with government, was usually, as in the case of John Mackenzie of Bechuanaland, an embarrassment to government and ignored by imperialists with preoccupations of a more material kind.[7]

It was suggested in chapter 3 that imperial enthusiasm was not the sole, nor necessarily the most important, influence behind the high levels of missionary recruitment in late Victorian Britain. If some recent historiography is correct to propose that a truly popular enthusiasm for the ideals and values of the British empire was actually stronger in the early twentieth century than in the Victorian era,[8] then the apparent decline in missionary recruitment after the First World War poses a further question mark against any simplistic equation between missionary motivation and imperial enthusiasm.

The continuing (and possibly growing) strength of popular imperialism well into the twentieth century does nonetheless imply that missionaries serving 'under the flag' in British colonial territories found it even harder than their Victorian predecessors to shake off attitudes of racial and cultural superiority. What has made the greatest negative impression on the collective memory of Christians in the former colonies is not the role played by missionary opinion in the process of imperial annexation, but the countless instances where individual missionaries have displayed arrogance, insensitivity and lack of trust in non-European capacity to discharge responsibility in the church. These failings must be taken seriously by all involved in world mission today, for they are sadly still to be found among Western Christians working overseas. To identify this crucial area of missionary failure is, however, only to acknowledge that missionaries, no less than any other Christians, have been fallible men and women of their time, sharing in the prejudices of the social groups from which they came. The failure of the missionary movement was less a failure in motivation than a failure in holiness: missionaries who were acutely conscious of their need to be radically distinctive from the 'pagan' people to whom they were sent, were insufficiently aware of the equal need for them to be distinctive from the racial and cultural assumptions of their own social background.

4. Is Christianity an inherently 'imperial' religion?

Much of the dynamic of the Protestant missionary movement was supplied by the conviction that Christianity was the exclusive self-revelation of God to the world, and hence the only way of salvation for mankind. Missionaries believed that they possessed the truth, and that the 'heathen' did not. They generally presumed that men and women were lost until they were found by Christ through the communication of the gospel. Non-Christian peoples were thus in a state of massive spiritual deprivation, and were absolutely dependent on the activity of Christians (initially from the Western world) in bringing the message of salvation to them.

It is these features of the missionary movement, above all others, which many late twentieth-century observers find wholly unacceptable. On this basis, Western missions could not do anything other than create a dependent relationship between the Western and non-Western worlds – a relationship that provided the ideological context for imperialism. The apparent spiritual arrogance implicit in the missionary claim to absolute truth has long been uncongenial to those without Christian commitment. Only in the twentieth century, however, has criticism of this theological position become widespread within the church itself. The permanence, acceptability and indeed desirability of religious pluralism have become axiomatic for most Christian theologians. Wishing to affirm, not merely that God is at work in other faiths, but further that his activity therein must be deemed sufficient for salvation, they have been compelled to adopt one of two conclusions. Either they have concluded that the exclusivity of the New Testament's presentation of Christ as the only way of salvation must simply be rejected as incompatible with reason and modern knowledge; or they have attempted to argue that almost all Christian theology from the early church to the modern era has been grossly mistaken in its reading of the Scriptures. Thus Kenneth Cracknell openly confesses:

> Any way the contemporary church may find to speak affirmatively about God's activity in and through other communities of faith must in itself deny important themes in the history of Christian theology. There is unhappily no avoiding such a negation. Our forebears were simply mistaken.[9]

It is no part of the brief of this book to engage in a full-scale theological discussion of the validity or otherwise of the exclusive truth claims which most generations of Christians have believed to be intrinsic to their faith. It is, however, appropriate for an historian to ask whether an assertion that the great majority of the Christian tradition has been so fundamentally misled in its biblical interpretation is not more likely to reflect the presuppositions of its own day than any genuinely new hermeneutical insight. To ask the question is not to deny that Christians in the past have been too ready to dismiss other religions as entirely devoid of the grace of God. The categorization by both Catholic and Protestant missionary traditions of other religions as idolatry can be defended from the Bible, but relatively few missionaries before the twentieth century followed the example of Paul in Athens in Acts 17 in combining that categorization with a non-confrontational evangelistic approach which acknowledges the seriousness of humanity's quest for God.

The suspicion remains, however, that much contemporary writing on the relationship of Christianity to other faiths is attempting to minimize that absolutist element in Christian theology that may properly be labelled 'imperial'. Christianity is an inherently imperial religion in the sense that it claims that the revealed truth of God was incarnated uniquely in the person of Jesus Christ, that all men and women are called to respond in repentance and faith to that revelation, and that the kingdom of God inaugurated in the coming of Christ makes absolute demands upon all people and all cultures. Precisely because the love of God is universal in its scope, there can be no exclusions from or exceptions to the invitation to submit to the liberating lordship of Jesus Christ.

The missionaries who have been the subject of this book had a clear and compelling grasp of the 'imperial' demands of the gospel. Their vision was frequently clouded by national and racial pride, and in certain essential respects was distorted by the mechanistic world-view which they had inherited from Enlightenment thought. As a result, they sometimes failed to apply the ethical demands of the kingdom of God as rigorously to their own nation as they did to the non-Western societies to which they were sent. Their relationship to the diverse forces of British imperialism was complex and ambiguous. If it was fundamentally misguided, their error was not that they were indifferent to the cause of justice for the oppressed, but that their perceptions of the demands of justice were too easily moulded to fit the contours of prevailing Western ideologies. In this respect, our predecessors reflect our own fallibility more closely than we care to admit.

Notes

Chapter 1

1 N. Pityana, 'What is Black Consciousness?', in B. Moore (ed.), *Black Theology: The South African Voice* (London, 1973), p. 59.
2 For 'Muntu' see D. M. Paton (ed.), *Breaking Barriers Nairobi 1975: The Official Report of the Fifth Assembly of the World Council of Churches* (London, 1976), p. 18; H. T. Hoekstra, *Evangelism in Eclipse: World Mission and the World Council of Churches* (Exeter, 1979), pp. 127-130.
3 T. Balasuriya, 'Towards the liberation of theology in Asia', in V. Fabella (ed.), *Asia's Struggle for Full Humanity* (New York, 1980), pp. 20-21; see also S. Torres and V. Fabella (eds.), *The Emergent Gospel* (New York, 1984), p. 266.
4 O. Costas, *Christ Outside the Gate: Mission Beyond Christendom* (New York, 1982), pp. 13-14, 62, 63.
5 S. Neill, *Colonialism and Christian Missions* (London, 1966), p. 13.
6 W. E. Hocking (ed.), *Re-thinking Missions: A Laymen's Inquiry after One Hundred Years* (New York, 1932), pp. 77, 251-253.
7 *Ibid.*, p. 251.
8 P. A. Cohen, *China and Christianity: The Missionary Movement and the Growth of Chinese Antiforeignism 1860-1870* (Cambridge, Mass., 1963), pp. 4-60.
9 *Ibid.*, pp. 265-267.
10 Chinese Communist hostility to the missionary presence became uncompromising after the outbreak of the Korean War in 1950; see B. Whyte, *Unfinished Encounter: China and Christianity* (London, 1988), pp. 220-227.
11 S. Neill, *Colonialism and Christian Missions*, p. 113.
12 D. M. Paton, *Christian Missions and the Judgment of God*, (London, 1953), p. 25.
13 E. S. Fife and A. F. Glasser, *Missions in Crisis: Rethinking Missionary Strategy* (British edn., London, 1962), p. 89 and also pp. 23, 66-90.
14 K. M. Panikkar, *Asia and Western Dominance: A Survey of the Vasco Da Gama Epoch of Asian History 1498-1945* (new edn., London, 1959), p. 293.
15 R. K. Orchard (ed.), *The Ghana Assembly of the International Missionary Council* (London, 1958), p. 148.
16 See A. Hastings, *A History of African Christianity 1950-1975* (Cambridge, 1979), pp. 95-97, 150-151; L. B. Greaves, *Carey Francis of Kenya* (London, 1969), p. 199.
17 R. Oliver and A. Atmore, *Africa since 1800* (Cambridge, 1967), p. 264.
18 *Ibid.*, pp. 257-269.
19 C. Morris, *The End of the Missionary?* (London, 1962), p. 61.
20 M. Warren, *The Missionary Movement from Britain in Modern History* (London, 1965), p. 166.
21 *Ibid.*, pp. 170-180.
22 M. Warren, *Social History and Christian Mission* (London, 1967), p. 131.
23 S. Neill, *Colonialism and Christian Missions*, pp. 412-425. Warren had attempted an outline

'theology of imperialism' in his *Caesar, The Beloved Enemy* (London, 1955), pp. 10-41.

24 A. Hastings, *History of African Christianity*, pp. 151-152.

25 *Ibid.*, pp. 191-196.

26 *Ibid.*, pp. 184-185.

27 *Ibid.*, pp. 138, 143, 204, 214, 219.

28 See E. Mondlane, *The Struggle for Mozambique* (new edn., London, 1983), pp. x-xxix; *Eduardo Mondlane* (PANAF Great Lives series, London, 1972), p. 137. FRELIMO was an acronym for 'Frente de libertação de Moçambique'.

29 A. Hastings, *History of African Christianity*, p. 213.

30 *Ibid.*, p. 219.

31 W. W. Rostow, *The Stages of Economic Growth* (Cambridge, 1960). On the history of development economics see C. Simmons, 'Economic development and economic history', in B. Ingham and C. Simmons (eds.), *Development Studies and Colonial Policy* (London, 1987), pp. 3-99.

32 See R. Nurkse, *Problems of Capital Formation in Under-Developed Countries* (Oxford, 1953); G. Myrdal, *Development and Underdevelopment* (Cairo, 1956); P. A. Baran, *The Political Economy of Growth* (New York, 1957).

33 K. Nkrumah, *Neo-Colonialism: The Last Stage of Imperialism* (London, 1965). For some account of the growth of the concept see B. Crozier, *Neo-Colonialism* (London, 1964).

34 See P. T. Bauer, *Dissent on Development* (London, 1971), *Equality, the Third World and Economic Delusion* (London, 1981), *Reality and Rhetoric: Studies in the Economics of Development* (London, 1984); and, for a Marxist critique of dependency theory, B. Warren, *Imperialism: Pioneer of Capitalism* (London, 1980).

35 E. W. Fasholé-Luke, 'The quest for an African Christian theology', *Ecumenical Review*, XXVII (1975), pp. 266-267.

36 A. Hastings, *History of African Christianity*, pp. 231-232.

37 See B. Moore (ed.), *Black Theology*, pp. 1, 48-58; G. S. Wilmore and J. H. Cone (eds.), *Black Theology: A Documentary History, 1966-1979* (New York, 1979), pp. 221, 223, 481.

38 B. Moore (ed.), *Black Theology*, pp. 42-44, 59-60, 79.

39 M. M. Thomas, *The Christian Response to the Asian Revolution* (London, 1966), pp. 32-33, 93-94, 101.

40 See G. H. Anderson (ed.), *Asian Voices in Christian Theology* (New York, 1976); D. J. Elwood (ed.), *Asian Christian Theology: Emerging Themes* (Philadelphia, 1980); V. Fabella (ed.), *Asia's Struggle for Full Humanity* (New York, 1980).

41 See T. C. Bruneau, *The Political Transformation of the Brazilian Catholic Church* (Cambridge, 1974), pp. 70-79.

42 E. Dussel, *A History of the Church in Latin America* (Grand Rapids, 1981), pp. 245-246; O. Costas, *Christ Outside the Gate*, p. 125; J. A. Kirk, *Liberation Theology: An Evangelical View from the Third World* (London, 1979), pp. 23-28, 46, 160-161, 223. For an evangelical assessment of the importance of Marcuse and Fanon to the 'New Left' of the 1960s see O. Guinness, *The Dust of Death* (London, 1971), pp. 128-131, 143-147, 161-163.

43 O. Costas, *Christ Outside the Gate*, p. 125; J. A. Kirk, *Liberation Theology*, pp. 27-28; E. R. Norman, *Christianity and the World Order* (the BBC Reith Lectures, Oxford, 1979), p. 52.

44 E. R. Norman, *Christianity and the World Order*, p. 52; see also M. Nash, *Ecumenical Movement in the 1960s* (Johannesburg, 1975), p. 334.

45 O. Costas, *Christ Outside the Gate*, pp. 122-123.

46 M. Nash, *Ecumenical Movement in the 1960s*, pp. 236, 249.

47 *Ibid.*, pp. 261-262, 326.

48 *Ibid.*, pp. 264-270; M. M. Thomas and P. Abrecht (eds.), *World Conference on Church and Society, July 12-26 1966: The Official Report* (Geneva, 1967); see also W. A. Visser't Hooft, *Memoirs* (London, 1973), pp. 293-294.

49 N. Goodall, *Second Fiddle: Recollections and Reflections* (London, 1979), pp. 113-114.

50 For a serious evangelical critique see H. T. Hoekstra, *Evangelism in Eclipse: World Mission*

and The World Council of Churches (Exeter, 1979).

51 W. A. Visser't Hooft, *Memoirs*, p. 367; N. Goodall, *Second Fiddle*, pp. 113–114.

52 See *Third Way*, VI, no. 9 (Oct. 1983), pp. 5–6; *International Review of Mission* LXXII, no. 288 (Oct. 1983), pp. 596–599.

53 For the moratorium debate see E. Kendall, *The End of an Era: Africa and the Missionary* (London, 1978), pp. 86–107.

54 H. T. Hoekstra, *Evangelism in Eclipse*, pp. 90, 94–95, 97; E. Kendall, *The End of an Era*, pp. 91–92; E. Castro, 'Bangkok, the New Opportunity', *International Review of Mission* LXII, no. 246 (April 1973), pp. 140–143. Castro is renowned in the ecumenical movement for his passionate commitment to evangelism; see *International Review of Mission* LXXIII, no. 289 (Jan. 1984), pp. 86–97, 106–123.

55 E. Kendall, *The End of an Era*, pp. 93–97.

56 A. Hastings, *A History of African Christianity*, p. 225.

57 J. D. Douglas (ed.), *Let the Earth Hear His Voice* (Minneapolis, 1975), p. 6; C. R. Padilla (ed.), *The New Face of Evangelicalism* (London, 1976), p. 165.

58 D. M. Paton (ed.), *Breaking Barriers Nairobi 1975*, pp. 57, 64; see also pp. 18, 251.

59 P. Clements-Jewery, 'Your Kingdom Come', *Baptist Quarterly*, XXIX (1981), p. 31; see *Your Kingdom Come: Mission Perspectives* (Geneva, 1980).

60 D. Gill (ed.), *Gathered for Life: Official Report VI Assembly World Council of Churches* (Geneva, 1983), pp. 31–32.

61 O. Costas, *Christ Outside the Gate*, pp. 58–69.

62 See J. F. A. Ajayi, *Christian Missions in Nigeria 1841–1891: The Making of a New Elite* (London, 1965); E. A. Ayandele, *The Missionary Impact on Modern Nigeria 1842–1914: A Political and Social Analysis* (London, 1966); A. Temu and B. Swai, *Historians and Africanist History: A Critique* (London, 1981).

Chapter 2

1   D. K. Fieldhouse, *Colonialism 1870–1945: An Introduction* (London, 1981), p. 1.

2   W. L. Langer, *The Diplomacy of Imperialism, 1890–1902* (2nd edn., New York, 1951), p. 67.

3   This distinction between colonization and colonialism is taken from D. K. Fieldhouse, *Colonialism 1870–1945*, pp. 4–6.

4   See chapter 1, p. 22.

5   D. K. Fieldhouse, *Colonialism 1870–1945*, p. 6.

6   R. Koebner and H. D. Schmidt, *Imperialism: The Story and Significance of a Political Word, 1840–1960* (Cambridge, 1964), p. xiii.

7   *Ibid.*, pp. 1–29.

8   *Ibid.*, pp. 107–165.

9   *Ibid.*, p. 194.

10 *Ibid.*, pp. 218–219; C. C. Eldridge, *Victorian Imperialism* (London, 1978), pp. 190–191.

11 R. Koebner and H. D. Schmidt, *Imperialism*, pp. 226–228, 250–256; B. Porter, *The Lion's Share: A Short History of British Imperialism 1850–1970* (London, 1975), pp. 168–169.

12 R. Koebner and H. D. Schmidt, *Imperialism*, pp. 265–266; D. K. Fieldhouse, *Economics and Empire 1830–1914* (new edn., London, 1976), pp. 41–43.

13 V. I. Lenin, *Imperialism, the Highest Stage of Capitalism*, in *V. I. Lenin: Collected Works* (Moscow, 1964), vol. XXII, pp. 266–267.

14 *Ibid.*, p. 255.

15 See E. Stokes, 'Late nineteenth-century colonial expansion and the attack on the theory of economic imperialism: a case of mistaken identity?', *Historical Journal*, XII (1969), pp. 285–301; R. Koebner and H. D. Schmidt, *Imperialism*, p. 270.

16 E. Stokes, 'Late nineteenth-century colonial expansion', pp. 299–301.

17 D. K. Fieldhouse, *Economics and Empire*, pp. 46–53.

18 C. C. Eldridge, *Victorian Imperialism*, p. 132.
19 D. K. Fieldhouse, *Economics and Empire*, pp. 53–62.
20 B. Porter, *The Lion's Share*, p. 122.
21 C. C. Eldridge, *Victorian Imperialism*, p. 132.
22 See D. C. M. Platt, *Finance, Trade, and Politics in British Foreign Policy 1815–1914* (Oxford, 1968), pp. 362–367; W. G. Hynes, *The Economics of Empire: Britain, Africa and the New Imperialism* (London, 1979), *passim*; B. Porter, 'Imperialism and the Scramble', *Journal of Imperial and Commonwealth History*, IX (1980), pp. 76–81.
23 J. Gallagher, *The Decline, Revival and Fall of the British Empire* (Cambridge, 1982), p. 74.
24 J. Gallagher and R. Robinson, 'The imperialism of free trade', *Economic History Review*, 2nd series, VI (1953), pp. 1–15, reprinted in J. Gallagher, *The Decline ... of the British Empire*, pp. 1–18.
25 J. Gallagher, *The Decline ... of the British Empire*, p. 15.
26 See their *Africa and the Victorians* (London, 1961) and 'The partition of Africa', *New Cambridge Modern History*, vol. XI (edited by F. H. Hinsley, Cambridge, 1962), pp. 593–640, reprinted in J. Gallagher, *The Decline ... of the British Empire*, pp. 19–72.
27 J. Gallagher, *The Decline ... of the British Empire*, p. 90.
28 R. Robinson, 'Imperial theory and the question of imperialism after Empire', *Journal of Imperial and Commonwealth History*, XII (1984), p. 43.
29 J. Gallagher, *The Decline ... of the British Empire*, pp. 98, 102, 137–141.
30 See R. A. Austen and W. D. Smith, 'Images of Africa and British slave-trade abolition: the transition to an imperialist ideology, 1787–1807', *African Historical Studies*, II (1969), pp. 69–83.
31 B. Porter, *The Lion's Share*, pp. 22–23, 270–275.
32 See R. Robinson, 'Imperial theory'. p. 43.
33 Compare R. Robinson, 'Imperial theory', p. 43 and C. C. Eldridge, *Victorian Imperialism*, pp. 64–67.
34 For two diametrically opposed interpretations of this process see J. Gallagher, *The Decline ... of the British Empire*, pp. 145–148 and B. Freund, *The Making of Contemporary Africa: The Development of African Society since 1800* (London, 1984), pp. 192–202, 232. The Marxist Freund still insists (p. 232) that the causes of decolonization lay partly in 'structural alterations in the needs of capital'.
35 D. K. Fieldhouse, *Economics and Empire*, pp. 463–464.
36 B. Porter, 'Imperialism and the scramble', pp. 79–80.
37 B. Porter, *The Lion's Share*, pp. 132–133; C. C. Eldridge, *Victorian Imperialism*, p. 143.
38 D. K. Fieldhouse, *Economics and Empire*, p. 462.
39 See B. Porter, *The Lion's Share*, pp. xi, 117–118, 134.
40 J. R. Seeley, *The Expansion of England* (London, 1883), p. 8, cited in C. C. Eldridge, *Victorian Imperialism*, p. 123.
41 C. C. Eldridge, *Victorian Imperialism*, pp. 149–150, 157; see J. Gallagher and R. Robinson, 'The partition of Africa' in J. Gallagher, *The Decline ... of the British Empire*, pp. 28–29.
42 B. Porter, *The Lion's Share*, p. 111.
43 D. K. Fieldhouse, *Colonialism 1870–1945*, pp. 41–42.
44 D. K. Fieldhouse, *Economics and Empire*, pp. 460–461, 468.
45 J. Gallagher, *The Decline ... of the British Empire*, p. 141.
46 D. K. Fieldhouse, *Colonialism 1870–1945*, p. 42.
47 D. K. Fieldhouse, *Economics and Empire*, pp. 75–76; J. Gallagher, *The Decline ... of the British Empire*, p. 80.
48 See J. M. Mackenzie, *Propaganda and Empire: The Manipulation of British Public Opinion 1880–1960* (Manchester, 1984); and J. M. Mackenzie (ed.), *Imperialism and Popular Culture* (Manchester, 1986).
49 J. Morley, *The Life of Richard Cobden* (new edn., 2 vols., London, 1896), II, pp. 206–214; see D. W. Bebbington, *The Nonconformist Conscience: Chapel and Politics, 1870–1914* (London,

1982), pp. 106–109.

50 J. Gallagher, *The Decline ... of the British Empire*, pp. 83, 105–106, 146–147.

51 See B. Stanley, '"Commerce and Christianity": Providence theory, the missionary movement, and the imperialism of free trade, 1842–1860', *Historical Journal*, XXVI (1981), pp. 74–75, 87.

52 J. Gallagher, *The Decline ... of the British Empire*, p. 78.

53 B. Porter, 'Imperialism and the scramble', p. 80.

54 The foregoing section is based on R. Robinson, 'Imperial theory', pp. 44–47.

55 See D. K. Fieldhouse, *Colonialism 1870–1945*, pp. 20–24.

56 J. Gallagher, *The Decline ... of the British Empire*, pp. 100–103, 145–148.

57 R. Robinson, 'Imperial theory', p. 47; D. K. Fieldhouse, *Colonialism 1870–1945*, pp. 34–35.

58 J. Gallagher, *The Decline ... of the British Empire*, pp. 101, 147–148.

59 *Ibid.*, p. 145; R. F. Holland, *European Decolonization 1918–1981: An Introductory Survey* (London, 1985), p. 128.

60 B. Freund, *The Making of Contemporary Africa*, pp. 216–217; R. Oliver and A. Atmore, *Africa since 1800*, pp. 230–231, 245–250.

61 See A Porter, 'The balance sheet of empire, 1850–1914', *Historical Journal*, XXXI (1988), pp. 685–699.

62 See D. K. Fieldhouse, *Colonialism 1870–1945*, pp. 104–105.

Chapter 3

1 H. P. Thompson, *Into All Lands: The History of the Society for the Propagation of the Gospel in Foreign Parts 1701–1950* (London, 1951), p. 17.

2 J. Van den Berg, *Constrained by Jesus's Love* (Kampen, 1956), pp. 55–56; E. A. Payne, 'Doddridge and the missionary enterprise' in G. F. Nuttall (ed.), *Philip Doddridge 1702–1751* (London, 1951), pp. 79–101.

3 J. Vickers, *Thomas Coke: Apostle of Methodism* (London, 1969), pp. 132–137, 151–154, 172.

4 See B. Semmel, *The Methodist Revolution* (London, 1974), ch. 6, and S. Piggin, 'Halévy revisited: the origins of the Wesleyan Methodist Missionary Society', *Journal of Imperial and Commonwealth History*, IX (1980), pp. 17–37.

5 Also involved in the preparation of the *Proposal* was Grant's friend William Chambers, interpreter in the Supreme Court at Calcutta; see H. Morris, *The Life of Charles Grant* (London, 1904), pp. 103–107.

6 M. Horne, *Letters on Missions; Addressed to the Protestant Ministers of the British Churches* (Bristol, 1794), pp. 21–22.

7 See R. H. Martin, *Evangelicals United: Ecumenical Stirrings in Pre-Victorian Britain, 1795–1830* (Metuchen, N. J., and London, 1983), pp. 41–47.

8 E. Stock, *The History of the Church Missionary Society* (4 vols., London, 1899–1916), I, pp. 60–63.

9 E. G. K. Hewat, *Vision and Achievement 1796–1956* (London, 1960), pp. 8–9.

10 J. M. Calder, *Scotland's March Past: The Share of Scottish Churches in the London Missionary Society* (London, 1945), p. 5.

11 R. H. Martin, *Evangelicals United*, p. 14.

12 P. J. Marshall and G. Williams, *The Great Map of Mankind: British Perceptions of the World in the Age of Enlightenment* (London, 1982), p. 67.

13 E. Carey, *Memoir of William Carey D.D.* (London, 1836), p. 18.

14 A. S. Wood, *Thomas Haweis 1734–1820* (London, 1957), pp. 170, 197–202; N. Gunson, *Messengers of Grace: Evangelical Missionaries in the South Seas 1797–1860* (Melbourne, 1978), p. 12.

15 R. Anstey, *The Atlantic Slave Trade and British Abolition, 1760–1810* (London, 1975); S. Drescher, *Econocide: British Slavery in the Era of Abolition* (Pittsburgh, 1977); see also H.

Temperley, 'Capitalism, slavery and ideology', *Past and Present*, LXXV (May 1977), pp. 94–118.

16 W. Carey, *An Enquiry into the Obligations of Christians to Use Means for the Conversion of the Heathens* (new edn., edited by E. A. Payne, London, 1961).

17 The best account of the Prayer Call remains E. A. Payne, *The Prayer Call of 1784* (London, 1941).

18 W. Carey, *An Enquiry*, pp. 79–80. Carey included among his 'tokens for good' the 'diminution of the spirit of popery', the campaign against the slave trade, and the founding of the colony of Sierra Leone.

19 For Edwards' influence on the missionary awakening see J. Van den Berg, *Constrained by Jesus's Love*, pp. 92–93; J. A. de Jong, *As the Waters Cover the Sea: Millennial Expectations in the Rise of Anglo-American Missions 1640–1810* (Kampen, 1970), pp. 124–137, 157–158, 167, 176–177.

20 M. Horne, *Letters on Missions*, p. 20.

21 J. Rippon, *The Baptist Annual Register*, vol. I (1790–93), pp. 438–439.

22 M. Vereté, 'The restoration of the Jews in English Protestant thought 1790–1840', *Middle Eastern Studies*, VIII (1972), pp. 3–50.

23 H. E. Hopkins, *Charles Simeon of Cambridge* (London, 1977), pp. 179–180.

24 J. A. James, *The Attraction of the Cross: A Sermon* (London, 1819), p. 17, cited in N. Gunson, *Messengers of Grace*, p. 268.

25 See H. Willmer, 'Evangelicalism 1785 to 1835' (Hulsean Prize Essay, University of Cambridge, 1962); R. Anstey, *The Atlantic Slave Trade*, ch. 7; G. M. Marsden, *Fundamentalism and American Culture: The Shaping of Twentieth Century Evangelicalism 1870–1925* (New York, 1980), parts I and II; D. Rosman, *Evangelicals and Culture* (London, 1984), ch. 2; and now, most notably, D. W. Bebbington, *Evangelicalism in Modern Britain: A History from the 1730s to the 1980s* (London, 1989), ch. 2.

26 D. W. Bebbington, *Evangelicalism*, pp. 141–152, 181–188.

27 Most nineteenth-century evangelicals regarded Roman Catholicism as 'popish idolatry' and thus little better than 'heathen' idolatry.

28 Genesis 11:1–9.

29 See P. J. Marshall and G. Williams, *The Great Map of Mankind*, pp. 113–114; N. Gunson, *Messengers of Grace*, pp. 199, 206–207.

30 *Wesleyan Methodist Magazine*, 5th ser. II (1856), p. 894.

31 *Ibid.*, p. 738.

32 *Ibid.*, pp. 433–434.

33 H. A. C. Cairns, *Prelude to Imperialism: British Reactions to Central African Society 1840–1890* (London, 1965), p. 100.

34 *Baptist Magazine*, XLI (1849), p. 394.

35 J. Campbell (ed.), *The Farewell Services of Robert Moffat in Edinburgh, Manchester, and London* (London, 1843), p. 109.

36 D. Livingstone, *Missionary Travels and Researches in South Africa* (London, 1857), p. 90; H. A. C. Cairns, *Prelude to Imperialism*, p. 291; G. Seaver, *David Livingstone: His Life and Letters* (London, 1957), pp. 49, 65–66, 138–139, 242.

37 H. Venn to J. S. H. Stewart, 23 Feb. 1850, G/AC 1/8 (1849–50), pp. 97–99, CMS archives, University of Birmingham; see W. R. Shenk, *Henry Venn – Missionary Statesman* (New York, 1983), p. 27.

38 E. Stock, *History of the CMS*, I, pp. 76–77.

39 See G. Rowell, *Hell and the Victorians* (Oxford, 1974). Rowell shows (pp. 180–207) that the doctrine of conditional immortality became an increasingly attractive option for those who wished to modify traditional eschatology without espousing universalism.

40 G. A. Oddie, 'India and missionary motives 1850–1900', *Journal of Ecclesiastical History*, XXV (1974), p. 69.

41 H. A. C. Cairns, *Prelude to Imperialism*, pp. 202, 292n.; C. P. Williams, 'The recruitment

and training of overseas missionaries in England between 1850 and 1900' (University of Bristol M. Litt. thesis, 1976), p. 195.

42 C. P. Williams, 'The recruitment and training', pp. 196, 198.

43 Dr and Mrs Howard Taylor, *Hudson Taylor and the China Inland Mission: The Growth of a Work of God* (London, 1918), pp. 30–31; C. P. Williams, 'The recruitment and training', pp. 193–194, 196, 199, 222. It is not clear how Taylor arrived at his figure of a million deaths a month; for some indication see A. J. Broomhall, *Hudson Taylor and China's Open Century. Book Four: Survivors' Pact* (London, 1984), pp. 53–54.

44 See H. Kraemer, *The Christian Message in a Non-Christian World* (London 1938), ch. IV.

45 See for example J. Milner, 'Observations on the use of history' in I. Milner (ed.), *A Selection of Tracts and Essays, Theological and Historical, from the Miscellaneous Writings of the Late Rev. Joseph Milner, A. M.* (London, 1810), p. 457.

46 W. Paley, *Natural Theology*, in *The Works of William Paley, D.D.* (7 vols., London, 1825), V, pp. 2, 10–11, and *The Principles of Moral and Political Philosophy* in *ibid.*, IV, p. 46.

47 *Evangelical Magazine*, new ser. XXI (1843), p. 90.

48 *Wesleyan Methodist Magazine*, 4th ser. V. (1849), pp. 770–771; see also 5th ser. III (1857), pp. 564–565.

49 See R. Coupland in *Cambridge History of the British Empire*, vol. II (Cambridge, 1940), p. 193; K. E. Knorr, *British Colonial Theories 1570–1850* (Toronto, 1944), pp. 246, 376; G. R. Mellor, *British Imperial Trusteeship 1783–1850* (London, 1951), pp. 22–23.

50 See D. R. Muller, 'Josiah Strong and American nationalism: a re-evaluation', *Journal of American History*, LIII (1966–67), pp. 487–503.

51 *Speeches on Missions: By the Right Reverend Samuel Wilberforce, D.D., late Bishop of Winchester* (edited by H. Rowley, London, 1874), p. 97.

52 W. Clarkson, *India and the Gospel: or, an Empire for the Messiah* (2nd edn., London, 1850), pp. 296, 302.

53 W. Monk (ed.), *Dr Livingstone's Cambridge Lectures* (London, 1858), p. 24.

54 I originally argued this case in my article '"Commerce and Christianity": Providence theory, the missionary movement, and the imperialism of free trade, 1842–1860', *Historical Journal*, XXVI (1983), pp. 71–94. For a critical response see A. Porter, '"Commerce and Christianity": the rise and fall of a nineteenth-century missionary slogan', *Historical Journal*, XXVIII (1985), pp. 597–621. For an older exposition of the theme see H. A. C. Cairns, *Prelude to Imperialism*, pp. 189–230.

55 *Parliamentary Register*, XXVI (1789), p. 150; cited in P. D. Curtin, *The Image of Africa: British Ideas and Action, 1780–1850* (London, 1965), p. 69.

56 S. Jakobsson, *Am I not a Man and a Brother?: British Missions and the Abolition of the Slave Trade and Slavery in West Africa and the West Indies 1786–1838* (Uppsala, 1972), pp. 69–70, 75.

57 W. Carey, *An Enquiry*, pp. 68, 80.

58 J. Tucker, *Four Tracts, Together with Two Sermons, on Political and Commercial Subjects* (Gloucester, 1774), Sermon I, pp. 15–19, and Sermon II, p. 32; see W. E. Clark, *Joseph Tucker: Economist. A Study in the History of Economics* (New York, 1903), pp. 50–51, 230–232.

59 *Periodical Accounts Relative to the Baptist Missionary Society*, vol. I (Clipstone, 1800), pp. 96–97.

60 N. Gunson, *Messengers of Grace*, pp. 119–121.

61 See D. Forbes, 'Sceptical Whiggism, commerce and liberty' in A. S. Skinner and T. Wilson (eds.), *Essays on Adam Smith* (Oxford, 1975), pp. 190, 194–201.

62 A Porter, 'Commerce and Christianity', pp. 602–606; A. T. Embree, *Charles Grant and British Rule in India* (London, 1962), pp. 168–169.

63 D. Coates, J. Beecham and W. Ellis, *Christianity, the Means of Civilization: Shown in the Evidence Given Before a Committee of the House of Commons, on Aborigines* (London, 1837), pp. 52–54 and *passim*.

64 See P. D. Curtin, *The Image of Africa*, pp. 300–302; and T. F. Buxton Papers for 1838, vol. 17 (Rhodes House, Oxford).

65 M. A. C. Warren (ed.), *To Apply the Gospel: Selections from the Writings of Henry Venn* (Grand

Rapids, 1971), p. 193; W. R. Shenk, *Henry Venn*, pp. 67–77; J. F. A. Ajayi, 'Henry Venn and the policy of development', *Journal of the Historical Society of Nigeria*, I (1959), pp. 331–342.

66 I. Schapera (ed.), *Livingstone's Missionary Correspondence 1841–1856* (London, 1961), pp. 301–302.

67 See O. Chadwick, *Mackenzie's Grave* (London, 1959), *passim*.

68 *E.g.* the Sudan United Mission. See J. H. Boer, *Missionary Messengers of Liberation in a Colonial Context* (Amsterdam, 1979), pp. 134–135, 175–177.

69 *BMS Periodical Accounts* I, pp. 175, 71–72.

70 W. Clarkson, *India and the Gospel*, pp. 224–225.

71 A typical example is H. E. Nichol's (pseudonym Colin Sterne) 'We've a story to tell to the nations', written in 1896.

72 Matthew 24:14.

73 See my article, 'The miser of Headingley', in W. J. Sheils and D. Wood (eds.), *The Church and Wealth* (*Studies in Church History*, vol. 24, Oxford, 1987), pp. 371–382.

74 E. Stock, *History of the CMS*, III, pp. 288–290; see A. Porter, 'Cambridge, Keswick, and late-nineteenth-century attitudes to Africa', *Journal of Imperial and Commonwealth History*, V (1976–77), pp. 5–34.

75 See C. Irvine, 'Notes on the origins of the watchword: "The evangelization of the world in this generation"', *Bulletin of the Scottish Institute of Missionary Studies* n.s. 3–4 (1985–87), pp. 7–9.

76 See C. J. Phillips, 'The Student Volunteer Movement and its role in China missions, 1886–1920', in J. K. Fairbank (ed.), *The Missionary Enterprise in China and America* (Cambridge, Mass., 1974), pp. 93–95.

77 Cited in A. Porter, 'Evangelical enthusiasm, missionary motivation and West Africa in the late nineteenth century: the career of G. W. Brooke', *Journal of Imperial and Commonwealth History*, VI (1977–78), p. 38.

78 J. Harris, *The Great Commission: or, the Christian Church charged and constituted to convey the Gospel to the world* (London, 1842), pp. 124–125.

79 See D. W. Bebbington, *Evangelicalism*, pp. 183–184, 191–194.

80 B. Stanley, 'Home support for overseas missions in early Victorian England c. 1838–1873' (University of Cambridge Ph.D. thesis, 1979), p. 26. The section which follows is based on chapter 1 of my thesis.

81 LMS Board Minutes, box 33, p. 551, Council for World Mission archives, School of Oriental and African Studies, London.

82 Register of Candidates, 1850–1859 (C/A Tm 5), CMS archives.

83 E. Stock, *History of the CMS*, II, p. 337.

84 *Ibid.*, II, p. 357.

85 B. Stanley, 'The miser of Headingley', pp. 377–378; W. Y. Fullerton, *The Christ of the Congo River* (London, n.d.), pp. 22–28.

86 Register of Candidates, 1873–1888 (C/A Tm 5), CMS archives. No figures are available for the years before 1850, but it is inconceivable that applications in this period were ever of a similar order of magnitude.

87 Figures compiled from the CMS *Register of Missionaries and Native Clergy from 1804 to 1904* (privately printed, n.d.) indicate that numbers of missionaries accepted from Great Britain and Ireland reached a peak of 86 in 1896. E. Stock, *History of the CMS*, IV, p. 22, mentions a peak of 103 in 1900, which is hard to reconcile with the Register.

88 A. F. Walls, 'British missions' in T. Christensen and W. R. Hutchison (eds.) *Missionary Ideologies in the Imperialist Era: 1880–1920* (Aarhus, 1982), pp. 159–160.

89 Sources of information: *Church Missionary Society. Register of Missionaries and Native Clergy from 1804 to 1904. In two parts* (privately printed, n.d.); Register of Candidates, 1850–1900 (C/A Tm 5), CMS archives.

90 See E. Stock, *History of the CMS*, II, pp. 397–399, III, pp. 321, 369–370.

91 S. C. Potter, 'The social origins and recruitment of English Protestant missionaries in the nineteenth century' (University of London Ph.D. thesis, 1974), p. 156; for the percentage of candidates accepted by the CMS in sample years see Williams, 'The recruitment and training', Appendix A, Table 7.

92 See E. Stock, *History of the CMS*, III, pp. 327, 354, 374.

93 C. P. Williams, 'The recruitment and training', pp. 15–16 and Appendix A.

94 J. Sibree, *London Missionary Society: A Register of Missionaries, Deputations, etc. from 1796 to 1923* (London, 1923); C. P. Williams, 'The recruitment and training,' pp. 12–13, 188, 214–215; *idem*, 'Healing and evangelism: the place of medicine in later Victorian Protestant missionary thinking' and A. F. Walls, ' "The heavy artillery of the missionary army": the domestic importance of the nineteenth-century medical missionary' in W. J. Sheils (ed.), *The Church and Healing (Studies in Church History*, vol. 19, Oxford, 1982), pp. 278, 290.

95 This paragraph is dependent on C. P. Williams, 'The recruitment and training,' pp. 17–22, 311 and Appendix A.

96 A. C. Ross, 'Scottish missionary concern 1874–1914: a golden era?', *Scottish Historical Review*, LI (1972), pp. 52–72.

97 K. S. Latourette, *A History of the Expansion of Christianity* (7 vols., London 1938–47), IV, title page and pp. 1, 7.

98 J. S. Dennis, *Centennial Survey of Foreign Missions* (Edinburgh and London, 1902), pp. 257–258. Dennis suggests (p. 22) that some adjustment should be made to eliminate the large proportion of SPG missionaries who were not engaged in work amongst non-European races; his proposed adjustment would reduce the British total to 8,623.

99 D. B. Barrett (ed.), *World Christian Encyclopedia* (Nairobi, 1982), p. 803; *idem*, 'Annual Statistical Table on Global Mission: 1989', *International Bulletin of Missionary Research*, vol. 13, no. 1 (Jan. 1989), p. 21. Barrett's estimates for 1989 do not distinguish Protestants from Roman Catholics, although he estimates that 81,700 of the 273,700 are Pentecostal or charismatic.

Chapter 4

1 S. Jakobsson, *Am I not a Man and a Brother?*, p. 287.

2 *BMS Periodical Accounts*, V (1813), pp. 292–293.

3 S. Jakobsson, *Am I not a Man and a Brother?*, pp. 301–302.

4 J. H. Hinton, *Memoir of William Knibb, Missionary in Jamaica* (London, 1847), pp. 149–150.

5 See S. Jakobsson, *Am I not a Man and a Brother?*, pp. 483–485; *Evangelical Magazine*, new ser. I (1859), pp. 561–562.

6 M. Turner, *Slaves and Missionaries: the Disintegration of Jamaican Slave Society, 1787–1834* (Urbana, 1982), pp. 8–10, 25, 76–77.

7 S. Jakobsson, *Am I not a Man and a Brother?*, pp. 315–316, 467; see also W. F. Burchell, *Memoir of Thomas Burchell*, (London, 1849). p. 256.

8 S. Jakobsson, *Am I not a Man and a Brother?*, pp. 306–317; *cf*. M. Turner, *Slaves and Missionaries*. pp. 86–87.

9 See C. Northcott, *Slavery's Martyr: John Smith of Demerara and the Emancipation Movement* (London, 1976).

10 M. Turner, *Slaves and Missionaries*, p. 102.

11 *Ibid.*, p. 112.

12 *Ibid.*, pp. 114–116; S. Jakobsson, *Am I not a Man and a Brother?*, pp. 389–394.

13 J. H. Hinton, *Memoir of William Knibb*, pp. 95–96; M. Turner, *Slaves and Missionaries*, pp. 134–142; S. Jakobsson, *Am I not a Man and a Brother?*, pp. 416–438.

14 In addition to the accounts in Jakobsson and Turner see K. R. M. Short, 'Jamaican Christian missions and the great slave rebellion of 1831–32', *Journal of Ecclesiastical History*,

XXVII (1976), pp. 57-72.

15 J. H. Hinton, *Memoir of William Knibb*, pp. 141-142, 148, 150-151; *Baptist Magazine*, XXIV (1832), p. 325; W. F. Burchell, *Memoir of Thomas Burchell*, p. 256.

16 *Baptist Magazine*, XXIV (1832), p. 325; for a fuller record of this speech see J. H. Hinton, *Memoir of William Knibb*, pp. 145-148.

17 J. H. Hinton, *Memoir of William Knibb*, pp. 151-152; K. R. M. Short, 'Jamaican Christian Missions', pp. 63-65; *Baptist Magazine*, XXIV (1832), p. 419.

18 R. Anstey, 'The pattern of British abolitionism in the eighteenth and nineteenth centuries', in C. Bolt and S. Drescher (eds.), *Anti-Slavery, Religion and Reform* (Folkestone, 1980), pp. 27-28.

19 See I. S. Rennie, 'Evangelicalism and English public life 1823-1850' (University of Toronto Ph.D. thesis, 1962, copy in Cambridge University Library), ch. IV.

20 J. H. Hinton, *Memoir of William Knibb*, pp. 469-473; S. Jakobsson, *Am I not a Man and a Brother?*, pp. 558, 565-567.

21 See J. H. Hinton, *Memoir of William Knibb*, pp. 48-49, 136-137.

22 See J. S. Galbraith, *Reluctant Empire: British Policy on the South African Frontier 1834-1854* (Berkeley and Los Angeles, 1963), ch. 1, and A. Ross, *John Philip (1775-1851): Missions, Race and Politics in South Africa* (Aberdeen, 1986), pp. 11-32, 81-87.

23 W. M. Macmillan, *The Cape Colour Question: A Historical Survey* (London, 1928), p. 215.

24 A. Ross, *John Philip*, pp. 105-111.

25 *Ibid*, pp. 105-108.

26 See B. A. Le Cordeur, *The Politics of Eastern Cape Separatism 1820-1854* (Cape Town, 1981), pp. 67-68.

27 J. S. Galbraith, *Reluctant Empire*, p. 86.

28 A. Ross, *John Philip*, pp. 127-129; W. M. Macmillan, *Bantu, Boer and Briton: The Making of the South African Native Problem* (revised edn., Oxford, 1963), pp. 96-101.

29 J. S. Galbraith, *Reluctant Empire*, p. 111.

30 A. Ross, *John Philip*, pp. 137-139.

31 W. D. Hammond-Tooke (ed.), *The Journal of William Shaw* (Cape Town, 1972), pp. 13-14; C. Sadler, *Never a Young Man: Extracts from the Letters and Journals of the Rev. William Shaw* (Cape Town, 1967), pp. 157-160.

32 W. Shaw, *The Story of My Mission in South-Eastern Africa: comprising some account of the European colonists; with extended notices of the Kaffir and other native tribes* (London, 1860), pp. 137-138.

33 Wesleyan *Missionary Notices*, No. 240 (Dec. 1835), p. 178; cited in W. Shaw, *The Story of My Mission*, pp. 155-156.

34 See for example W. M. Macmillan, *Bantu, Boer and Briton*, pp. 95-96.

35 *Ibid.*, pp. 145-148; A. Ross, *John Philip*, pp. 140-141.

36 W. M. Macmillan, *Bantu, Boer and Briton*, pp. 162-164.

37 *Ibid.*, pp. 166-167; J. S. Galbraith, *Reluctant Empire*, pp. 123-129; A. Ross, *John Philip*, pp. 139-140.

38 W. Shaw, *The Story of My Mission*, p. 143; C. Sadler, *Never a Young Man*, pp. 163-165.

39 Parliamentary Papers, 1836, VII (538), *Report from the Select Committee on Aborigines (British Settlements)*, pp. 70-71, 100-101, 501-502, sections 749-757, 1070, 4311; see also J. S. Galbraith, *Reluctant Empire*, p. 105.

40 W. Shaw, *A Defence of the Wesleyan Missionaries in Southern Africa: Comprising Copies of a Correspondence with the Reverend John Philip, D.D.* (London, 1839).

41 Compare G. G. Findlay and W. W. Holdsworth, *The History of the Wesleyan Methodist Missionary Society* (5 vols., London, 1922), IV, pp. 269-274, with R. Lovett, *The History of the London Missionary Society 1795-1895* (2 vols., London, 1899), I, pp. 554-560.

42 W. M. Macmillan, *The Cape Colour Question*, pp. 176-177, 216-217; idem, *Bantu, Boer and Briton*, p. 371; A Ross, *John Philip*, p. 225.

43 E. A. Walker, *A History of Southern Africa* (3rd edn., London, 1957), pp. 174, 183; W. M.

Macmillan, *The Cape Colour Question*, p. 174.

44 J. S. Galbraith, *Reluctant Empire*, p. 105; W. M. Macmillan, *Bantu, Boer and Briton*, pp. 146–148, 165–166, 235, 258; A. Ross, *John Philip*, p. 140.

45 W. M. Macmillan, *Bantu, Boer and Briton*, p. 242; A. Ross, *John Philip*, pp. 218–219.

46 (W. B. Boyce), *Memoir of the Rev. William Shaw, Late General Superintendent of the Wesleyan Missions in South-Eastern Africa, edited by his oldest surviving friend* (London, 1874), p. 176; B. A. Le Cordeur, *The Politics of Eastern Cape Separatism*, pp. 90, 105.

47 (W. B. Boyce), *Memoir of the Rev. William Shaw*, pp. 177–178.

48 A. Mayhew, *Christianity and the Government of India* (London, 1929), pp. 29–37.

49 E. D. Potts, *British Baptist Missionaries in India 1793–1837* (Cambridge, 1967), p. 171; J. C. Marshman, *The Life and Times of Carey, Marshman, and Ward* (2 vols., London, 1859) I, pp. 93–95.

50 A. Mayhew, *Christianity and the Government of India*, p. 22.

51 A. K. Davidson, 'The development and influence of the British missionary movement's attitudes towards India, 1786–1830' (University of Aberdeen, Ph.D. thesis, 1973), pp. 292–294.

52 *53 Geo. 3 c.* 155, sections 33 and 49; see E. D. Potts, *British Baptist Missionaries*, p. 200.

53 J. Marshman, 1807, cited in E. D. Potts, *British Baptist Missionaries*, p. 202.

54 *Ibid.*, p. 146.

55 *Ibid.*, pp. 144–157; K. Ingham, *Reformers in India 1793–1833* (Cambridge, 1956), pp. 44–54.

56 Hence the entry into the English language of the word 'juggernaut' to describe a large wheeled vehicle.

57 Cited in E. D. Potts, *British Baptist Missionaries*, p. 164.

58 K. Ingham, *Reformers in India*, p. 38.

59 I. S. Rennie, 'Evangelicalism and public life', pp. 352–356; E. D. Potts, *British Baptist Missionaries*, p. 166.

60 Parliamentary Papers, 1857–58, XLII, *East India: Correspondence Relating to Missionaries and Idolatry*, pp. 329–332.

61 B. Stanley, 'Christian responses to the Indian mutiny of 1857' in W. J. Sheils (ed.), *The Church and War (Studies in Church History*, vol. 20, Oxford, 1983), pp. 283–284.

62 *Ibid.*, p. 280.

63 *Wesleyan Methodist Magazine*, 5th ser. III (1857), p. 1036; see A. Mayhew, *Christianity and the Government of India*, pp. 158–159.

64 Cited in B. Stanley, 'Christian responses to the Indian mutiny', p. 286.

65 Cited in *ibid.*, p. 286.

66 *Ibid.*, pp. 287–288.

67 *Church Missionary Intelligencer*, XI (1860), p. 151.

68 This paragraph summarizes the argument of my ' "Commerce and Christianity": Providence theory, the missionary movement, and the imperialism of free trade, 1842–1860', *Historical Journal*, XXVI (1983), pp. 87–90.

69 (George Smith), *Our National Relations with China: being two speeches delivered in Exeter Hall and in the Free-Trade Hall, Manchester, by the Bishop of Victoria* (London, 1857), pp. 5–7; *The Times*, 28 Feb. 1853, cited in J. S. Galbraith, *Reluctant Empire*, p. 3.

70 See for example LMS Newcastle auxiliary, minute book, 1827–44, p. 149, Congregational Library MSS, now in Dr. Williams's Library, London.

71 See G. A. Oddie, *Social Protest in India: British Protestant Missionaries and Social Reforms 1850–1900* (New Delhi, 1979), pp. 21–24.

72 *Ibid.*, p. 245.

73 *Ibid.*, p. 245.

74 *Ibid.*, pp. 250–251.

75 See M. Greenberg, *British Trade and the Opening of China 1800–42* (Cambridge, 1951), p. 196 and *passim*.

76 J. K. Fairbank, *Trade and Diplomacy on the China Coast* (new edn., Cambridge, Mass., 1964), pp. 66–70; A. J. Broomhall, *Hudson Taylor and China's Open Century. Book One: Barbarians at the Gates* (London, 1981), pp. 185–210.

77 See H. Schlyter, *Der China-Missionar Karl Gützlaff und seine Heimatbasis* (Studia Missionalia Upsaliensia XXX, Uppsala, 1976), pp. 27–37.

78 E. Hodder, *The Life and Work of the Seventh Earl of Shaftesbury, K.G.* (3 vols., London, 1886), I, p. 440.

79 *Evangelical Magazine*, new ser. XXI (1843), p. 40; *LMS Annual Report for 1842–43*, pp. xciv–xcv.

80 B. Stanley, 'Commerce and Christianity', pp. 76–79.

81 See S. C. Miller, 'Ends and means: missionary justification of force in nineteenth-century China', in J. K. Fairbank (ed.), *The Missionary Enterprise in China*, pp. 251–277.

82 *Speeches on Missions* (ed. Rowley), p. 98.

83 M. Horne, *Letters on Missions*, pp. 77–78.

84 *Church Missionary Intelligencer*, I, 19 (Nov. 1850), p. 444.

85 *Evangelical Magazine*, new ser. XXII (1844), p. 602; J. A. James, *God's Voice from China to the British and Irish Churches*, in *The Works of John Angell James, edited by his son* (17 vols., London, 1862), XVI, p. 481.

86 J. S. Gregory, 'British missionary reaction to the Taiping movement in China', *Journal of Religious History*, II (1963), pp. 204–218; *idem*, *Great Britain and the Taipings* (London, 1969), ch. 4.

87 *Wesleyan Methodist Magazine*, 5th ser. II (1856), p. 906: J. A. James, *God's Voice from China*, p. 522.

88 (G. Smith), *Our National Relations with China*, p. 21; see B. Stanley, 'Commerce and Christianity', p. 80.

89 *Record*, 6 March 1857, p. 2; *Wesleyan Methodist Magazine*, 5th ser. III (1857), p. 16.

90 E. Stock, *History of the CMS*, II, pp. 301, 304; J. A. James, *God's Voice from China*, p. 481; *Baptist Magazine*, LI (1859), p. 333; for divisions among Congregationalists see *Evangelical Magazine*, new ser. XXXV (1857), p. 385, and G. I. T. Machin, *Politics and the Churches in Great Britain 1832 to 1868* (Oxford, 1977), pp. 281–282.

91 See the comments of Bishop G. Smith in *Our National Relations with China*, p. 6.

92 J. A. James, *God's Voice from China*, pp. 495, 552–553; S. C. Miller, 'Ends and means', p. 281.

Chapter 5

1 See D. W. Bebbington, *The Nonconformist Conscience: Chapel and Politics 1870–1914* (London, 1982), pp. 13, 59–60.

2 G. S. Rowe (ed.), *Fiji and the Fijians* (2 vols., London, 1858) II, pp. 1–2, 432–433; P. McOwan to G. Osborn, 9 Feb. 1858, Box 17, Home Letters, and W. Wilson to WMMS General Secretaries, 12 Oct. 1858, Box 532, Methodist Church, Overseas Division (hereafter MMS) archives, School of Oriental and African Studies, London; T. McCullagh, *Sir William McArthur K.C.M.G.* (London, 1891), pp. 143–145.

3 N. Gunson, *Messengers of Grace*, pp. 144–145.

4 See G. S. Rowe (ed.), *Fiji and the Fijians*, II, pp. 433–435.

5 J. Royce to G. Osborn, 7 Sept. 1858, Box 532, MMS archives.

6 J. Royce to G. Osborn, 7 Sept. 1858, postscript dated 22 Oct. 1858; see K. L. P. Martin, *Missionaries and Annexation in the Pacific* (London, 1924), pp. 47–49.

7 W. Wilson to WMMS General Secretaries, 12 Oct. 1858; see also J. Royce to G. Osborn, 7 Sept. 1858, J. S. Fordham to J. Eggleston, 18 Oct. 1858, and J. Binner to J. Calvert, 29 Oct. 1858; Box 532, MMS archives.

8 W. Arthur, *What is Fiji, the Sovereignty of which is offered to Her Majesty?* (London, 1859), p. 8.

9 W. Wilson to G. Osborn, 3 Nov. 1859, Box 532, MMS archives.

10 See J. D. Legge, *Britain in Fiji 1858-1880* (London, 1958), pp. 29-31.

11 *Ibid.*, pp. 41-42; see W. J. Smythe (ed.), *Ten Months in the Fiji Islands* (Oxford, 1864), pp. 198-199.

12 N. Gunson, *Messengers of Grace*, p. 145; J. Waterhouse to WMMS General Secretaries, 18 Oct. 1860, Box 532, MMS archives.

13 J. Calvert to WMMS General Secretaries, 14 July 1862, Box 532, MMS archives.

14 J. D. Legge, *Britain in Fiji*, pp. 44-45.

15 J. Calvert to Vice-Admiral Erskine, 5 March 1869, Box 532, MMS archives.

16 J. Nettleton to Rev. G. Perks, 23 Oct. 1869, Box 532, MMS archives.

17 Parliamentary Papers 1868-69, XLIII, *Correspondence Respecting the Deportation of South Sea Islanders*, pp. 1106-1107.

18 J. D. Legge, *Britain in Fiji*, pp. 116-121.

19 *Ibid.*, pp. 55-56; T. McCullagh, *Sir William McArthur*, pp. 147-148.

20 F. Langham and others to British Consul for Fiji and Tonga, 12 March 1874, Box 532, MMS archives.

21 T. McCullagh, *Sir William McArthur*, p. 182.

22 The concept of a protectorate was developed by the European powers in the last thirty years of the nineteenth century to describe arrangements made between a European power and a native ruler designed to exclude other European powers from any interference in the ruler's territory. See W. R. Johnston, *Sovereignty and Protection: A Study of British Jurisdictional Imperialism in the Late Nineteenth Century* (Durham, N. C., 1973).

23 See Parliamentary Papers, 1874, XLV, *Fiji Islands: Copy of a Letter Addressed to Commodore Goodenough, R. N., and E. L. Layard, Esq. . . .*, p. 302.

24 A. J. Dachs, 'Missionary imperialism – the case of Bechuanaland', *Journal of African History*, XIII (1972), pp. 647-658.

25 Cited in *ibid.*, p. 650.

26 *Ibid.*, p. 658.

27 *Ibid.*, p. 652.

28 See A. Holmberg, *African Tribes and European Agencies: Colonialism and Humanitarianism in British South and East Africa 1870-1895* (Göteborg, 1966), pp. 173-174.

29 See I. Schapera, *Tribal Innovators: Tswana Chiefs and Social Change 1795-1940* (London, 1970), pp. 43, 119-121.

30 Resolution passed at the October 1882 meeting of the Congregational Union of England and Wales, cited in J. Mackenzie, *Austral Africa: Losing it or Ruling it* (new edn., 2 vols., New York, 1969), I, p. 143.

31 Mackenzie to Frere, 10 Dec. 1879, in A. J. Dachs (ed.), *Papers of John Mackenzie* (Johannesburg, 1975), pp. 135-136.

32 Mackenzie to Lanyon, 24 Sept. 1878, in A. J. Dachs (ed.), *Papers of John Mackenzie*, pp. 124-125.

33 Mackenzie to Whitehouse, 3 June and 25 Sept. 1879, in A. J. Dachs (ed.), *Papers of John Mackenzie*, pp. 127-128, 130-133.

34 Whitehouse to Mackenzie, 27 Nov. 1879, in A. J. Dachs (ed.), *Papers of John Mackenzie*, pp. 133-134.

35 Mackenzie to Whitehousse, 10 Feb. 1880, in A. J. Dachs (ed.), *Papers of John Mackenzie*, pp. 136-137.

36 See A. Holmberg, *African Tribes and European Agencies*, pp. 5-11, 71-73, 89-105.

37 A. J. Dachs, 'Missionary imperialism', p. 653; A. J. Dachs (ed.), *Papers of John Mackenzie*, pp. 136-137.

38 J. Mackenzie, *Austral Africa*, I, pp. 142-143; Parliamentary Papers, 1882, XLVII, *Further Correspondence Respecting the Affairs of the Transvaal and Adjacent Territories*, pp. 1037, 1048-1050; and 1883, XLIX, *Further Correspondence Respecting the Affairs of the Transvaal and Adjacent Territories*, p. 201.

39 J. Mackenzie, *Austral Africa, passim*; A. Sillery, *John Mackenzie of Bechuanaland 1835–1899* (Cape Town, 1971), pp. 49–56.

40 A. Holmberg, *African Tribes and European Agencies*, pp. 86–87.

41 *Ibid.*, pp. 89–105.

42 *Ibid.*, pp. 145–146; A. J. Dachs (ed.), *Papers of John Mackenzie*, p. 152.

43 A. J. Dachs (ed.), *Papers of John Mackenzie*, p. 152.

44 J. McCracken, *Politics and Christianity in Malawi 1875–1940* (Cambridge, 1977), p. 175.

45 K. N. Mufuka, *Missions and Politics in Malawi* (Kingston, Ontario, 1977), pp. iii–iv.

46 See S. Brock, 'James Stewart and David Livingstone', in B. Pachai (ed.), *Livingstone Man of Africa: Memorial Essays 1873–1973* (London, 1973), pp. 86–110.

47 J. Wells, *The Life of James Stewart* (London, 1919), pp. 124–126. The Free Church of Scotland originated in the 'Disruption' of 1843, when about one-third of the ministers of the Church of Scotland seceded in protest against secular control of church patronage.

48 A. C. Ross, 'Livingstone and the aftermath', in B. Pachai (ed.), *Livingstone*, p. 191.

49 J. McCracken, *Politics and Christianity*, p. 30: J. S. Galbraith, *Mackinnon and East Africa 1878–1895* (Cambridge, 1972), pp. 67–70.

50 See A. C. Ross, 'Livingstone and the aftermath', pp. 196–204.

51 J. McCracken, *Politics and Christianity*, pp. 39–42.

52 *Ibid.*, pp. 58–59, 79–84.

53 R. Oliver, *The Missionary Factor in East Africa* (2nd edn., London, 1965), pp. 94–116.

54 See D. K. Fieldhouse, *Economics and Empire 1830–1914* (London, 1973), pp. 372–375.

55 R. Oliver, *The Missionary Factor*, p. 116.

56 *Ibid.*, p. 121; J. McCracken, *Politics and Christianity*, p. 158.

57 J. McCracken, *Politics and Christianity*, pp. 158–159; W. P. Livingstone, *A Prince of Missionaries: The Rev. Alexander Hetherwick* (London, 1931), pp. 49–52.

58 D. K. Fieldhouse, *Economics and Empire*, pp. 352–354.

59 R. Oliver, *The Missionary Factor*, p. 127.

60 J. McCracken, *Politics and Christianity*, p. 161.

61 *Ibid.*, pp. 162–167.

62 *Ibid.*, p. 167.

63 *Ibid.*, pp. 164–165.

64 Although J. McCracken, *Politics and Christianity*, pp. 163–164, sees some distinction in social class and education between Blantyre and Livingstonia.

65 R. Oliver, *The Missionary Factor*, p. 38n.

66 J. McCracken, *Politics and Christianity*, p. 173.

67 K. N. Mufuka, *Missions and Politics in Malawi*, p. 197.

68 J. V. Taylor, *The Growth of the Church in Buganda* (London, 1958), p. 51.

69 The best accounts of the complex evolution of Bugandan politics in this period are M. Wright, *Buganda in the Heroic Age* (Nairobi, 1971) and H. B. Hansen, *Mission, Church and State in a Colonial Setting: Uganda 1890–1925* (London, 1984).

70 R. Oliver, *The Missionary Factor*, p. 134.

71 J. S. Galbraith, *Mackinnon and East Africa*, pp. 13–15, 192–193.

72 See M. Wright, *Buganda in the Heroic Age*, pp. 121–122.

73 A. R. Tucker, *Eighteen Years in Uganda and East Africa* (2 vols., London, 1908), I, p. 42, cited in R. Oliver, *The Missionary Factor*, p. 140. Tucker was the third bishop; the second had died *en route* to Buganda.

74 J. S. Galbraith, *Mackinnon and East Africa*, p. 197; A. R. Tucker, *Eighteen Years*, I, p. 149.

75 J. S. Galbraith, *Mackinnon and East Africa*, pp. 211–212.

76 E. Stock, *History of the Church Missionary Society*, III, p. 439.

77 J. S. Galbraith, *Mackinnon and East Africa*, pp. 212–213. Galbraith sees this letter as the result of the Hutchinson-Kemball meeting, and makes no mention of the Tucker-Mackinnon meeting, which must have taken place earlier in September.

78 E. Stock, *History of the CMS*, III, p. 440.

79 D. A. Low, *Buganda in Modern History* (London, 1971), pp. 57-59.
80 For a full account see *ibid.*, pp. 55-83.
81 *Ibid.*, pp. 79-80.
82 A. P. Shepherd, *Tucker of Uganda: Artist and Apostle 1849-1914* (London, 1929), p. 88; see also pp. 93-94.
83 See D. K. Fieldhouse, *Economics and Empire*, pp. 380-382.
84 D. W. Bebbington, *Nonconformist Conscience*, p. 114; A. R. Tucker, *Eighteen Years*, I, pp. 145-146; E. Stock, *History of the CMS*, III, p. 444.
85 A. R. Tucker, *Eighteen Years*, I, pp. 146-151.
86 *Ibid.*, I, p. 127.
87 *Ibid.*, I, p. 127.
88 M. Perham (ed.), *The Diaries of Lord Lugard*, (vols. I-III, London 1959), III, pp. 167-170, 215-216; M. Wright, *Buganda in the Heroic Age*, pp. 127-129.
89 R. H. Walker, 5 March 1890, cited in H. B. Hansen, *Mission, Church and State*, pp. 16-17.
90 E. Tucker, *Eighteen Years*, I, p. 126.
91 See D.A. Low, *The Mind of Buganda: Documents of the Modern History of an African Kingdom* (London, 1971), pp. 30-31; M. Wright, *Buganda in the Heroic Age*, pp. 123, 127-129.

Chapter 6

1 K. S. Latourette, *A History of Christian Missions in China* (London, 1929), pp. 765-766.
2 D. M. Paton, *Christian Missions and the Judgment of God* (London, 1953), p. 43; A. F. Walls, 'British Missions', in T. Christensen and W. R. Hutchison (eds.), *Missionary Ideologies in the Imperialist Era: 1880-1920* (Struer, Denmark, 1982), p. 159.
3 See M. L. Pirouet, 'East African Christians and World War I', *Journal of African History*, XIX (1978), pp. 117-130.
4 K. S. Latourette, *History of Missions in China*, pp. 687-688.
5 See J. A. Gallagher, *The Decline, Revival and Fall of the British Empire* (Cambridge, 1982), pp. 141-144.
6 A. Hastings, *A History of English Christianity 1920-1985* (London, 1986), p. 491.
7 A. F. Walls, 'British missions', p. 165; J. H. Boer, *Missionary Messengers of Liberation in a Colonial Context: A Case Study of the Sudan United Mission* (Amsterdam, 1979), pp. 73-74, 211-213.
8 See E. S. Wehrle, *Britain, China and the Antimissionary Riots 1891-1900* (Minneapolis, 1966), pp. 4-6, 16-18; and B. Whyte, *Unfinished Encounter: China and Christianity* (London, 1988), p. 124.
9 This paragraph is based on E. S. Wehrle, *Britain, China ...*, pp. 107-118.
10 See P. R. Bohr, *Famine in China and the Missionary: Timothy Richard as Relief Administrator and Advocate of National Reform, 1876-1884* (Cambridge, Mass., 1972). For other missionaries who arrived at conclusions similar to those of Richard see S. S. Garrett, *Social Reformers in Urban China: the Chinese Y.M.C.A., 1895-1926* (Cambridge, Mass., 1970), pp. 9-23.
11 See R. G. Collingwood, *The Idea of History* (new edn., Oxford, 1961), pp. 145-146.
12 T. Richard, *Conversion by the Million in China: Being Biographies and Articles* (Shanghai, 1907).
13 See J. K. Fairbank, *The Great Chinese Revolution: 1800-1895* (London, 1987), pp. 132-133.
14 There is some doubt over the precise totals; see K. S. Latourette, *History of Missions*, pp. 512-513, 516-517.
15 K. S. Latourette, *History of Missions*, p. 522; M. Broomhall, *The Jubilee Story of the China Inland Mission* (Philadelphia, 1915), p. 257.
16 *China Centenary Missionary Conference: Records* (Shanghai, 1907), p. 743.
17 *World Missionary Conference*, 1910 (Edinburgh and London, 1910), vol. IX, p. 246.
18 Statistics drawn from K. S. Latourette, *History of Missions*, pp. 606, 675, 680, 768, 773.
19 S. S. Garrett, *Social Reformers in Urban China*, pp. 89-92; K. S. Latourette, *History of*

Missions, p. 588; C. H. Hopkins, *John R. Mott 1865–1955* (Grand Rapids, 1979), pp. 396–397.

20 J. Reed, *The Missionary Mind and American East Asia Policy, 1911–1915* (Cambridge, Mass. and London, 1983), pp. 35–39.

21 D. W. Treadgold, *The West in Russia and China, Vol. 2: China, 1582–1949* (Cambridge, 1973), p. 93.

22 G. Hewitt, *The Problems of Success: A History of the Church Missionary Society 1910–1942* (2 vols., London, 1971, 1977), II, p. 216.

23 D. W. Treadgold, *The West in Russia and China*, p. 97. In Britain, however, Christian sympathizers with the Soviet State were rare before 1933; see A. Hastings, *History of English Christianity*, pp. 319–320.

24 K. S. Latourette, *History of Missions*, pp. 621–622; J. K. Fairbank, *Great Chinese Revolution*, pp. 183–194; V. Hayward, *Christians and China* (Belfast, 1974), p. 34.

25 The best accounts of the anti-Christian movement of 1922–27 are J. G. Lutz, 'Chinese nationalism and the anti-Christian campaigns of the 1920s', *Modern Asian Studies*, X (1976), pp. 395–416, and Ka-che Yip, *Religion, Nationalism and Chinese Students: The Anti-Christian Movement of 1922–1927* (Washington, 1980).

26 J. G. Lutz, 'Chinese nationalism', p. 407; K. Yip, *Religion, Nationalism and Chinese Students*, p. 33; P. A. Varg, 'The missionary response to the Nationalist Revolution', in J. K. Fairbank (ed.), *The Missionary Enterprise in China and America* (Cambridge, Mass., 1974), p. 316.

27 H. R. Williamson, *British Baptists in China 1845–1952* (London, 1957), pp. 123–124; K. S. Latourette, *History of Missions*, p. 811; P. A. Varg, 'Missionary response', pp. 311–315.

28 B. Whyte, *Unfinished Encounter*, pp. 125–127; H. S. C. Nevius, *The Life of John Livingston Nevius* (New York, 1895), pp. 402–405.

29 K. S. Latourette, *History of Missions*, pp. 795–805.

30 See B. Whyte, *Unfinished Encounter*, pp. 188–189, 203–205, 214–215.

31 On Kikuyu 1913 see especially J. J. Willis, *et al.*, *Towards a United Church* (London, 1947), pp. 17–74.

32 R. W. Strayer, *The Making of Mission Communities in East Africa* (London, 1978), p. 103; G. Hewitt, *The Problems of Success*, I, p. 122.

33 A. J. Temu, *British Protestant Missions* (London, 1972), pp. 118–119.

34 W. E. Owen, 'Empire and Church in Uganda and Kenya', *Edinburgh Review*, CCXLV (1927), p. 51.

35 Leys's letter is printed in J. W. Cell (ed.), *By Kenya Possessed: the Correspondence of Norman Leys and J. H. Oldham 1918–1926* (Chicago and London, 1976), pp. 91–136.

36 A. J. Temu, *British Protestant Missions*, pp. 94–101.

37 J. W. Cell, *By Kenya Possessed*, p. 92.

38 *Ibid.*, p. 39; A. J. Temu, *British Protestant Missions*, p. 122; G. Hewitt, *The Problems of Success*, I, p. 164.

39 R. W. Strayer, *The Making of Mission Communities*, p. 108.

40 A. J. Temu, *British Protestant Missions*, pp. 123–125.

41 H. M. Smith, *Frank Bishop of Zanzibar* (London, 1926), p. 251; G. Hewitt, *The Problems of Success*, I, pp. 164–165.

42 R. W. Strayer, *The Making of Mission Communities*, p. 107.

43 A. Hastings, *History of English Christianity*, p. 95.

44 See R. Oliver, *The Missionary Factor in East Africa* (2nd edn., London, 1965), pp. 252–255.

45 R. Oliver, *The Missionary Factor*, pp. 261–262.

46 See J. W. Cell, *By Kenya Possessed*, pp. 43–62.

47 A. J. Temu, *British Protestant Missions*, p. 132.

48 The contrasting responses of Hooper and McGregor are described in R. W. Strayer, *The Making of Mission Communities*, pp. 125–128.

49 This paragraph is based on R. W. Strayer, *The Making of Mission Communities*, pp. 128–133.

50 See J. M. Lonsdale, 'European attitudes and African pressures: missions and government in Kenya between the wars', *Hadith*, 2 (edited by B. A Ogot, Nairobi, 1970), pp. 235-236; R. W. Strayer, *The Making of Mission Communities*, p. 107.

51 The following account of the female circumcision controversy is based on R. W. Strayer, *The Making of Mission Communities*, ch. VIII.

52 T. F. C. Bewes, *Kikuyu Conflict: Mau Mau and the Christian Witness* (London, 1953), p. 45; A. J. Temu, *British Protestant Missions*, pp. 163-164.

53 R. W. Strayer, *The Making of Mission Communities*, p. 102.

54 J. W. Cell, *By Kenya Possessed*, pp. 103-109.

55 J. H. Oldham, *Christianity and the Race Problem* (London, 1924), pp. 98-99.

56 W. E. Owen, 'Empire and Church', p. 57.

57 See A. Hastings, *History of African Christianity*, p. 102; T. F. C. Bewes, *Kikuyu Conflict*, pp. 47-48.

58 See A. Hastings, *History of African Christianity*, p. 53; also my 'The East African Revival: African initiative within a European tradition', *Churchman*, XCII (1978), pp. 6-22.

59 J. Murray, *Proclaim the Good News: a short history of the Church Missionary Society* (London, 1985), pp. 244-245.

Chapter 7

1 See chapter 3, p. 64.

2 N. Gunson, *Messengers of Grace* (Melbourne, 1978), pp. 195-199, 206-207, 272-273.

3 *Ibid.*, p. 276.

4 *Ibid.*, pp. 274-278.

5 See chapter 4, pp. 100-101.

6 *Periodical Accounts Relative to the Baptist Missionary Society*, I (Clipstone, 1800), p. 126.

7 Carey to Fuller, 30 Jan. 1795, BMS archives, Regent's Park College, Oxford.

8 See E. A. Nida, *Customs, Culture and Christianity*, (London, 1963), pp 14-16.

9 E. D. Potts, *British Baptist Missionaries in India, 1793-1837* (Cambridge, 1967), p. 91.

10 *BMS Periodical Accounts*, III (London, 1806), p. 208.

11 William Ward's Journal, 15 Nov. 1802, BMS archives.

12 D. Coates, *et al.*, *Christianity the Means of Civilization* (London, 1837), pp. iii-iv, 174-175. (See above, chapter 3, p. 72).

13 W. O. Chadwick, *The Victorian Church* (3rd edn., 2 vols., London, 1971), I, p. 1.

14 For a review of the idea of progress in history see D. W. Bebbington, *Patterns in History*, (Leicester, 1979), pp. 68-91.

15 See P. D. Curtin, *The Image of Africa*, (London, 1965), pp. 62-65, 252-253; P. J. Marshall and G. Williams, *The Great Map of Mankind* (London, 1982), pp. 146-147, 213-214.

16 See D. A. Lorimer, *Colour, Class and the Victorians*, (Leicester, 1978), pp. 131-161; N. Stepan, *The Idea of Race in Science* (London, 1982), pp. 1-3, 44-46, 83-84.

17 This paragraph is based on A. F. Walls, 'Black Europeans, White Africans: Some Missionary Motives in West Africa', in D. Baker (ed.), *Religious Motivation* (*Studies in Church History*, vol. 15, Oxford, 1978), pp. 339-348.

18 *Ibid.*, p. 341.

19 H. H. Johnston, *George Grenfell and the Congo*, (2 vols., London, 1908), I, pp. 382-407, 480.

20 See J. F. A. Ajayi, *Christian Missions in Nigeria, 1841-1891* (London, 1965), pp. 250-251, 260-264; C. P. Williams, 'From Church to Mission ... the Church Missionary Society on the Niger, 1887-93', in W. J. Sheils and D. Wood (eds.), *Voluntary Religion* (*Studies in Church History*, vol. 23, Oxford, 1986), pp. 391-409.

21 J. H. Boer, *Missionary Messengers of Liberation* (Amsterdam, 1979) p. 147.

22 *Ibid.*, p. 125.

23 Hence the title of the magazine of the Sudan United Mission, first published in 1904.

24 Grenfell to Baynes, 13 May 1901, BMS archives.
25 See G. Rowell, *Hell and the Victorians* (Oxford, 1974), pp. 79–89, 190–192; E. J. Sharpe, *Faith Meets Faith* (London, 1977), pp. 13–15.
26 See E. J. Sharpe, *Faith Meets Faith*, pp. 19–32; *idem, Not to Destroy but to Fulfil* (Uppsala, 1965); D. B. Forrester, *Caste and Christianity* (London, 1980), pp. 136–149; J. N. Farquhar, *The Crown of Hinduism* (London, 1913).
27 See E. J. Sharpe, *Not to Destroy*, pp. 329–345.
28 Holman Bentley to Baynes, 24 April 1888, BMS archives.
29 *The Lightbearer*, March 1911, p. 59, cited in J. H. Boer, *Missionary Messengers of Liberation*, p. 171.
30 Other missionaries had assumed Chinese dress as a 'disguise' during occasional forays inland, but Taylor was the first to do so on a permanent basis; see A. J. Broomhall, *Hudson Taylor and China's Open Century, Book II* (London, 1982), pp. 278–287, 293–294.
31 C. P. Williams, 'The recruitment and training of overseas missionaries in England between 1850 and 1900' (Univ. of Bristol M. Litt. thesis, 1976), pp. 227–228.
32 A. F. Walls, 'Black Europeans, White Africans', pp. 346–347.
33 See A. Porter, 'Cambridge, Keswick, and late nineteenth-century attitudes to Africa', *Journal of Imperial and Commonwealth History*, V (1976–77), pp. 23–28.
34 Grenfell to Baynes, 13 May 1901, BMS archives.
35 See K. Robbins, 'Britain, 1940 and "Christian civilization"', in D. Beales and G. Best (eds.), *History, Society and the Churches: Essays in Honour of Owen Chadwick* (Cambridge, 1985), pp. 279–299.
36 R. W. Strayer, *The Making of Mission Communities in East Africa* (London, 1978), pp. 14–20.
37 Lorna Bowden, cited in *ibid*, p. 89.
38 T. F. C. Bewes, *Kikuyu Conflict: Mau Mau and the Christian Witness* (London, 1953), pp. 18–19, cited in *ibid*., p. 90.
39 R. W. Strayer, *The Making of Mission Communities*, p. 86.
40 See D. B. Barrett, *Schism and Renewal in Africa* (Nairobi, 1968), pp. 9, 12–13, 132, 258; F. B. Welbourn and B. A. Ogot, *A Place to Feel at Home* (London, 1966), pp. 39–71.
41 Cited in J. R. W. Stott and R. Coote (eds.), *Down to Earth: Studies in Christianity and Culture* (London, 1980), p. 313.
42 *Ibid.*, p. 1.
43 L. Newbigin, *Foolishness to the Greeks: The Gospel and Western Culture* (Geneva, 1986), p. 4.
44 See D. Whiteman, *Melanesians and Missionaries* (Pasadena, 1983), pp. 429–431.
45 See L. Newbigin, *The Other Side of 1984: Questions for the Churches* (Geneva, 1983).
46 *Ibid.*, pp. 22, 35–36; *idem, Foolishness to the Greeks*, pp. 19, 101–102.
47 D. Whiteman, *Melanesians and Missionaries*, pp. 418–419.
48 L. Newbigin, *The Other Side of 1984*, pp. 28–37.
49 See, for example, J. Wimber, *Power Evangelism: Signs and Wonders Today* (London, 1985), pp. 74–96.

Chapter 8

1 For a recent Christian discussion of nationalism see B. Thorogood, *The Flag and the Cross: National Limits and the Church Universal* (London, 1988).
2 Paul's reference in Acts 17:26 to God having determined the boundaries of human habitation may refer to the geographical boundaries between land and sea rather than to political frontiers.
3 D. W. Bebbington, *Patterns in History* (Leicester, 1979), p. 184.
4 Melvill Horne's phrase (see above, chapter 4, p. 107).
5 See R. A. Markus, *Saeculum: History and Society in the Theology of St Augustine* (Cambridge, 1970), *passim*.

6 B. Stanley, 'Christian responses to the Indian mutiny of 1857', in W. J. Sheils (ed.), *The Church and War* (*Studies in Church History*, vol. 20, Oxford, 1983), pp. 281–282.

7 On this theme see especially A. Holmberg, *African Tribes and European Agencies: Colonialism and Humanitarianism in British South and East Africa, 1870–1895* (Göteborg, 1966).

8 J. M. Mackenzie (ed.), *Imperialism and Popular Culture* (Manchester, 1986), pp. 5–8.

9 K. Cracknell, *Towards a New Relationship: Christians and People of Other Faith* (London, 1986), p. 9.

Index

African National Congress 17
African theology 23-24
Ajayi, J. F. A. 30
All Africa Conference of Churches 28
Alliance High School 16, 153
Alves, Rubem 25
America, Latin 12, 21-25, 40
America, North *see* Canada, United
  States of America
American missions 13-14, 28, 29, 55,
  57-58, 67, 69, 83-84, 107, 135,
  138, 140, 144-145
Anderson, Rufus 145
Anglican Church 43, 55-57, 61, 66,
  68, 71, 79, 85-86, 90-91, 99,
  102, 108, 112, 162, 169, 182. *See
  also* Evangelical Anglicans,
  Anglo-Catholics
Anglo-Catholics 61, 74, 146
Angola 17, 20
Anstey, Roger 59
anthropology 160, 162
Anti-Christian Student Federation
  15, 143
anti-slavery 42, 43, 59, 72, 73, 78,
  86-91, 103-104, 115, 122-125,
  130, 132, 182
Argentine, the 40
Arthington, Robert 76, 80, 103
Arthur, J. W. 148, 151, 152
Arthur, William 114
Asian theology 23, 24
Assyrian empire 177, 181
Attlee, Clement 50, 135
Augustine of Hippo 180
Australia 34, 40, 57, 58, 176

Ayandele, E. A. 30

Babylonian empire 177
Baker, Thomas 115
Balasuriya, Tissa 11
Banda, Dr Hastings 19
Baptist Missionary Society (BMS)
  20, 56, 60, 65, 71, 72, 76, 80,
  86-91, 97, 99, 108-109, 138,
  159-160, 163, 165
Baptists 56, 59, 60, 61, 66, 86-91,
  99-101,102, 108, 138, 159-160
Baran, Paul 22
Barbados 85, 86
Barrett, D. B. 83
Basel Mission 58
Bashford, Bishop James 140
Bauer, Lord P. T. 22
Bechuanaland 112, 116-121, 130,
  132, 178, 182
Beecham, John 97
Belgium 17, 39, 40, 163
Bentinck, Lord William 100-101
Bentley, W. Holman 165
Berlin Society 58
Bewes, T. F. C. 152, 168-169
Beyerhaus, Peter 27
Bible Union of China 145
Binns, H. K. 168
Bismarck, Count Otto von 45, 124
black theology 23-24
Blantyre Mission 79, 83, 123-127
Botswana (formerly Bechuanaland)
  17, 117, 121. *See also*
  Bechuanaland
Bowring, Sir John 108

Boxer rising 139-140, 142
Boyce, William 97, 98
Brainerd, David 55
Brazil 25
Brethren movement 76, 165
British South Africa Company 40, 118, 121, 125, 126
Brockman, Fletcher 141
Brooke, Graham Wilmot 77
Brown, David 56, 58
Buchanan, Claudius 58
Buganda 79, 111, 127-132
Burchell, Thomas 89, 91
Burke, Edmund 58, 68
Burton, Richard 162
Butler, Bishop Joseph 68
Buxton, Sir Thomas Fowell 73, 78, 87, 88, 94, 96, 97

Cakobau 113-115
Calvinism 56, 59-60, 63
Camara, Dom Helder 25
Cambridge, University of 18, 45, 70, 81-83
Canada 34, 40, 55, 90, 162
candidates, missionary 66, 78-84, 135, 140, 165-166
Cape Colony 43, 85, 90, 91-98, 120, 178
capitalist imperialism, theory of 37-41, 143
Carey, William 55, 56, 58, 60, 71, 72, 75, 99, 100, 159
caste 103, 104, 159, 164
Castro, Emilio 28
Castro, Fidel 38-39
Catholic Church see Roman Catholic Church
Catholic missions see Roman Catholic missions
Chadwick, W. O. 161
Chiang K'ai-shek 143-144
China 14-16, 29, 38, 51, 65, 67, 72, 79, 83, 85, 104-109, 110, 133, 136-146, 147, 148, 153, 154-155, 165, 172, 179-180
China Inland Mission (CIM) 67, 76, 83, 109, 137, 140, 145, 153, 155,

165-166
Chinese Communist Party (CCP) 143-144
Ch'ing (Manchu) dynasty 16, 51, 104, 107, 109, 136, 139, 142
Church Missionary Society (CMS) 18, 57, 59, 66-67, 76-82, 86, 103, 106, 108, 109, 112, 127-132, 137, 142, 146-148, 150, 152, 163, 166, 168
Church of Christ in Africa 169
Church of Christ in China 145
Church of England see Anglican Church, Anglo-Catholics, Evangelical Anglicans
Church of Scotland - missions of 57, 79, 83, 112, 121-127, 146, 148, 150, 151
circumcision controversy 151-153
Ciskei 92, 96, 97
civilization 21, 36, 67, 69, 72, 74, 75, 77, 82, 96, 98, 114, 123, 125, 130, 134, 135, 138, 148, 154; chapter 7, passim.
Clapham Sect 57, 71
Clarkson, Thomas 71
Clarkson, William 70, 75
Cobden, Richard 47, 108
Coke, Thomas 56
Colombia 25
colonialism - definitions 34-35, 46
Colonial Office 43, 48, 88, 94, 96, 147, 149, 153
colonization 34, 43, 44, 114, 146
Comely, John 152
commerce and Christianity 70-74, 82, 97, 103, 108, 122-123, 128
communism 15-16, 21, 29, 136, 142-145, 154, 180
Comintern 136, 142, 143
Cone, James 24
Conference of British Missionary Societies 144, 148
Congo 80, 163, 165. See also Zaire
Congregationalists 57, 59, 60, 66, 82, 90, 107, 112, 120, 158. See also London Missionary Society
Cook, Captain James 58

Costas, Orlando 12, 30
Cracknell, Kenneth 183
Crowther, Bishop Samuel 162, 163
culture 23-26, 126, 135, 147, 151,
    154, 155; chapter 7, *passim.*
  - definition 170

Dachs, Anthony J. 117-118
Dale, R. W. 79
Darwin, Charles 142, 161
Davidson, Archbishop Randall 149
decolonization 16-17, 44, 50, 180
Demerara 86-88
dependency theory 21-23, 27
Disraeli, Benjamin 36, 45, 47, 115
Doddridge, Philip 55
Drescher, Seymour 59
Dublin, Trinity College 81
D'Urban, Sir Benjamin 96
Dutch Reformed Church 21

East African Revival 27, 154
East India Company 56, 58, 69, 85,
    98-101, 105, 110
ecumenism 26-29, 57, 134, 140, 145,
    146. *See also* International
    Missionary Council, World
    Council of Churches
Edinburgh, University of 82
Eddy, George Sherwood 141
education, missionary 16-17, 48, 49,
    52, 72, 77, 132, 133-134,
    140-143, 171
Edwards, Jonathan 59-60
Egypt 45, 61
Ellis, William 96, 160
Enlightenment 62-63, 67-68, 71, 73,
    74, 77, 86, 154, 161, 171, 172,
    173, 181, 184
Erskine, John 57
eschatology 60-61, 63, 65-67, 74-78,
    82, 109, 164, 166
Evangelical Revival 55, 59-60, 77
Evangelical Anglicans 57, 59, 62,
    66-67, 71, 79, 81, 90-91, 101,
    108, 112, 129, 131

Fanon, Frantz 25, 39

Farquhar, J. N. 164
Fieldhouse, D. K. 34, 45, 46
Fife, Eric 15
Fiji 112-116, 130, 132
finance capitalism 37, 39
Fleming, W. S. 137
FNLA (Frente National de
    Libertaçao de Angola) 20
Fountain, John 99
France 16, 23, 25, 35, 39, 40, 58, 61,
    91, 99, 112, 113, 114, 123, 127,
    130, 131, 137
Francis, Carey 153
Free Church of Scotland - missions
    of 16-17, 79, 112, 121-127
FRELIMO (Frente de Libertaçao de
    Moçambique) 20, 26
French Revolution 61, 86, 99
Fuller, Andrew 59-60
Fung, Raymond 24

Gallagher, J. A. 41-42, 44, 46, 49, 70
Gambia 17
Gatu, John 27, 29
George, Henry 142
Germany 37, 39, 40, 78, 121,
    124-125, 128, 131, 133, 137
Ghana 16-17, 19
Gibson, John Campbell 145
Gladstone, W. E. 36, 45, 47, 115,
    120, 130
Glasgow Missionary Society 57
Glasser, Arthur 15
Glenelg, Lord (Charles Grant the
    younger) 96, 101
Goodall, Norman 26, 27
Grant, Charles (the elder) 56, 58, 72
Great Trek, the 96, 98
Green, Francis 150
Grenfell, George 163, 167
Griqualand, West 117, 119
Guevara, Che 39
Guinea-Bissau 20
Gutiérrez, Gustavo 25
Gützlaff, Karl 105, 109
Guyana 86-88

Hankey, W. A. 87

Hannington, Bishop James 127, 131
Hastings, Adrian 20, 28, 148
Hastings, Warren 58
Havelock, Henry 102
Haweis, Thomas 56, 58
Hetherwick, Alexander 126
Heywood, Bishop R. S. 148, 152
Hick, John 23
Hilferding, Rudolf 37–38
Hinduism 65, 100–101, 159, 164
Hobson, J. A. 37–38
Hooper, Handley 148, 150
Horne, Melvill 56, 61, 71, 107
Huntingdon, Selina, Countess of 56
Hutchinson, General George 129

idolatry 63–65, 100–102, 104, 107,
    158, 161, 164, 184
Idowu, Bolaji 23
Imperial British East Africa
    Company (IBEAC) 40, 128–131
imperialism
  – definitions 34–35, 40–41, 50–51
  – cultural 24, 25–26, 52, 67, 143,
    145, 154; chapter 7, *passim*
  – economic 22, 37–40, 42, 44–45,
    51–52, 70–74, 79, 103, 105–109,
    119, 127. *See also* capitalist
    imperialism, theory of
  – origins of the term 35
  – popular 36–37, 46–47, 182
India 16, 18, 35, 36, 40, 42, 44,
    47–48, 49, 50, 55, 56, 57, 58, 65,
    69, 70, 72, 75, 79, 85, 91,
    98–104, 110, 111, 135, 148, 158,
    159–160, 161, 164, 176, 178, 181
Indian mutiny 69, 79, 101–103, 110,
    181
International Missionary Council 16,
    26
International Review of Missions 148
Irving, Edward 76
Islam 65, 124, 127–128, 131,
    135–136, 153, 168
Italy 39, 133

Jackson, F. J. 128
Jagannath temple (Puri) 101

Jamaica 85–91, 162
James, John Angell 62, 107–109
Japan 39, 137, 139, 144
Jehovah's Witnesses 19
John, Griffith 137
Johnston, Sir Harry H. 125–126

K'ang Yu-wei 139
Kaunda, Kenneth 17
Kemball, General Sir Arnold 129
Kemp, Johannes van der 93
Kennaway, Sir John 137
Kenya 16–17, 34, 43, 136, 146–155,
    168–169, 172
Kenya African Union 153, 154
Kenyatta, Jomo 16, 150, 153
Keswick movement 76, 82, 111, 154,
    165–166, 172
Khoisan 91–97
Kikuyu Association 149–150
Kikuyu Central Association (KCA)
    150, 151
Kipling, Rudyard 36
Kitamori, Kazoh 24
Knibb, William 87–91, 97, 132
Koebner, R. 35
Koyama, Kosuke 24
Kraemer, Hendrik 67
Kuang-hsu, Emperor 139, 140
Kumm, Karl 163
Kuomintang (KMT) 141, 143–144
Kwama 118

Labour party 47, 50, 135
Langer, W. L. 34
Latourette, K. S. 83
Lausanne Congress on World
    Evangelization 28–29
Laws, Robert 126
Lenin, V. I. 15, 38, 39, 143
Leopold II, King of the Belgians 163
Lesotho (formerly Basutoland) 17
Leys, Norman 147, 153
liberalism, theological 61, 66–67, 75,
    77, 134, 142, 145, 164–165, 166
liberation theology 23, 24–26
Livingstone, David 57, 66, 70–71,
    73–74, 79, 83, 122–123, 128

Livingstonia Mission 16-17, 79, 123-127
London Missionary Society (LMS) 56-57, 58, 60, 65, 66, 71, 72, 76, 78-80, 82-83, 86-88, 93-98, 99, 102, 106, 109, 111, 112, 113, 117-120, 137, 158, 160, 164
Lugard, Lord 48, 128, 131, 132
Luo 169
Luthuli, Albert 17
Lutley, A. F. 142

McArthur, Sir William 115-116
McCracken, John 121
McGregor, A. W. 150-151
Machel, Samora 20
Mackay, A. M. 127, 128
Mackenzie, Bishop C. F. 74
Mackenzie, John 117-121, 182
Mackenzie, Robert 138
Mackinnon, Sir William 123, 128-129
Macmillan, Harold 17
McOwan, Peter 64
M'afu 113, 115
Malawi (formerly Nyasaland) 16-17, 19, 79, 112, 121-127, 130, 132, 147
Mao Tse-tung 38
Maqoma 95
Marcuse, Herbert 25
Marshman, Joshua 159
Martyn, Henry 55
Marx, Karl 22-23, 37, 142
Marxism 12, 14, 20-23, 25, 34, 35, 37-39, 41, 45. See also communism
Mateer, Calvin 138
Mau Mau 152, 154
Maurice, F. D. 66, 164
Mauritius 90
Maxwell, James Lowry 163
Mbiti, John 23
medical missions 48, 77, 82, 171
Methodists 56, 59, 64, 66, 76, 82, 86, 88-91, 94-98, 102, 108, 112-116, 144, 158. See also Wesleyan Methodist Missionary Society
Mfecane 93
Mlozi 124
Mobutu, Sese Seko 19
Moffat, J. S. 118
Moffat, Robert 57, 65, 78, 98, 117, 118
Moghul empire 51
Mondlane, Eduardo 20, 26, 27
Moody, D. L. 82, 83
moratorium debate 27-29
Moravians 93
Morris, Colin 17-18
Morrison, Robert 105
Mott, John R. 76, 141
MPLA (Movimento Popular de Libertaçao de Angola) 20
Mozambique 17, 20
Mutesa I, Kabaka of Buganda 79, 127
Mwanga, Kabaka of Buganda 127-128
Myrdal, Gunnar 22

Namibia (formerly South-West Africa) 121
Nanking, Treaty of (1842) 79, 106
Napoleon Bonaparte, Emperor 35, 61
Napoleon, Louis (Emperor Napoleon III) 35
Natal 97
National Christian Council (of China) 145
nationalism 16-21, 24, 49-50, 51, 52, 126, 132; chapter 6, passim; 172, 176, 182
Ndebele 111, 118
Neill, Stephen 13, 18, 170
neo-colonialism 22-23, 27, 35
Nevius, John L. 145
Newbigin, Lesslie 170, 172, 173
New Caledonia 113
Newton, Isaac 63, 68
New Zealand 34, 40, 43, 58, 176
Ngcqika 93
Ngoni 124
Nigeria 17, 48, 72, 73, 78, 136, 163,

166, 168
Nkrumah, Kwame 16, 19–20, 22
Nonconformists 43, 47, 55–61, 76,
    82, 86–87, 89–90, 98–99, 102,
    103, 112, 116, 131, 158
Northern Rhodesia *see* Zambia
Nova Scotia 162
Nurkse, Ragnar 22
Nyasaland *see* Malawi
Nyerere, Julius 20

Oldham, J. H. 148–149, 153, 154
Oliver, Roland 124
opium wars 85, 104–109, 179
Orsmond, John 158
Owen, W. E. 147, 149, 151, 153,
    154, 169
Oxford, University of 81–82

Pacific, South 46, 58, 72, 78, 111,
    112–116, 158–159, 161
Pakistan 50
Paley, William 68
Palmerston, Lord 108, 114
Panikkar, K. M. 15–16, 27
Parrinder, Geoffrey 23
Paton, David M. 15
Peace Society 102, 108
Peggs, James 100–101
Peking, Convention of (1860) 108
Persian empire 177
Peters, Karl 124, 128
Philip, John 57, 93–98, 110
Pierson, A. T. 76
Pilkington, George 131
Pius VI, Pope 61
Portal, Sir Gerald 130
Portugal 12, 17, 20–21, 25, 28, 39,
    124–125
postmillennialism 60, 63, 74–76, 109
premillennialism 76–77, 82, 166
Presbyterians 138, 145. *See also*
    Church of Scotland – Missions
    of, Free Church of Scotland –
    Missions of
Pretoria, Convention of (1881) 120
Pritchard, W. T. 113–114
protectorates 48, 116, 120–121,

124–126, 146, 147
providence 60, 63, 67–70, 74, 103,
    107, 108, 109, 179–181
P'u-yi, Emperor 140

race 36, 97, 102, 119, 162–163, 167,
    172, 182–183
Rampley, W. J. 152
Reid, Gilbert 138–139
Re-thinking Missions (1932) 14
Rhodes, Cecil 37, 40, 118, 119–121,
    125–127
Rhodesia *see* Zimbabwe
Richard, Timothy 138–139, 142,
    154, 164, 166
Ridgeway, Joseph 108
Robertson, C. H. 141
Robinson, Ronald 41–42, 44, 70
Roman Catholic Church 19–20, 25,
    28, 43, 61, 128, 131, 132
Roman Catholic missions 12, 14, 16,
    25, 84, 112, 113, 127–128, 139,
    184
Roman empire 98, 177–178, 180
Romanticism 63, 77
Rosebery, Lord 36, 130
Rostow, W. W. 22
Rowe, John 86
Royce, James 113
Russell, Bertrand 143
Russia 38, 39, 51, 136, 137. *See also*
    Soviet Union
Rwanda 17, 154
Ryland, John 61

Salisbury, Lord 125, 129, 137
sati, 100–101, 104, 159
Sawyerr, Harry 23
Schmidt, H. D. 35
Scott, David 125
Scott, Thomas 66
Scottish Missionary Society 57
Scottish Society for the Propagation
    of Christian Knowledge 55
Sebituane 66
Sechele I 118
Seeley, Sir J. R. 45
Serampore 100, 159–160

Shaftesbury, Lord 106
Shaw, William 94–98
Shipman, John 88
Sidmouth, Lord 99
Sierra Leone 17, 56, 71, 162
Simeon, Charles 57, 62, 67
slave emancipation (1834) 78, 88, 89–90
slave trade *see* anti-slavery
Smith, Adam 71, 72, 97
Smith, Edwin 23
Smith, George, Bishop of Victoria 108
Smith, Ian 17, 21
Smith, John 86–88
Smythe, Colonel W. J. 114
Society for Promoting Christian Knowledge (SPCK) 55, 98
Society for the Diffusion of Christian and General Knowledge among the Chinese 138
Society for the Propagation of the Gospel in Foreign Parts (SPG) 55, 61, 86, 87, 107
Somaliland 17
Somerset, Lord Charles 93
Song, C. S. 24
South Africa 11, 17, 21, 23–24, 26, 36–37, 40, 78, 85, 91–98, 102, 103, 110, 117, 121, 146. *See also* Cape Colony
Southern Rhodesia *see* Zimbabwe
South Seas *see* Pacific, South
Soviet Union 22, 51, 136, 142, 176
Spain 12, 33
Spurgeon, C. H. 66
Stanley, H. M. 79–80
Steane, Edward 108
Stephen, James 94
Stewart, James 122–123
Stock, Eugene 129, 131
Strong, Josiah 69
Studd, C. T. 83
Student Volunteer Missionary Union 76, 82
Stumpf, Hulda 152
Sudan United Mission 163
Suez Canal 79, 123

Sun Yat-sen 16, 141–144
Swaziland 17
Swiney, Sam 88

Tahiti 113
Taiping rebellion 107, 109
Tanzania (formerly Tanganyika) 17, 20, 124
Taylor, James Hudson 67, 76, 109, 140, 165
Temu, Arnold 152
Thomas, M. M. 24
Three-Self Patriotic Movement 145, 154–155
Thuku, Harry 150
Tientsin, Treaty of (1858) 108–109
Tonga (Malawi) 124
Transvaal Republic 119–120
treaty ports 106, 137, 144
trusteeship 36, 47, 49, 51, 68–69, 98, 146, 147, 149, 179
Tswana 117–121
Tucker, Bishop Alfred 128–131
Tucker, Joseph 71

Uganda 17, 79–80, 111, 112, 127–132, 146, 178, 182
United Methodist Free Church Mission 146
Universities' Mission to Central Africa (UMCA) 61, 74, 122
United States of America 23, 24, 25, 27, 29, 35, 38, 39, 40, 44, 59, 69, 71, 83–84, 113, 114, 135, 140–142, 176, 181

Venn, Henry 66, 67, 73, 79, 145
Venn, John 57
Visser 't Hooft, W. A. 27

Walls, A. F. 162
Ward, William 99, 100, 160
Warren, Max A. C. 18
Watts, Isaac 55
Wellesley, Lord 99
Wesley, John 55, 56
Wesleyan Methodist Missionary Society (WMMS) 56, 64, 82,

86, 88, 91, 94–98, 112–116
West Indies 43, 56, 59, 78, 85–91,
    103–104, 110
Weston, Bishop Frank 146, 148
White Fathers 112, 127–128
Wilberforce, Bishop Samuel 69, 107
Wilberforce, William 71, 99, 132
Williams, John 78
Willis, Bishop J. J. 148
Willmer, Haddon 62
World Council of Churches 11,
    26–29
World Missionary Conference,
    Edinburgh 1910 140
World Student Christian Federation
    141, 143
World War, First 38, 42, 47, 67, 83,
    134–135, 146–147, 149, 165,
    167, 182
World War, Second 42, 49, 135, 167

Wu, Y. T. 145

Xhosa 93–97

Yao 124
Young Kikuyu Association (YKA)
    150
Young Men's Christian Association
    (YMCA) 140–143, 145, 148,
    164
Yuan Shih-k'ai 141

Zaire (formerly Belgian Congo) 17,
    19
Zambia (formerly Northern
    Rhodesia) 17–18
Zanzibar 124, 130, 146
Zimbabwe (formerly Rhodesia,
    Southern Rhodesia) 17, 21, 28,
    34, 111, 118, 146, 167

The Apostolic Fathers
Second Edition

Translated by J. B. LIGHTFOOT and
J. R. HARMER
Edited and Revised by
MICHAEL W. HOLMES

Recent years have witnessed an upsurge of interest in
the writings of the apostolic fathers – a primary source
for the study of the development of Christianity in the
immediate post-apostolic period. Unlike some
collections this volume includes all the writings
entitled to be classed as from the apostolic fathers.

This second edition includes the English text which is a
revision of the Lightfoot-Harmer translation of 1891.
Dr Holmes has made changes 'only as seemed required
by considerations of clarity, readability and
contemporary . . . English usage'. Significant revisions
of the original translations are indicated in footnotes.

Dr Holmes has used the opportunity of revision to take
into account new discoveries, such as some fragments
of Papias which have come to light in recent years. He
has written both a new general introduction and
introductions to each of the writings of the apostolic
fathers. These provide an assessment of each work's
historical context and of its theological themes. Since
many significant passages in *The Apostolic Fathers*
continue to be the subject of scholarly debate, the
editor has also included extensive textual notes. The
value of this volume is enhanced by up-to-date
bibliographies.

352 pages   *Hardback*

APOLLOS

Approaches to Old Testament Interpretation
Updated Edition
JOHN GOLDINGAY

In this book, Dr Goldingay examines five different approaches to the Old Testament: as a faith to be believed; a way of life; the story of salvation; a witness to Christ; and Scripture.

He devotes a chapter to each approach and interacts with the views of the main advocates of each. He discusses a number of key issues such as the law, the use of the Old Testament by the writers of the New, and the relationship between the two Testaments.

The book has now been updated by the addition of a Postscript which surveys books published since 1981 and sketches three important new developments: the sociological analysis of the Old Testament, literary studies (especially of the narratives) and canonical criticism.

208 pages   *Large paperback*

APOLLOS

Christianity and Western Thought
A History of Philosophers,
Ideas and Movements
Volume One: From the Ancient World to the Age of Enlightenment
COLIN BROWN

This book is an introductory survey of Western
thought from Socrates and the early Greeks to the
eighteenth century. It is about the dramatic changes
in the ways in which people have thought about
faith, particularly Christianity.

All the leading philosophers are discussed, but so
also are the dominant patterns of thought at
particular times which shaped discussion and
discourse, and which influenced both private and
public behaviour.

This book is useful for the non-specialist student
and general reader as well as the beginning student
of philosophy, and those who undertake theological
or religious studies.

Volume Two, now in preparation, will continue the
survey into the nineteenth and twentieth centuries.

352 pages   *Hardback*

APOLLOS

Contextualization
Meanings, methods and models

DAVID J. HESSELGRAVE and EDWARD ROMMEN

The Christian church is not only under obligation to be faithful to the gospel. It is also required to communicate the gospel meaningfully in a whole variety of different cultures. In other words, the gospel must be contextualized if it is to be understood properly.

The authors begin by sketching in the historical background to contextualization and then they discuss a number of different approaches to it. In the third part of the book they analyse the concept from a number of perspectives and conclude by outlining different models which can be used to convey the gospel to people as different as tribals in remote areas to nominal Christians in Europe.

244 pages   *Large paperback*

APOLLOS

Interpreting the Parables

CRAIG BLOMBERG

Many Christians have heard the parables of Jesus expounded in rather strange ways. This book will help towards a saner and more satisfying way of interpreting them.

Dr Blomberg shows, contrary to received scholarly opinion, that the parables do contain allegorical elements because they symbolize spiritual realities, and that they are meant to make more than one main point. Furthermore, the Gospel parables are authentic in the sense that they accurately represent our Lord's teaching.

All who have to study and teach the parables will find this book of immense help.

330 pages   *Large paperback*

APOLLOS

Theology of the Reformers

TIMOTHY GEORGE

This book, an introduction to Reformation theology, presents the thought of Martin Luther, Huldrych Zwingli, John Calvin and Menno Simons, the Anabaptist leader. Each is largely allowed to speak for himself by means of a judicious selection of quotations from his writings. Though he does not ignore social and political factors, Dr George concentrates upon the theology of the reformers because for him the Reformation is primarily a religious event. Because of its exceptional clarity and readability, this book will appeal not only to students and lecturers, but to the general reader as well.

338 pages 　　　*Hardback*

APOLLOS